'An amazing East-West German story of life and love…'
Die Welt

'So much more than a regular biography... [a] unique account
of life behind the Iron Curtain when the Berlin Wall was up
and the Cold War was at its chilliest.'
road cc

'A gripping book. Was as unputdownable as the best espionage novels.'
Seven Day Cyclist

'A fascinating tale.'
Bikes Etc

'The story of Dieter Wiedemann is an intriguing tale,
encompassing a potent combination of politics, sport, love and
betrayal. Herbie Sykes impressively balances the political and the
personal, making *The Race Against the Stasi* an enjoyable,
compelling and highly recommended read.'
The View East

'A window into a world that no longer exists but which conditioned the
lives of millions of people… most definitely a book worth reading.'
The Jersey Pocket

'A hugely rewarding read and a tour de force of excellent journalism.'
TourofBritain.co.uk

'More than the story of a cyclist, more than a story about cycling…
it's the story of a man forgotten by history but who deserves to
be remembered, not just for the life he lived, but for the way the
story of that life has been told.'
Podium Cafe

'A great book that mixes a variety of source materials to tell the
story of a cyclist… a story that deserves to be told.'
INRNG.com

'Incr vork of great credit
to its ial parts social and
spo f the finest books

Herbie Sykes is a journalist and writer.
He lives in Italy, and is the author of a number
of books about cycling.

The Eagle of the Canavese, a biography of Franco Balmamion,
was published in 2008. It was described by *Cycling Weekly* as
"a gem of a book". In 2011 Sykes released **Maglia Rosa**.
The first historical examination of the Giro d'Italia in the
English language, it received widespread critical acclaim.
It was the podiumcafe.com book of the year, and is regarded
by cycling historians as a seminal work.

Coppi, a pictorial biography of the campionissimo with
supporting testimony from his contemporaries, was shortlisted
at the 2012 British Sports Book of the Year Awards.

Sykes has written for a number of publications,
notably *Rouleur*, *Pro Cycling* and *Mondial*.

HERBIE SYKES

THE RACE
AGAINST
THE STASI

THE INCREDIBLE STORY OF DIETER WIEDEMANN, THE IRON CURTAIN AND THE GREATEST CYCLING RACE ON EARTH

Aurum
Press

Quarto is the authority on a wide range of topics.

Quarto educates, entertains and enriches the lives of
our readers—enthusiasts and lovers of hands-on living.
www.QuartoKnows.com

First published in Great Britain
2014 by Aurum Press Ltd
74–77 White Lion Street
Islington
London N1 9PF
www.aurumpress.co.uk

This paperback edition first published in 2016 by Aurum Press

A catalogue record for this book is available from the British Library.

ISBN 978 1 78131 536 1

1 3 5 7 9 10 8 6 4 2
2016 2018 2020 2019 2017

Typeset in Minion Pro by Carrdesignstudio.com
Printed and bound by CPI Group (UK) Ltd, Croydon, CR0 4YY

In memory of Ian Steel

28 December 1928 – 20 October 2015

CONTENTS

'The Peace Race was an oasis, and through it we were able to dream. It was about different peoples, from different countries, crossing borders and coming together. It was about genuine fellowship, and that was its beauty and virtue. For two weeks a year it offered us a window on worlds we were denied access to. It was a huge paradox, obviously, but for me it remains something beautiful. It was the race of peace.'

Horst Schäfer, Curator, Peace Race Museum

NOTES ON THE TEXT

Documents prefixed MfS (Ministry for State Security) are reproduced from Stasi files. Those prefixed MfS383/65 are reproduced from Wiedemann's file. Where the prefix includes a number other than 383/65, they are reproduced from the files of the informants who reported on him.

Many persons are redacted in the Stasi files. People referred to as (?) are either protected under current legislation, unknown to the author, or have chosen to remain anonymous. In some instances addresses and other indicators are also redacted, in order to help conceal their identity. Some blocks of text have been redacted from the Stasi files. In these instances the text is either indecipherable or is not germane to Dieter Wiedemann. In translating the Stasi files I have attempted to be as faithful as possible to the original documents. On occasion, therefore, the grammar may be less than perfect.

This work is not intended as an examination of Stasi structure or methodology, but twenty-five secret informants are believed to have compiled reports on or including Dieter Wiedemann. Most were submitted to one of the following four Stasi offices:

Berlin: Seat of the vast Stasi headquarters and of the GDR Cycling Federation. From here, main department V sought to recruit Wiedemann as an informant in 1962.

Chemnitz (previously known as Karl-Marx-Stadt): One of the fifteen regional 'area command units'.

Flöha: A 'district service unit' in Wiedemann's home town, subordinate to Chemnitz Area Command Unit.

'W': A division responsible for the Wismut uranium mining company and its assets, including the sport club it ran.

Staff or informants from the following Stasi departments compiled reports on Wiedemann at one time or another:

Main Department II: Counterintelligence

Department M: Postal surveillance

Main Department VI: Passport control, Tourism

Main Department VII: Ministry for the Interior, People's Police

Main Department VIII: Economy

Main Department XX: Apparatus of the State, Culture (including sport), Church, 'Underground'

Main Department V: As Main Department XX, prior to 1964

The Stasi files use various terms to describe the unofficial informants. Most commonly these are 'GI' (*Geheimer Informator*), the term used throughout the 1950s, and 'IM' (*Inoffizieller Mitarbeiter*), adopted in 1969 but already prevalent beforehand. For the purposes of simplicity, however, I have used the term 'informant' throughout the text. Equally, where other Stasi abbreviations appear (for example 'KW'; conspiratorial dwelling), I have taken the liberty of translating them.

All of the interviews in this book were carried out *before* the Stasi files were accessed.

The text includes a number of articles reprinted from *Neues Deutschland*, the official organ of the ruling communist party. No free press existed in the GDR, and as such the articles represent, *de facto*, Politburo press releases.

Witnesses

Dieter: Dieter Wiedemann

Sylvia: Sylvia Wiedemann, wife of Dieter

Nicole, Alex and Nina: Daughters of Dieter and Sylvia

Eberhard: Eberhard Wiedemann, brother of Dieter

Rainer: Rainer Müller, best friend of Dieter

Klaus: Klaus Huhn, sports editor, *Neues Deutschland*

Täve: Täve Schur, racing cyclist with DHfK

Immo: Immo Rittmeyer, racing cyclist with SC Karl-Marx-Stadt

Manfred: Manfred Weissleder, racing cyclist with SC Karl-Marx-Stadt

Ian: Ian Steel, British racing cyclist

Frank: Frank Seal, British racing cyclist

Axel: Axel Peschel, racing cyclist with Dynamo Berlin

Gerhard: Gerhard Richter, Wiedemann family friend

Udo: Udo Richter, son of Dieter's trainer, fellow cyclist and defector

In absentia

Emil: Emil Reinecke, racing cyclist with DHfK

Werner: Werner Scharch, former president of GDR cycling and defector

Informants

'Fritzsche': Cycling trainer, SC Karl-Marx-Stadt, born 1915

'Hildebrand': Cycling trainer, SC Dynamo Berlin, born 1929

'Jonni': Worker, SDAG Wismut, born 1926

'Kaufmann': Neighbour of Dieter Wiedemann, born 1897

'Orion': Classmate of Dieter Wiedemann, born 1941

'Radler': Cycling trainer, SC Dynamo Berlin, born 1913

'Seppel': Retired cyclist, trainer at BSG Wismut, born 1927

'Ursel': Worker, SDAG Wismut, born 1928

CENTRAL
EUROPE
1964

DENMARK

Berlin
Wall

W ⟶ E

Berlin

NETHERLANDS

EAST GERMANY

Flöha
Chemnitz

Giessen

BELGIUM

WEST GERMANY

Mitterteich

LUXEMBOURG

FRANCE

SWITZERLAND

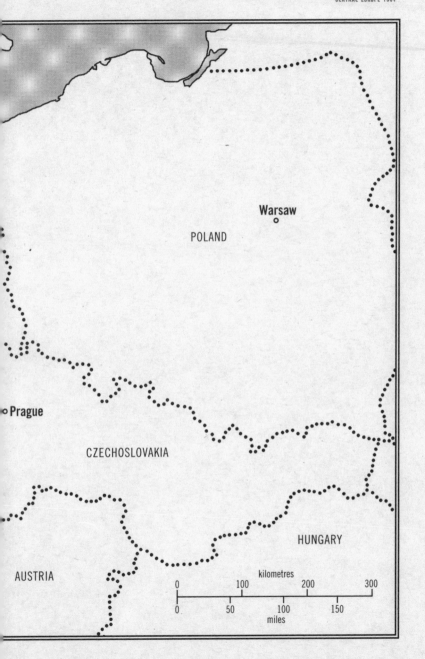

Warsaw

POLAND

Prague

CZECHOSLOVAKIA

HUNGARY

AUSTRIA

kilometres
0   100   200   300
0   50   100   150
miles

THE RACE FOR PEACE

Arguably the most efficient of the Warsaw Pact dictatorships, East Germany (the GDR) is invariably portrayed as the cruellest and most oppressive. In the broad-brush historical way of things, it's come to be characterised by little more than the Berlin Wall, and by the secret police force known as the Stasi. In a sporting context it's synonymous with a grotesque, state-orchestrated doping programme, with Olympic fraud on a mammoth scale.

Immediately Stalin bludgeoned it into being in 1949, the GDR was declared a rogue state by the western allies. Two years later, when the GDR formed its own National Olympic Committee, the IOC refused to recognise its legitimacy. Instead it was invited to participate in the 1952 Olympics as part of a combined German team, with predictable consequences; no East German athletes made the trip to Helsinki. Between 1956 and 1964 a deeply politicised all-German 'alliance' competed at both summer and winter games. Not until 1965 did the IOC recognise the GDR and the Mexico games hosted, for the first time, its national team.

For twenty years thereafter the country, a socialist totalitarian state of around seventeen million people, achieved astounding, unprecedented results at the Olympics. GDR athletes out-ran, -jumped, -lifted and -swam all but those of the USSR. The 'GDR sports miracle', driven by systematic, state-run anabolic steroid abuse, saw the country's weightlifters, skiers, athletes and gymnasts routinely finish second in the Olympic medal table. It was entirely as ordered by the ruling SED party,* for whom sports were a crucial propaganda instrument. In performing so spectacularly, they apparently underscored the moral and political supremacy of communism to their countrymen, but also to the capitalist west.

At the Montreal games of 1976, East German teenagers won eleven of the thirteen female swimming competitions. All told, the GDR accumulated no fewer than forty golds at those games, six more than the USA, a country of 220 million people. Meanwhile, West Germany (the FRG), with its sixty-one million citizens, took home ten. Eight years on, at the winter games in Sarajevo, the GDR actually topped the medal table, winning a quarter of all the available prizes.

Huge doses of Oral-Turinabol, the testosterone-filled 'blue bean' developed by the state-owned pharmaceutical company VEB Jenapharm, were administered under Stasi supervision. Stories of the hideous physical and psychological damage it visited upon the country's teenage swimmers and gymnasts are legion, but no less horrific for it. They tell of liver damage, hirsuteness and infertility among the girls, of testicular cancer and of appalling emotional and corporal deformation. Particularly shocking was the testimony of Hans-Georg Aschenbach, a former ski-jumping champion. Doped from the age of sixteen, he claimed that the drugs, combined with the massive physical workload, saw to it that for every East German Olympic gold medallist there were 350 invalids.

---

* The Socialist Unity Party. The GDR was notionally a multi-party state, with SED leading a coalition. In reality, however, the four so-called 'Bloc Parties' had no power. Communist rule was written into the constitution, and only once did Parliament fail to rubberstamp the dictates of the Politburo. That was in 1972, an issue of conscience over abortion.

The man who oversaw the programme, code-named 'Stateplan 14.25', was a former Nazi named Manfred Ewald. As head of the hugely successful German Gymnastics and Sport Federation (DTSB) he was one of the first recipients of the Olympic Order, an honour he shared with Jesse Owens and Pope John Paul II. Two years later, GDR First Minister Erich Honecker was given one, as was the Romanian dictator Nicolae Ceauşescu. The latter was summarily executed for genocide in December 1989, while Honecker escaped to Chile. Ewald was convicted for the intentional bodily harm of twenty elite athletes, all of whom had been administered anabolic steroids without their knowledge. He was sentenced to twenty-two months. Suspended.

All of the above is a matter of public record, but what of East German cycling, a sport with a notoriously troubled relationship with doping? I'd always been intrigued by the subject, and I'd learned that bike racing had been extremely popular there, particularly in the 1950s and 1960s. At its vanguard was the mythical *Friedensfahrt*, the Peace Race. The so-called 'Tour de France of the East', it ran each May between Berlin, Warsaw and Prague, and by common consent had once been a much bigger event than the Tour. I wanted to understand just *how* big, and to gain an appreciation of its significance culturally, politically and socially. I'd heard from British participants about the vast crowds, but had no understanding of the quotidian reality for those for whom it was the highlight of the sporting calendar. Where did it sit within the GDR sporting milieu, and within that of the Eastern Bloc as a whole? Who were East Germany's cycling heroes, and how politicised were their lives? How much was controlled and orchestrated by the state, and to what degree did political conviction (or otherwise) materially condition cycling achievement? What was it like to be a bike racer in a supposedly tyrannous state, and how did the sport's practitioners fare at the hands of the Stasi?

Like many cycling people I was familiar with the story of Wolfgang Lötzsch. The most talented rider of his generation, he had earned selection for a 1972 Olympic training camp aged just nineteen. His father, however, had criticised the absence of a free press in the GDR, and Wolfgang failed to denounce him. In so doing, and in his refusal to join the party, he made himself an enemy of the state. For all his extravagant talent he would never represent his country, never travel to the west, never ride the Peace Race or the World Championships.

The problem for the dictatorship was that Lötzsch routinely trounced those who did, ridiculing the hypocrisy at its root. Wolfgang Lötzsch was easily the best rider in the GDR, but his career became an ideological *cause célèbre*. Support for him inferred opposition to the party, and as he won and won again so his 'fan base' grew. Simple bike rider or otherwise, he became synonymous with the 'passive resistance' movement, and so the Stasi declared all-out war on him.

Twelve full-time agents and fifty secret informants hounded him relentlessly, and eventually he cracked. In articulating his support for the dissident musician Wolf Biermann, he presented them with the pretext they needed. He served ten months in solitary confinement and, upon his release, had his racing licence revoked. He later agreed to conform but, licence back in hand, simply resumed hostilities. His life and career started to resemble a political chess match, albeit one played out in public. A part-time cyclist denied access to decent equipment and training facilities, he continued to humiliate the full-time, state-sponsored riders and their paymasters.

In 1979 he lined up with the elite of the national team at the Tour of Berlin. It was biggest single-day race in the GDR, and one of the few to be televised. Before a huge audience he rode away 150 kilometres from home, and soloed to victory. It was the apogee of his 'career', and the symbolism of it was lost on nobody. Lötzsch claimed to be apolitical, but being apolitical, or even ambivalent, wasn't remotely good enough in the GDR: either you were with socialism or you were against it. Therefore in winning a simple bicycle race, Lötzsch had rubbed their noses in it. From there on in his training would be curtailed further still, the chances of a repeat performance all but eradicated.

Wolfgang Lötzsch, though, was one of thousands of racers in the GDR. I therefore assumed that his case couldn't be representative of all GDR cyclists, and nor of sport there as a whole. Could it?

In 2012 I was working with Timm Kölln, a Berlin-based photographer. Travelling extensively through eastern Germany, we met former cyclists, journalists and officials. In addition, we mined the vaults at the Peace Race Museum, tucked away amidst the agricultural communities of Saxony-Anhalt. We did so in the hope of exhuming something of the GDR cycling landscape and, gradually but unequivocally, an extraordinary story revealed itself. It was ostensibly that of a two-week stage race, but it would inform all of GDR sport for the thick end of four decades.

As a child of the capitalist west I'd had no real understanding of the degree to which politics – *all* twentieth-century politics – directly influenced the careers of those who rode the Peace Race, and those who didn't. Equally, I had totally underestimated the sheer political resonance of GDR bike racing, particularly in the 1950s and 1960s. Nowhere, not even in Nazi Germany, has sport been so influential in shaping the way a society acted and thought.

From the outset, western politicians and diplomats viewed the GDR as an illegitimate pariah state, unlawfully created and propped up both militarily and politically by the USSR. Stalin, however, didn't much trouble himself with the platitudes of diplomacy. Rather, he charged his East Berlin serfs with the creation of a dynamic new country, and with persuading a population of 18.9 million to buy into it. Somehow they had to be convinced that they were stakeholders in a progressive new society, that they were fashioning an alternative to the imperialism which had decimated their continent.

The political rhetoric of the nascent GDR project was therefore characterised not only by stereotypical communist sloganeering, but also by a unique optimism. Through a huge propaganda machine the party set about convincing East Germans that they were building the model socialist state. As ever in these circumstances they fostered the idea of a common enemy – capitalism – and gave it a flesh and blood embodiment: Chancellor Konrad Adenauer and the Bonn government of the FRG. The rationale for so doing was manifest. In Leipzig, Dresden and East Berlin, ordinary Germans had suffered appalling, incalculable hardship as a direct consequence of Nazism. The party therefore sought to prove to them that the FRG remained a fascist rampart and a class enemy. If they could be convinced, it reasoned, they would be unburdened of moral, emotional and political responsibility for the war. That in turn would lead to national unity, and ultimately to the utopia of communism. Meanwhile, the opposition parties were systematically disembodied, the police and the judiciary neutered, religious institutions marginalised.

West German politicians lobbied for reunification. They also claimed that in the meantime theirs was the only legitimate Germany, that the GDR was simply a Soviet foil. The east ostensibly sought repatriation, too, but as a socialist state. Many believed it was entirely disingenuous, a pretext upon which to pin the supposed intransigence of the west. For all their diplomatic bluster it was never going to happen, but that really wasn't the point. The point was the successful creation and manipulation of East German (as distinct to German) sentiment. The party apparatchiks knew full well that the business at hand wasn't reconciliation at all, but, rather, quite the opposite. Their objective was the unification of *East*

Germans, and they'd achieve it first and foremost through the systematic portrayal of western politicians as implicitly corrupt, morally bankrupt. Through total media control – and many would say outright lies and obfuscation – they set about creating an entirely new German identity, to building the GDR.

◯

Against this political backdrop, the leaders of the Czech and Polish cycling federations sat down to discuss a complex problem in 1950. Two years earlier a coalition of sports journalists had conceived a cross-border bike race for national amateur teams. It would be run off between Warsaw and Prague, and would be organised and promoted by the respective party newspapers, *Trybuna Ludu** and *Rudé Právo*. Its genesis had lain in the idea of using sport to promote solidarity between two populations which had suffered immeasurable damage during the war, and which were now being rebuilt under communist dictatorships.

The event, circumventing Germany (the common enemy), had been inaugurated on 1 May 1948, International Workers' Day. It had finished, by design, eight days later on VE Day, and had immediately captured the public imagination. At the second edition, finishing in Warsaw, the great Czech rider Jan Veselý had triumphed, while Polish riders won two of the stages. Later that year Germany's division became permanent and the Soviet Occupation Zone became the GDR, ostensibly a communist ally.

Notwithstanding – or perhaps because of – its inherent nationalism, the event was rebranded 'The Peace Race'† in 1950, and assumed Picasso's white dove as its symbol. According to its precepts any nation, regardless of political orientation, creed, sporting prowess or wealth, would be at

---

* The first edition was organised by *Głos Ludu*.
† *Wyścig Pokoju* in Polish, *Závod Míru* in Czech.

liberty to send a team. The previous year a team of French communists had competed alongside their brethren from behind Churchill's 'Iron Curtain'. So, too, had a group from neutral Finland, and all had been generously received. Their presence hardly represented a groundswell of geopolitical goodwill, but it was a start. The Peace Race, unencumbered by the monetary inducements which compromised the integrity of professional sport, was simply an open invitation to come and ride. While the Tour de France and the Giro d'Italia were professional events constructed around commercial interest, this was something else entirely. It was cycling as a metaphor for community among all the world's peoples.

Except that at the cessation millions of ethnic Germans had remained in Poland and Czechoslovakia. The Sudetenland, for example, lay within the Czech border, but over three million German speakers had been resident there at the outbreak. Though the vast majority had never set foot in Germany itself, the Potsdam Conference of 1945 decreed that they be expelled. With no infrastructure and little or no practical governance, however, it would be a monumental task. In the meantime they were subject to horrific reprisals by the indigenous Slavic populations, made scapegoats for the atrocities committed in the name of the Fatherland. Raped and massacred and interned into concentration camps every bit as inhuman as those with which the Nazis had defiled the human condition, they were among the first victims of post-war ethnic cleansing.

In Poland, where German speakers were stripped of citizenship rights, an estimated 250,000 were interned. So barbaric were conditions that up to 60,000 are thought to have perished. The regimes, often run by local militia squads, were arbitrary and invariably gratuitous. No reliable statistics exist, but it's believed that in six post-war years from 1944, 10–12 million German speakers were displaced across Europe. Upwards of a million of them were simply lost, presumed killed. By 1950 their slaughter, allied to one of the biggest diasporas in twentieth-century history, had all but purged Poland and Czechoslovakia of German ethnicity.

For all that eighteen million of them were now apparently allies in the anti-imperialist war, Germans – all of them – remained an irreconcilable enemy in millions of Polish and Czech hearts and minds. When, therefore, it was announced that the GDR had issued a request to field a team at the 1950 Peace Race, it provoked outrage. Many found the idea abhorrent, but ultimately the ideals of the event (and by extension those of communism) were upheld; for the first time, the GDR sent a team of its own.

The GDR riders were well beaten, but it mattered not. The delicacy of the geopolitical situation meant that victory would in all probability have been counterproductive anyway, and besides the wider implications of having taken part outweighed issues around performance. In itself participation represented *de facto* acceptance of the country's legality, something its diplomats were ill-equipped to deliver. This was the Peace Race, and there was far more at stake than stage wins, hearts and flowers.

Neues Deutschland, the SED party newspaper, largely ignored the hostility of the Czech and Polish roadside public. Instead it seized upon the story of Otto Friesse, the team mechanic. The race began in Warsaw, but such was the shortage of resources – and this five years on from the cessation – that the team officials were obliged to share cars. The hosts were detailed, symbolically, to share with the Germans. And so it was that Friesse was given a driving tour of a city still pretty much in ruins, alongside the Polish mechanic.

They watched on as the local population toiled to rebuild its broken town, but the Pole was having none of it. Incandescent that he be obliged to spend ten days with the sworn enemy, he directly cross-referenced the devastation with Friesse himself. On and on he baited him, jabbing his finger and shouting, 'Nazis — you!'

At the conclusion of the stage a crestfallen Friesse informed the German delegation that he was packing his bags. He was no Nazi, he said, and nor was he in any way responsible for the destruction of Warsaw. He wasn't prepared to endure further harassment for a doctrine he too abhorred, for the accidents of his birth. Eventually, however, he was persuaded to stay (quite how was never made clear), and he saw out the race in the company of the Pole.

After the final stage Friesse is purported to have gone AWOL in Prague. Klaus Huhn, a twenty-two-year-old sports journalist working for *Neues Deutschland*, was dispatched to find him. Huhn searched long and hard, and eventually snared his man in the small hours. He was found, stociously drunk and having a high old time of it, in a bar with the Polish mechanic. As metaphors go it was just about perfect, and Huhn saw to it that the story was riveted hard into the East German psyche and cultural lexicon. The Peace Race had been as good as its word, and the Otto Friesse story became part of its warp and weft. Within two years Klaus Huhn would become sports editor of *Neues Deutschland*, and ultimately one of its chief ideologues.

Warsaw–Prague had delivered in ten days what the party functionaries and their Soviet paymasters had singularly been failing to achieve for years. Recognition of its status as a bona-fide sovereign nation would be pivotal in creating a new East German identity, and in engendering patriotism among a population bewildered by two decades of ideological brutality. That the beginnings of it had been conferred by a humble bike race (as distinct from some faceless diplomat) was lost on nobody, least of all the party itself. The notion that GDR athletes might become sporting ambassadors began to germinate in East Berlin. The idea, later branded 'diplomats in tracksuits', would inform the next manoeuvre in this rapidly escalating sporting cold war.

In 1951 a move of unprecedented brinkmanship saw the formation of a GDR National Olympic Committee (NOC). The objective, notionally at least, was to prepare a GDR team for the Helsinki games the following year, but there was much more to it than that. Two years earlier the IOC had welcomed the construction of an all-German NOC, one which didn't distinguish between athletes from Dresden and Düsseldorf. With post-war sanctions now lifted, Germany had been accepted back into the fold, another small step on the road to Central European equanimity. In moving to overthrow it, however, the GDR drew Adenauer's government further into ideological and diplomatic battle. They in turn resolved that Berlin be denied the chance to engender patriotism through sporting events, and set to persuading the IOC to outlaw its new 'neighbour'. Persuaded it duly was, and the existing agreement held; GDR athletes would be permitted to compete in Finland only as part of a united team. Their politicians refused even to contemplate the idea (so much for German unification), but the IOC told them to take it or leave it.

So that was that. In carrying the fight, the GDR had declared itself an opponent of the Olympic movement. All international sporting bodies under its auspices were notified accordingly, rendering Berlin a sporting heretic. It had upped the stakes, lost disastrously, and now its athletes found themselves out in the cold.

The Peace Race, however, was different. Conceived in the Soviet Bloc, it hadn't been sanctioned by the International Cycling Union (UCI), and therefore remained outside of the IOC's sphere of influence. Berlin applied to become an anchor city, and in 1952 Warsaw–Prague became Warsaw–Berlin–Prague. The perfect opportunity to disseminate East German unity, values and identity, it would be the first major international sporting event to be hosted on socialist German soil. In light of the IOC snub it would also be the best opportunity to generate serious political traction through sports.

Klaus Huhn would be installed as co-organiser of the four German stages. He would take the innate passion for cycling, harness it to his own ideological zeal and set about placing the race right at the heart of the East German sporting map.

Enthusiasm for the race was unprecedented, still more so because of the sanctions. As regards international sports it was just about the only show in town, and *Neues Deutschland* stoked it for all it was worth. In the event the best amateurs from Italy, Belgium and Holland were too good, and the GDR 'collective' was outmuscled once more. For the third Peace Race in succession the GDR failed to land even a stage, as the English (of all people) helped themselves to the team prize and, through Ian Steel, the yellow jersey.

Shortly afterwards FIFA, the governing body of world football, accepted the GDR into the fold, though it would be five years before a ball was kicked meaningfully. In the meantime the GDR played a slew of friendly matches with communist Poland (three times), Bulgaria (three) and Romania (four). Football's administrators had led their horses to water, but they were damned if they were about to share it with the class enemy. Moreover, the Peace Race was played out against a backdrop of continual westward migration. It was a dazzling festival of colour, speed and community, but it was at variance with the prevailing mood.

By 1953 some 700,000 – a catastrophic 4 per cent of the population – had already left, the GDR brain-drain a matter of everyday fact. From the outset it had been clear even to the party stalwarts that building communism would be tough. However, the haemorrhage, allied to ongoing war reparations to the Soviets and the totemic absence of inward investment, was having a profound effect. Those who defected were portrayed as ideologically decadent by the party, but the consumer goods and cars they bought in the west constituted handsome recompense.

They were declaring themselves satisfied with the benefits of materialism, while those left behind worked more and received less.

Ordinary East Germans very well understood that theirs was a Soviet satellite in all but name. They had been promised peace, and yet some 11 per cent of the country's budget was being spent on militarisation. A further 10 per cent went directly to Moscow in the form of reparations, while the 'sovietisation' of society saw farms and small businesses collectivised. With the emphasis placed on heavy industry, shops had nothing to sell. Food shortages ensued, and even basics like electricity were rationed. Communism, the antidote to imperialist land-grabbing and to genocide, required of them very real sacrifice. The price they were paying, much like tension on their factory floors, was high, but more depressing still was the growing feeling that they'd been conned. Denuded of self-determination, they'd become Stalin's marionettes. By the time the 'Gardener of human happiness' died in March, the seeds of popular disillusionment were bearing acrid fruit in East German soil. By the eve of the sixth Peace Race it was clear that something good needed to happen, and soon.

Stage eight would travel 226 hugely emblematic south-easterly kilometres. Rolling out of Berlin, it would conclude in the border town of Görlitz, on the River Neisse. During the war the city had been the site of the wretched Stalag VIII-A POW camp, where thousands of Poles and Russians had perished through malnutrition and dysentery. When its eastern borders had been redrawn at the cessation, however, Germany had lost all points east of the Neisse, 23.8 per cent of its pre-war territory. The right bank of the city was thus annexed to Poland, and renamed Zgorzelec. Those ethnic Germans who escaped with their lives were expelled, and replaced for the most part by Greek and Macedonian refugees. The figurative importance of the stage was therefore impossible to overstate. The Peace Race, the sporting embodiment of communism and the new Central European *realpolitik*, had been created explicitly to promote reconciliation. On VE Day 1953 it would unite a city – and its people – torn apart by fascism.

Denmark's Hans Andresen led the race from a team-mate, Christian Pedersen. The Danes also led the team event, while the GDR lay second. Meanwhile, one of them, young Gustav-Adolf 'Täve' Schur, stood third overall at 7'31". None of the above were present when a break of six went, but Bernhard Trefflich, a GDR racer with a very tidy sprint, made it on. Before a massive crowd in (of all places) Görlitz, Trefflich delivered a GDR stage win at long, long last.

East Germany finally had something to cheer about. Furthermore, the remaining stages saw the two Danes, hammer and tongs for the GC win, dump the rest of their colleagues. As such the combined efforts of Trefflich, Schur and Lothar Meister saw the GDR overtake them in the race for the team prize. The winner of the Peace Race wore yellow, just as he did at the Tour, but beyond that the culture and substance of the two events were as different as night and day. At the Peace Race the winning team wore a blue jersey, and its import was colossal. Not only did it signify primacy on the road, but also unity, shared purpose and self-sacrifice – the very best values of communism. Prior to the 1951 race there had been serious talk of abolishing the yellow jersey altogether. The notion was that its presence was a catalyst for individualism, anathema to the socialist sporting model.

The blue jersey, allied to Täve's engaging personality, fired the public imagination as never before. The hard cases of the party took note, and *Neues Deutschland* went into hyperbolic overdrive. An internal Sports Committee report deduced that 'Almost the entire population was under the spell of the Peace Race, and of the patriots fighting for the GDR … For the first time people were laying claim to ownership of the country, speaking of the GDR as *our* team …'

Nobody could have imagined the outpouring of national pride that ensued, but it would be short-lived. The following month work quotas were increased by 10 per cent. There would be increases in taxation, too, and those who failed to meet their quotas would simply have their salaries cut. Berlin's construction workers downed tools, and the strike escalated into an uprising on 17 June. Then Russian tanks rolled into the capital, Leipzig and Dresden, as innocents were slaughtered in scenes every bit as horrific as those which Budapest and Prague would subsequently witness.

These two events, the 17 June uprising and the Peace Race, would significantly shape the lives of generations of East Germans. When the dust settled the latter had proved itself, once more, infinitely more effective in creating social ballast than ideology. While people had had a gutful of politics and politicians, they couldn't get nearly enough of sport. The questions, therefore, were essentially two: how best to make more of it, and how best to capitalise on it?

Socialist canon made little distinction between work and free time. It was the responsibility of all citizens to create communism, wherever they were and whatever the context. Unlike in bourgeois capitalist societies, 'leisure' wasn't regarded as an autonomous entity, but as a contributory element to the whole. The party was of the opinion that 'Everyone, everywhere, should play sports', but the significance of organised sporting activities extended beyond simple physical wellbeing.

Under communism viewing sport wasn't a passive, pejorative exercise, and wasn't limited simply to individual spectatorship. Instead it involved participatory activities, and social responsibility at communal level. When, therefore, the Peace Race travelled through East German towns and villages, the local populations were expected to mobilise around its appearance. Schools would organise events weeks in advance, their syllabuses reconfigured in anticipation. Pupils would learn not only about the riders and tactics, but also the inherent symbolism of 100 disparate cyclists coming together from around the globe. Teachers were expected to articulate the communist context in which it was set, and to teach their children that only through socialism could it be possible. Favourable comparison would be made with the Tour de France, a race conceived purely as a commercial entity and disfigured by sponsorship and professionalism.

The Peace Race was a perfect vehicle for cultivating both patriotism and social control. Schools and factories piped radio broadcasts of the race around their buildings, and took pride in contributing prizes for the cyclists. On the day of their stage entire towns and villages would engage, pupils and workers bussed to the roadside to form part of the spectacle. Everybody felt an obligation to attend, because to do otherwise was perceived as an abrogation of civic responsibility. Community leaders would will their constituents into formation in the hope of creating the most colourful show of support. Though doubtless people were corralled into being involved, the race quickly became synonymous with fun, togetherness and civic pride. Whole communities were mobilised, the event the undoubted highlight of the sporting calendar. Not for nothing was the *Friedensfahrt* known as 'the Race of Millions'.

Previously the global sporting community had wanted nothing to do with the GDR, but the Peace Race was becoming a catalyst for international recognition. So big had the event become that sixteen national teams took to the start in 1954. The UCI president, Achille Joinard, was invited to attend, and pronounced himself amazed by the ambition. Claiming that he'd never seen cyclists so well taken care of, he welcomed it enthusiastically into the fold. Only the Tour, he added, was comparable as regards pure spectacle, and even there only eight nations were represented. Furthermore nowhere had the sport – or for that matter *any* sport – aspired to such high moral principle.

The GDR wouldn't compete at the 1954 football World Cup, held in Switzerland. The West Germans, on the other hand, reached the final. They were huge underdogs against the all-conquering Hungarians, but somehow they won. The so-called 'Miracle of Bern', like the success of their estranged cousins at the Peace Race, was highly instrumental in creating the *idea* of nation. *Neues Deutschland* predictably (and shamefully) peddled the idea that theirs was a victory for fascism, but it made the Federal Republic of Germany a cultural and emotional reality for millions. By the autumn of 1955 the FRG had joined NATO, the GDR the Warsaw Pact. Whether the great unwashed liked it or not, 'Germany' was receding further into the distant past.

International sporting competitions were unequivocal, straightforward and absolute, and they were becoming authentic geopolitical battlegrounds. The party recognised the correlation between sporting success and political opportunity, and in that sense the 1955 Peace Race was a godsend. Täve Schur won it for the GDR, sealing emphatic victory before 100,000 Poles in Warsaw. That he became the most popular sportsman in GDR history is irrefutable. The best amateur cyclist in the world, he'd add another Peace Race four years later, in addition to successive World Championships. Nine times in succession he was voted his country's sportsman of the year, but the Täve phenomenon (and I use the word advisedly) could never be measured simply by the bike races he won.

For all that we construct myths around them, the likes of Fausto Coppi and Eddy Merckx were, when all is said and done, simply very famous cyclists. Though largely unknown in the west, Täve Schur was something else entirely. In winning that first Peace Race he became a pin-up boy not just for an entire population, but for the state itself. A committed, card-carrying communist, he was the perfect mascot for a unique socio-political experiment, the construction of the model socialist proletariat. They named a planet in his honour, wrote countless best-selling biographies, venerated his name and all that he stood for. Every May hundreds of thousands of German children would belt out his name as one. Täve was Karl Marx and Gino Bartali, Elvis Presley and Roy Rogers. Heart-throb and philosopher, diplomat and prole, he was all things to all men, the very personification of the *neue Mensch*. He was, quite simply, political gold dust; the living, breathing synthesis of socialism's great victory. The proof is to be found at the Peace Race Museum, where they retain several thousand letters sent to him by a gushing public. A great many of them come from German womanhood. Some are really quite wanton (at least by the standards of the puritanical GDR in the 1950s), and most constitute marriage proposals.

Nowhere in the world was sport more politicised than in the GDR, and Täve's ideological conviction and engaging character were among the most potent propaganda tools at the party's disposal. His victories belonged to everyone: to the farmers and factory workers, to the teachers and their children, to doctors, mothers and labourers. Above all they belonged to and were forged by revolutionary socialism, and both he and the party delighted in articulating the fact. While dictatorships of all hues have traditionally used outstanding sportsmen as political blunt instruments, none were exploited more effectively than Täve.

The winner of the 1956 Peace Race, Warsaw's Stanisław Królak, became a lifelong hero for allegedly having walloped a Russian rider with his bike pump. Unsubstantiated legend has it that the Russian riders were throwing their weight around in general, and threatening one of the Polish team in particular. Królak therefore defended his colleague (ergo Polish honour) with the only weapon at his disposal, his pump. All of Warsaw proclaimed his win, and the humble bike pump became *the* symbol of the Peace Race in Poland.

That the story of the pump has zero basis in fact is indicative of just how important the Peace Race was, and how persuasive its legend would remain. Królak was adamant that he never hit the guy, but his denials fell on deaf ears. The Polish public so *wanted* to believe that he'd stood up to the occupying force that he gave up arguing in the end.

Stanisław Królak would become a fabled figure in Polish sporting lore, but his yellow jersey, like the blue one of the 1953 GDR team, was also a major political happening. His triumphant return to Warsaw brought them out in their multitudes and, just as significantly, contributed to the groundswell of anti-Moscow sentiment already being fermented. Bolesław Bierut, Poland's 'Little Stalin', had died two months earlier, and the battle to succeed him was raging. The proletariat wanted the moderate Władisław Gomułka installed, but the party apparatchiks favoured a hard-line Stalinist named Edward Ochab. The country was headed towards tipping point, and Królak and his pump were a major contributory factor in what would follow. The Poznań uprising of 28–30 June allegedly cost the lives of more than a hundred Polish civilians, among them a thirteen-year-old boy named Romek Strzałkowski. Russian tanks smashed the revolution, and an atrocious twenty-five-year media embargo saw to it that the massacre was largely forgotten in the west. However, Stanisław Królak's name, like that of poor Romek Strzałkowski, became furniture in his countrymen's headspace. Later that autumn the Budapest uprising was similarly crushed, and five years later the Berlin Wall hermetically sealed the fate of millions of Central and Eastern Europeans.

The year 1972 saw Vlastimil Moravec win arguably the greatest, most emblematic Peace Race of all. With Czech hearts broken by the Prague Spring, he traded the yellow jersey four times with the Soviet Władisław Neljubin. Finally, aided by a coalition of the willing – and by the team-mate who brought Neljubin off as he sprinted for a prime which would likely have won him the race – he prevailed by just two seconds. The average speed of that Peace Race was 42.6kph. Meanwhile Eddy Merckx, crushing all comers at a turgid Giro, did so at 36.1kph. Cycling people are for ever invoking the great battles between him and Gimondi, Coppi and Bartali, Anquetil and Poulidor. However, as regards drama, malevolence and pure sporting theatre, nothing the west ever witnessed came remotely close.

As Moscow arm-wrestled Washington and subjugated Prague and Warsaw, and as Berlin squabbled with Bonn, the Peace Race, too, began to accumulate masses of geopolitical baggage. Though conceived in the spirit of détente, it had been predicated upon and rooted in the ideological battlegrounds of Central Europe. As such it evolved into their perfect sporting metaphor: a sporting cold war within the Cold War. A beautiful, utopian idea, it was no more than a mirror on the maelstrom which had created it, and which inevitably contaminated it. How, given the unique context in which it was set, could it be otherwise?

Though cycling's popularity would wax and wane over the decades, it's undeniable that the Peace Race was a towering sporting edifice. Further, the bike-racing culture which created great post-communism roadmen like Jan Ulrich, Eric Zabel and Tony Martin has its roots not in the reasoned, centralist unified Germany of the twenty-first century. Their successes, and those of dozens like them, were conceived in a very different time, in a very different country. They were made, emphatically and unequivocally, in the German Democratic Republic.

That, at least, was the bones of it. Or so it seemed.

In scanning the runners and riders of the 1964 Peace Race I stumbled across a familiar looking name. I had an idea I'd seen Dieter Wiedemann elsewhere, and so it was. Wiedemann, it transpired, was not only Wolfgang Lötzsch's cousin, but had ridden the 1967 Tour de France. He'd been supporting Hennes Junkermann, an outstanding stage racer from the Rhineland, and had been present when Tom Simpson rode himself to death on Mont Ventoux.

But the Tour, very obviously, had taken place on the other side of the Berlin Wall. It had been a national event, and Dieter Wiedemann had ridden it for the Federal Republic of Germany. He'd ridden it for capitalism and that, given that he was from the east, was a technical, practical and administrative impossibility. We set to trying to find him, and to finding out how he'd done it.

Eventually we tracked him down in a small village in northern Bavaria. In the first instance he told us that he doesn't speak to journalists about it. He said that he never has done and that, almost fifty years on, he wasn't about to start. This explained why there is virtually no information about him online, and nor, for that matter, in print. It also implied that he must have had a very great deal to talk *about*, and so I persevered. Eventually, after several phone calls and a great deal of back and forth in the Wiedemann family, Dieter agreed to meet me.

This is what happened next.

THE RACE
AGAINST
THE STASI

DIETER

You ask why, now, after fifty years?

My story is unusual and quite complicated. I wasn't prepared for it to be distilled down to a column in a tabloid newspaper or a page in a cycling magazine, because that would be to misrepresent what actually happened. The important thing for me is that we do it in its entirety, and that partly explains why I've never spoken about it before. I'll tell you the story, but I'm not interested in telling half of it.

When the Wall came down I thought about it quite a lot. The Stasi file was there in Berlin, available to view, but ultimately I decided it was best left behind. Sylvia and I reasoned that opening it could only cause more pain, and we'd had more than enough pain. I couldn't change what was in there, so we decided that no good could come of it.

So we got on with our lives, but then out of the blue you came along and said you wanted to do this book. We spoke about it as a family, and we came to the conclusion that it's time. The world is different now, and the context is different.

My problem is that I'm seventy-three years old, and I still don't know my history. I know a version of my life, but I also know that there's probably another one in a filing cabinet in Berlin. So in a sense the Stasi created another Dieter Wiedemann, and he and I existed in parallel. We knew the same people and places, and the truth of it is that I've never really been free of him. He's been shadowing me for over fifty years, and until I know his story I can never fully understand my own. Life goes on, yes, but if I'm honest you never truly leave it behind. You don't so much carry it around with you as it becomes part of who you are.

Regarding the file I have no idea what we'll find or who we'll find. I have an idea about what might be in there, and that one person in particular that I was very close to was informing on me. Equally I've no doubt that a lot of the people who passed through my life back then were Stasi. The law of averages suggests it can't realistically be otherwise, simply because of my circumstances. Again I have my suspicions about who, but until we see the file we won't know.

So the best thing is that we make a start. We'll tell you about our lives as we lived them back then, and when we finish we'll go to Berlin. We'll get the file and find out about my other life, the one I wasn't privy to.

THE FIRST LIFE OF
DIETER WIEDEMANN
(and the Fourth)

All I know is that my paternal grandparents came from Czechoslovakia. They were from Carlsbad, in the Sudetenland, but they were deported at the end of the war. All the ethnically German people were expelled from Czechoslovakia, so there were millions of homeless people roaming around. You hear terrible stories about families walking for hundreds of kilometres through the winter, killing squads, people starving to death and suchlike. I really don't know what happened to mine, though, because all the information from that time is lost.

What I do know is that they made their way to a town called Giessen, fifty kilometres north of Frankfurt. There was a big textile industry there, and my grandfather was a tailor. So it could be that somebody told my grandfather that it would be a good place for him to find work, but I really can't be sure.

Their son – my father – was called Peter Hermann. He was twenty-four when the war ended, but he didn't go as far north as Giessen. He stopped just across the Czech/German border, in a small town in Bavaria. The place is called Mitterteich, and as I understand it a lot of refugees stayed around there. I guess they were hoping they'd be allowed to go home, and they probably felt safer there because it was in the American Zone.

Anyway, that's where he met my mum. Her name was Ilse Potthast and she was a war widow. She'd married a guy from Cologne, but then he'd gone to the front and hadn't come home. When he was killed she'd been alone, so she'd gone back to Mitterteich to be with her family again.

During the war Cologne had been heavily bombed, and apparently my mum had been badly traumatised by it. They told her she'd never be able to have children, so I think that when she came home she just wanted to enjoy herself a little bit. I think she and my dad had some fun together, because she was much older than him. She was thirty and he was twenty-five, and I think it was a bit of a shock when I came along. I was born on 4 June 1946. It's an easy date to remember: 4-6-4-6.

The following May I got a little brother, and his name was Roland. One of my earliest memories is of being a bridesmaid, carrying my mum's veil. As far as I know she hadn't really wanted to marry, but if you had kids back then you had to. They didn't let unmarried couples rent, so it was the only way to get a place to live.

So I don't know much, but I know that I grew up in Mitterteich, with Roland and with my mum and dad. I also know that my destiny was written in Giessen, but I'll explain why later on.

DIETER

My mum was called Marianne Lang and my dad was called Karl Wiedemann. She was twenty-eight when I was born, but he was thirty-seven. My mum worked as a machinist in a textile factory, and my dad did coachworks.

I was born on 17 June 1941, in Flöha, a town of about 12,000 people near Chemnitz. We lived in a tiny two-roomed flat. We cooked, ate and washed in the kitchen, and we lived and slept in the other room. There were four families living in our building, and we shared two toilets. We had electricity and running water, but it wasn't hot water. It was the post-war GDR, so it was a very basic existence.

When I was four my brother was born, and his name was Eberhard. The flat was just too small then, and eventually they gave us a new one on Rudolf-Breitscheid-Strasse.* It still didn't have hot water, but it had a bedroom. We had a radio, but there was no TV back then. I was given one of those much later on.

One of the more vivid memories I have is of the whole class going out to the fields to collect Colorado beetles on my birthday. They told us that the Americans had dropped them because they wanted to destroy our crops so that we'd starve. There were no pesticides, so we picked the beetles off by hand. When we'd picked them off the potatoes we would put them in jars. We thought it was great.

---

* Rudolf Breitscheid was a social democrat politician and German patriot. He fled to France when Hitler came to power, but was interned first at Sachsenhausen and later at Buchenwald. He perished at Buchenwald in 1944, many believe murdered by an SS guard. The Nazis claimed he had died in a bombing raid.

NEUES DEUTSCHLAND
ORGAN DES ZENTRALKOMITEES DER SOZIALISTISCHEN EINHEITSPARTEI DEUTSCHLANDS

In the villages of Ahlbeck, Heringsdorf, Seabad Bansin, Zinnowitz, Zempin and Kölpin, Colorado potato beetles have recently been found washed up on the beach. Since the beetle is unable to survive in water, they could only have been dropped on to the coastal region overlooking the sea.

The discovery of potato beetles on the coast of the district of Usedom provides further proof, for those who have yet to recognise the common methods of the Anglo-American warmongers, of the enormity of their crime. The motives driving the US imperialists are not hard to recognise.

With the support of the Soviet Union and the people's democracies, the GDR has rebuilt from the chaos of 1945 on its own, and thereby obtained independence. The rapid upward trend in the economy, and increasing prosperity in the republic, has convinced more and more of the West German population that the path we are treading is the correct one. Thus the concept of the Anglo-American warmongers is thoroughly spoiled, and so they try to disrupt the forces of peace by resorting to the most reprehensible means. The gangsters will not achieve their objective.

Many hands clamour to take part in the fight against the 'Americabeetle', as the population has taken to calling it. Were it not for the American crime, they'd be free to perform other tasks. Moreover the 14.5 million marks which the government used to introduce measures against the Americabeetle could be used to benefit us, for kindergartens and recreation centres.

Reprinted from 'Crimes committed in the fear of peace', 17 June 1950

SYLVIA

At the beginning there was nothing to buy, and it was just a question of survival. It was a battle to put food on the table, but as I grew up it got better. My dad always said we had been lucky to be in the American Zone,* not the Russian one. The Americans had a big military base about forty kilometres away, at Grafenwöhr.

The American soldiers used to have huge cars ... Chevrolets I think they called them. Then sometimes they would drive through town in their jeeps. We'd run along after them and they'd throw chocolate and chewing gum to us. They'd laugh at us because they thought we were funny, and we would be laughing as well.

They had things we'd never seen before. There was cheddar cheese, hot-dog sausages in cans, ketchup ... We'd heard about ketchup before, but we'd never seen it. You could spread it on your bread and butter with sugar, and it was made by Heinz. We thought that was just fantastic, you know?

The American soldiers were much more handsome. They were always smiling, and their uniforms were much nicer than the German ones. Their kids always had the best clothes, and when we saw them sitting in the car with their parents we thought they looked perfect, like perfect little dolls.

Our neighbours had a daughter the same age as me, and we used to pretend we were the wives of American officers. They sounded funny, and we used to try to copy their accents.

---

* None of the four powers came remotely close to satisfying the specified 2,000 daily calories in post-war Germany. The American Zone came closest, at 1,330 calories, the Russians next, at 1,083. In the British Zone the average was 1,050, while adults in the French Zone were surviving – or not – on just 900 calories a day. The figures are illusory in the sense that the Russian Zone was largely agrarian, while the British Zone, for example, encompassed the crippled industrial heartlands of the Rhine and Ruhr. Devastated France, its own population subject to chronic shortages, struggled to reconcile the idea that it might be obliged to send aid to Germany.

DIETER

We were lucky because my father had inherited a smallholding. He grew fruit and vegetables in it, kept chickens and bred angora rabbits. My mum would sell or trade the eggs and wool. It may sound ridiculous today, but those rabbits were vital to our wellbeing.

There was rationing, and that created a barter economy. People would buy things they didn't need and use them to bargain for things they did. You mostly traded food with other families. So for example my mum might swap our salad for eggs, and then we had things like strawberries and raspberries. Things like that – the things you couldn't get in the shops – were quite valuable, so my mum used to do well out of them. Fruit was very scarce, and so was meat. That was the thing with the smallholding, and with the rabbits. It was because of them that we never went hungry. I knew a lot of kids who did, though.

So in answer to your question, yes, I think I had a settled childhood. We were quite a happy family, I enjoyed school and my grades were generally decent. We didn't really have anything, but that didn't matter because neither did anyone else.

SYLVIA

My dad's hobby was drumming, and he'd go off and play for the American soldiers in the officers' mess. He was also a sort of entrepreneur, which you had to be to make ends meet. He traded in coffee, and he combined that with the music. So he was always wheeling and dealing, and I guess that one way or another he was around clubs quite a lot.

My mum was a hairdresser, so she was on her feet all week. By the weekend she tended to be quite tired, and she wasn't much for staying out dancing. My dad was, though. They'd go out on a Saturday night, and she'd have to beg him to come home at a reasonable hour.

My grandparents didn't have a particularly good relationship with him. He wasn't the son-in-law they'd hoped for, but I was just a child and I didn't understand any of that. I got on well with him and we had fun together. On a Sunday afternoon we'd go to the café to dance. I'd dance with my little brother, and we used to make out that he was taking care of me.

So I think I had a good childhood, yes. I was happy at school and at home, and life was full of fun. I guess that was just my nature.

DIETER

I loved sport, and the two most popular sports were football and cycling. There was always a great bike-racing tradition around Chemnitz, and always lots of big champions. Twice a year they would hold a big evening criterium, and 30,000 would turn out to watch. All the best riders would be there, and they were heroes.

DIETER

Everybody followed the bike races, and the biggest of all was the Peace Race. It was a two-week stage race and it always started at the beginning of May. It ran between Berlin, Warsaw and Prague, and the route would be rotated annually. So one year it would start in Poland, the next Czechoslovakia, and then the GDR. It crossed the three borders, and that was the whole point of it. It was all about disseminating the message of peace, and demonstrating that through socialism different states could live side by side in harmony. In that sense it was much more important than a traditional bike race.

It had started in 1948. After the war there were tensions between Warsaw and Prague about how to manage their German populations. A group of sports journalists sat down and talked about how sport could help to resolve the problems. The idea had been to organise a boxing tournament, but blokes hitting each other didn't really work as a symbol of peaceful co-existence. Then somebody suggested a bike race linking the two capitals. They'd both been devastated by the war, but now the cyclists would act as couriers, delivering the message of peace. It was a beautiful idea.

That first year there were two races running simultaneously, Warsaw to Prague and vice versa. They started on International Workers' Day and they invited teams from other socialist countries as well. So Bulgaria, Romania, Hungary and Yugoslavia all took part. So what had started out as an idea to build bridges between the Poles and the Czechs was extended to all the countries of the Soviet Bloc.

The Peace Race riders were heroes to all the boys in my school, and the biggest hero of all was Täve Schur, our great champion.

TÄVE

I used to ride a bike, and I really enjoyed it. Then I learned about this race which went from Warsaw to Prague. I was fascinated by it, by the fact that they could ride so far and that a bike race could cross international borders. So in 1949 I started to enter races around Magdeburg, just on a regular bike. People started telling me I was good, and that I ought to get a racing bike. I'd say, 'But how am I going to be able to afford one of those?' You couldn't work more and get more, so I thought about it seriously and realised that if I saved I might be able to build one over time.

In 1950 the organisers renamed it the 'Peace Race', and it adopted Picasso's white dove as its emblem. The leader's jersey carried it as its symbol, and I remember thinking that was a beautiful idea. The basic tenet was that it didn't distinguish according to ideology, creed or religion, and that Europeans had to set history aside and find ways to forgive.

DIETER

The GDR Cycling Federation wasn't in the UCI, so they asked the organising committee if they could send a team. I'm not sure how popular that was in Poland and Czechoslovakia, but whether they liked it or not the GDR people were their comrades now. The event was about showcasing the humanistic values of communism to the entire world, and tolerance was at the heart of that. The English sent a team as well, and that was very significant.[*]

KLAUS

It was a Polish journalist who first had the balls to invite the GDR team to Prague–Warsaw. Prior to that Germans hadn't been welcome, and millions of Poles were saying they didn't want Germans there. It was a big problem for them, but this guy said, 'No! We have to make a start.'

When we were in Katowice there was a gala dinner. Somebody came up to me and said, 'Please Klaus, you have to leave the table immediately. Just go!' I didn't understand why, but I did as I was asked and went outside. Afterwards they came out and explained what had happened. There was a very well-known Polish actress there, who had survived Auschwitz. She had sworn never to sit at the same table as a German. If she had heard that I was German she'd have said, 'Either he goes or I go.'

That was what we were up against.

DIETER

In 1952 they announced that the Peace Race was coming to the GDR, and that from here on in it would be Warsaw–Berlin–Prague. They said there would be a stage finish in Chemnitz, and the following day the

---

[*] The English teams' involvement was used to underscore the inclusive nature of the race. The subtext was that, notwithstanding the intransigence of their capitalist governments, enlightened western athletes understood that communism was winning the argument.

race would actually pass through Flöha. Everybody was really looking forward to it, and I think that the anticipation of it coming is one of my first real cycling memories.

It fascinated me, just as it fascinated everybody else. At school we'd make prizes for the competitors, and have lessons about the countries they came from. Factories would contribute things as well, because everyone was expected to show their respect and solidarity for the riders. The GDR riders were superstars, real heroes. They were portrayed as shining examples of sportsmanship, and of understanding between different peoples.

The thing to bear in mind is that it was the first big international sporting event to be hosted in the GDR. So the reason that people were so passionate about it was linked to the popularity of cycling, but also to the fact that they were no longer pariahs. The Peace Race conferred legitimacy on the GDR as a state, and I suppose it made us feel like we belonged.

The race was jointly organised by the communist party newspapers in each country, and for us that was *Neues Deutschland*. They used it to disseminate the message that they were peaceful countries, that only socialism could deliver that peace, but that Bonn and Washington were intent on undermining it.

They wanted to demonstrate that the GDR people and government totally rejected capitalism, and were blameless for what the Nazis had done. The old Germany had been responsible for the war, and the people and values which had created fascism were still prevalent in the west. So in that sense it was paradoxical. It *was* a race about peace, but also about war. There was a new enemy now, NATO, and a new struggle. There was a propaganda war to be won, and to do that they needed powerful slogans.

People referred to it as the 'Tour de France of the East', and I suppose there were practical similarities. The Peace Race was much more important than the Tour to the local populations, though obviously the Tour was much bigger internationally.

There was nothing with the altitude or romance of the Alps and Pyrenees, but then again the race took place in Central Europe at the beginning of May. It crossed the Ore Mountains on the Czech/German border, and sometimes the Harz as well. You never knew what the weather would be like, and sometimes it would be absolutely atrocious, sub-zero. A lot of the roads were cobbled, and many of them were still in really poor condition. So you'd see higher instances of punctures and mechanical failures, and that made the racing really difficult to predict. Invariably it was a real battle, and it wasn't as tactical as professional racing in the west.

The main difference was that there was no professional sport in socialist countries, so it was an amateur event. Then it lasted two weeks as opposed to three, and the stages themselves tended to be shorter. Everyone was invited, and the general idea was that young people from each of the continents would ride in fellowship. You had the greatest champions from the three host countries riding alongside genuine amateurs from places like Finland and Albania. Some of them were absolutely hopeless, to be honest, and they'd lose hours on almost every stage. It didn't matter, though, because unlike the Tour there was no time limit.

DIETER

Anyway, the stage to Chemnitz took place on VE Day. It was a national holiday and so the crowds were huge, but it's most famous because it was the first time the race went up the 'Steep Wall of Meerane'. It was a wide, straight, cobbled hill of 340 metres, with an 11 per cent gradient. Thousands of people gathered there because you could see them approaching, and you could watch them ride pretty much all the way to the top. Meerane always blew the race to bits, and it became the most emblematic climb in the history of the Peace Race.

I suppose technically you could liken it to the Koppenberg or the Mur de Grammont, the big climbs in the Tour of Flanders. Bear in mind that they didn't have the bikes for climbs like that back then, and they certainly didn't have the gears. So the first challenge was just to get over it, and that was extremely hard for the genuine amateurs. Then you always had vast crowds, so psychologically it was a key moment. It became a symbol of the Peace Race in the same way the Stelvio was for the Giro, or Galibier for the Tour. Ask just about anybody from the GDR about the Peace Race and there are two things they will remember: the theme music and the Steep Wall of Meerane.

Jan Veselý had the jersey the day the race came to Chemnitz. There was a split in the peloton, though, and the English had three riders in the breakaway. Ian Steel* took the yellow jersey, and all the big favourites lost ten minutes. Steel kept the jersey all the way to Prague and the English won the team prize. They may have been just amateurs at home, but they were *extremely* famous in the GDR. In fact, Ian Steel was a household name.

---

* Though he was competing for England, Steel was actually a Glaswegian. Team-mate Ian Greenfield came from Edinburgh, while Bev Wood, Ken Jowett, Les Scales and Frank Seal were all from south of the border.

At the beginning of the stage the 'English' were already in possession of the blue jersey, their lead over seventeen minutes. Meanwhile, Steel began the day sixth, six minutes behind Veselý. The race-winning break comprised six riders, among them Steel, Greenfield and Jowett. Given that the first three riders qualified for the team classification on each stage, their lead grew to an unassailable forty-six minutes. Steel's advantage in the yellow jersey contest was only 1'42", but he came through the brutal Czech stages unscathed. By the finish he led runner-up Veselý by 2'35". The Scot never won a stage, but through his humility and outstanding sportsmanship became a Peace Race icon.

Jan Veselý was one of the greatest champions in the history of the race. He'd triumphed in 1949, and would win sixteen stages throughout his career. Though apolitical, his status at home was akin to that of Schur, at least among the populace. In 1957 he was selected to ride the tenth-anniversary Peace Race, despite having been ill in the run-up. He abandoned and was subsequently banned for two years by his own federation. They viewed the abandon as a form of treason, and Veselý, notwithstanding his huge popularity, was never invited to work for the federation.

Jan Stablinski, later World Professional Champion, was third. Like many French cyclists he was the son of émigré Polish parents, and was here competing for the 'Polish France' team. All told, ninety-four took part, among them teams from Trieste and Finland.

IAN

We were just six young British cyclists, and we had no understanding whatsoever of what we were getting into. None of us had ever flown before, so the idea of travelling to Warsaw and riding a stage race across Europe was magical.

We went to a big gala reception before the race, and that's where it dawned on us. All the Eastern Bloc teams were immaculately turned out. They were all in blazers and ties, but we were pretty much in our civvies. We looked like a bunch of tail-end Charlies.

I'd say that I have three abiding memories of the Peace Race. The thing that most struck us all was the fellowship between the riders. I rode the Tour and the Vuelta later on, but they were totally different. At the Peace Race you were competing against one another, but it was implicit that you also looked out for one another. There was no doping as far as I know, and there was a real sense of community and sportsmanship.

Then the amount of spectators; there seemed to be seas of people everywhere. I never saw anything like it in cycling, or in any other sporting event. I'd been used to riding amateur races in Britain, and as often as not there was nobody watching. People back home had not the slightest understanding of how big a race this was, and there were no British cycling journalists there to inform them. The only media was a guy from the *Socialist Worker*, the communist party newspaper.

Above all I remember Warsaw. It was seven years on from the war but most of it was still in ruins. Britain had never been invaded, so we'd had no perception whatsoever of the degree of devastation. It was almost total, and I think we were all genuinely shocked by what we saw there. They were at pains to show us what the Nazis had done, but also to demonstrate how they were building a new future. They took us to see a brand new cinema built entirely from rubble, and they were immensely proud of that.

So we hadn't imagined the sheer scale of it, but we soon realised how much it meant to the communist bloc teams. We had the best of every-thing, but at the same time there was also this terrible hardship. As I said, people in the west had absolutely no idea.

FRANK

We flew to Copenhagen, and then on to Warsaw. We were met off the plane by a great phalanx of people, given flowers, treated like kings. Then there was an armoured escort through Warsaw, and a very grand civic reception in a hotel. We all felt a bit out of place in our bomber jackets, but, we joined the queue to meet Marshal Rokossovsky, the Commander of the Soviet forces in Poland. The protocol was that he stood behind a desk, and when it was your turn you'd salute him. Then he'd knock back his Vodka, and off you went. He must have been pretty sloshed by the end, because there were sixteen teams!

Our problem was that we couldn't work out what you were supposed to say. They just seemed to bark something, then he'd knock the vodka back. Anyway Les Scales chirped up in his cockney accent. He said, 'Let's say "bollocks"', and so that's what we did. We said 'bollocks', with military precision, to the most dangerous man in Poland.

The opening ceremony was about the most impressive thing I've ever seen. The stadium was huge, and it was full of people. There were gymnastic displays, marching bands, flags … Then you had huge banners with Stalin on them, and the Polish guy, Bierut.* Everywhere we went in Poland he was there, and everywhere we went in Czechoslovakia there was another guy. Anyway, the ceremony seemed to go on for hours, and

---

* The communist director Joris Ivens produced a 45-minute documentary about the 1952 race. A Dutchman then based in Poland, his work has been likened to that of Leni Riefenstahl, Hitler's celebrated filmmaker. Certainly it bears many of the totali-tarian leitmotifs which characterised her output, and much of its imagery is extraor-dinarily beautiful. Ultimately though, the whole thing is a crass propaganda exercise. It vilifies the "fascist" west whilst likening Soviet work practices to those of the noble bike riders.

then suddenly they released 1,000 white doves and we were off. It was all a bit much to take in, to be honest. I was twenty-three years old and I'd been working as a plumber. I'd got a job in a bike shop so as I could get a bit more time off, and here I was being treated like a superstar!

The roads were long and straight, and as often as not they were lousy. They were usually brick, laid in a herringbone design. We'd come from the sedate world of British cycling, so we were a bit naïve. There was no quarter, and you'd to fight like hell for a wheel. Then there were echelons all over the road, and we'd never experienced them before. We learned very quickly that we had to race aggressively.

I seem to remember that there were always thousands of miners, their faces black with coal dust. One minute you'd be riding past these huge steelworks, or brickworks or whatever, and the next thing you'd be in the middle of nowhere on these pan-flat country roads.

FRANK

It was a huge shock to the Eastern Europeans that we won it. We didn't get any money, but there were prizes galore. Each team car had a two- to three-tonne truck with a wooden crate on top, and that was where they kept the prizes we'd won. I remember that everyone got a Carl Zeiss camera, and then there were radios, briefcases, crystal, you name it. We even won some sort of outboard motor, though I haven't the faintest idea why, even to this day. It was reported that Ian was going to get a car, and that we'd be getting a Jawa motorbike each for having won the blue jersey. That never materialised, though.

When we were in Prague there was this strange climate. There was a bloke working at the hotel who'd been in Edinburgh before the war. He was a real nice chap but he was really sheepish when he spoke with us, like he was always watching his back. We found out later that he'd been hauled in for interrogation. People were really friendly but they'd say,

'Things are terrible here. You're always being watched and you can be arrested just for talking to the wrong person.'*

---

* Stalin sought to make an example of Czechoslovakia, and as such terror reigned in early-1950s Prague. The infamous Slánský trials had seen eleven high-ranking party members executed the previous winter, all but two of them Jews. The Soviets were entreating the Arab states to adopt communism, so being seen to purge the party of so-called "Zionist" elements was a very useful construct. The Soviets understood that Anti-Semitism, in principle the very antithesis of the communist doctrine, remained a potent geopolitical tool.

MfS4458/69 BSTU0021

Chemnitz, 21.11.52

Chemnitz Area Command
Department VII
Re: Recruitment of People's Police Inspector
Lorenz, Carly, domiciled at (?), Chemnitz.

Application Report

At around 12.30 on 21.11.52, the above named was
brought up to our room in the People's Police
Station with the purpose of enlisting him as
an informant. Lorenz arrived punctually at
the agreed time and the meeting began with him
detailing his background. This he did without any
fuss.

As regards his sporting activity, he explained
that his life reached a crossroads in 1945. On
the one hand there was sport with its nice, easy
life, on the other there was hard service with the
People's Police.

He fought long and hard with himself, but
finished up in good hands. That's to say in a good,
comradely environment where he was convinced
by the righteousness of Marxist–Leninist study.
On the question of agent activities within
the GDR, Lorenz admitted that there were even
such elements within the People's Police. It was
explained to him that the mission of the MfS
was to expose these elements, and that the MfS
is placing trust in him to support us in this
mission. Lorenz agreed to this and the declaration
was placed before him for signing.

Once he had signed this a meeting was arranged
and he was assigned the mission of establishing
where the mother of (?) lives, and in what
circumstances.

Meeting duration ½ hour
Next meeting 25.11.52 at 16.00

Hauer

MfS4458/69 BSTU0019/0020

Chemnitz 21.11.52

Declaration

I, Carli Lorenz

am prepared to support the Ministry for State
Security in carrying out its operations. I know
that reactionary forces will use any means to
subvert progress in the GDR.

I therefore commit myself to report without
delay and prejudice to members of the MfS any
matters which could lead to the subversion of
democratic progress, any rumours and such like
which become known to me and any indications of
planned or already executed crimes.

Furthermore I commit myself to justify the
trust placed in me by maintaining unconditional
silence about my connection to the MfS and its
officers.

I am aware that by breaking this code of
silence I am endangering the work of the MfS
and progress in the GDR as well as aiding the
enemy and this will result in prosecution and
the removal of my freedom.

For all reports and activities I will use the
alias 'Radler'

Carli Lorenz
Born 27.11.13

NEUES DEUTSCHLAND
ORGAN DES ZENTRALKOMITEES DER SOZIALISTISCHEN EINHEITSPARTEI DEUTSCHLANDS

The race is organised as part of the celebrations for May Day, the international holiday of the working people, during which the peoples of Poland, Czechoslovakia and the German Democratic Republic celebrate the anniversary of the days when they were liberated from the hardship and misery of Nazi occupation by the invincible Soviet Army, led by Stalin's genius. Thus, besides the sporting mission of the race, it is also emphasised that its value lies in the strengthening of friendly relations not only between the participating countries, but in the consolidation of peaceful co-existence between all nations. 'In the name of fraternity of nations, friendship and peace' is the dominating slogan of the race. [...]

The importance of the race became even more prominent after the fifth edition, when the course led from Warsaw to Berlin to Prague, 2,050 kilometres long. Thus it passed for the first time through the GDR, where the working people, under the leadership of President Wilhelm Pieck, are building the foundations of a new, peace-loving Germany. Millions of working people, standing along the route throughout the GDR, clearly demonstrated that the overwhelming majority are for peace, for the democratic unity of the country, and against the revanchist policy of the Krupps and the former Hitlerite generals.

The importance of the race is further strengthened by the fact that progressive sportsmen from capitalist countries are annually strengthening the ranks of the racers. The history of the race is glorious. Both victory and participation therefore represent the highest distinction achievable in their sporting life [...]

Reprinted from 'Six years of the International Peace Race', 1 May 1953

FRANK

British cycling was split into two groups, the NCU and the BLRC. The NCU was affiliated to the UCI, but it was old-fashioned. They didn't agree with mass-start racing, and just rode time trials. The BLRC had started out as a splinter group for people who wanted to race our bikes like they did on the Continent. So our riding the Peace Race was nothing to do with politics, and we couldn't have cared less about them. We just wanted to ride our bikes, and we could only do that in non-UCI races.

KLAUS

I was born in Berlin in 1928, and I was born into communism. We hated the Nazis, hated what they stood for and hated what they'd done.

My mother and father were both founding members of the KPD, the German Communist Party, in 1918. My mother had been married before, to another of that group,* so I had a half-brother who was nine years older than me. My own father was the first president of the GDR Central Bank.

During the war I was sent to Saalfeld, near Jena. They wanted to evacuate Berlin, and my grandparents had a shoe shop there. So I was helping them in the shop, but then I was conscripted to anti-aircraft. It was 1943, and the British and American bombers were trying to bomb

---

* Hugo Eberlain was a victim of Stalin's purges. He was detained when the National Socialists came to power in 1933, and later exiled. He made his way to Russia in 1936, but was imprisoned the following year. Initially sentenced to fifteen years in the gulag at Vorkuta, he was sentenced to death and shot in Moscow in 1941.

  Huhn's half-brother was Werner Eberlein. At the cessation their mother lobbied Wilhelm Pieck, then co-chairman of the party (and subsequently president of the GDR) in an attempt to find him. Pieck in turn appealed to Stalin, and he was discovered working in a sawmill in Siberia. Despite his father's loss he had survived the war, and his communist conviction would survive Stalin. Returned to Berlin in 1948, he became Walter Ulbricht's Russian interpreter, translating Russian politicians' speeches on radio and TV. He became known as 'Khrushchev's Voice', and was highly skilled in softening the Soviet leader's doggerel. He later served in the Politburo, and became party chief secretary for Magdeburg.

the Carl Zeiss factory. You automatically assume that all German people were trying to protect their country, but it's not true.

So there I was, a fifteen-year-old boy being made to shoot at British aircraft. They were using Russian POWs as forced labour, and the prisoners would bring us the anti-aircraft grenades. They'd deliver canisters of hydrochloric acid, which they used to create a smokescreen. They made the Russians open them, but it was like a death sentence because exposure to the acid damaged their lungs.

One time they caught me giving one of the prisoners some bread. I was just giving a piece of bread to a hungry man, but for that I went without food myself for twenty-four hours. The next day I told them I was so hungry that I didn't have the energy to work.

NEUES DEUTSCHLAND

ORGAN DES ZENTRALKOMITEES DER SOZIALISTISCHEN EINHEITSPARTEI DEUTSCHLANDS

The manufacturing city of Chemnitz, the city with the great traditions of the German working class and of such revolutionary fighters as Fritz Heckert and Ernst Schneller, today receives the name of the greatest son of the German people, Karl Marx. Few cities in our country are so proud of the glorious struggles of the proletariat against capitalist exploitation and oppression, and of the liberation of working people from capitalism. Following the defeat of Hitlerism by the glorious Soviet Army, the working people of Chemnitz proved, through their exemplary performance in reconstructing their city and their businesses, that they possess the revolutionary momentum with which to fight against capitalist exploitation and oppression, and to create socialism in our country. Chemnitz will be called Karl-Marx-Stadt because its people, led by the working class and their party, have proved themselves worthy of this great German, and will continue to do so.

The workers of Karl-Marx-Stadt speak

At the centre of Chemnitz, in one of the liveliest squares, stands a bright circular building. Amidst the dark houses and ruins it acts, with its floral borders and the freshly mown lawn at the front, as a kind of clearing whose view relaxes the eyes. On its roof is a large, bright red star. It is the Soviet star.

The square in which it stands is called Stalinplatz, and the building is the Soviet Pavilion. Its construction was carried out by volunteer workers from the population of Chemnitz. 'It was necessary for us all to participate in this construction,' says worker Hans Werner. 'With the construction of this pavilion we wanted to document that the friendship with the Soviet Union is a matter of the heart for the workers of Chemnitz.' […]

Reprinted from 'Karl-Marx-Stadt – a centre of the German workers movement', 10 May 1953

DIETER

They renamed it, yes, but it wasn't like people suddenly started calling it 'Karl-Marx-Stadt'. Maybe they did in public, but it had been Chemnitz for hundreds of years! Karl Marx had never even been to Chemnitz!

These people were crazy.

NEUES DEUTSCHLAND

ORGAN DES ZENTRALKOMITEES DER SOZIALISTISCHEN EINHEITSPARTEI DEUTSCHLANDS

At the Army stadium in Warsaw, where GDR cyclists started the Peace Race for the first time three years ago, the evening of 14 May brought the greatest sporting triumph in the history of the movement of our republic. The four remaining riders of the GDR team, united as one, won the team competition of the sixth International Peace Race by over two minutes.

On the 2,230 kilometres to Warsaw, they left the best amateur cyclists in Europe in their wake. This great success was possible only because the athletes of the GDR enjoy assistance without parallel in the history of Germany.

The working people of the GDR have taken great pleasure in this success. On the evening of 14 May a flood of telegrams arrived in the Polish capital. Their joy is combined with the satisfaction that workers in all the socialist enterprises of our republic strive towards higher performance and thus pave the way for the wider promotion of sport. Here our team competed in peaceful competition with sixteen nations, and gave their all to produce a worthy characterisation of the GDR.

And yet the triumph of our team is but a victory for the movement for world peace. As America's lackeys in Europe continue their imperialist war against the Soviet Union and the people's democratic countries, the best cyclists from almost the whole of Europe were brought together in democracy. The great International Peace Race ran through the heart of Europe, demonstrating by example that peaceful and friendly understanding between its peoples is quite possible. Under the banner bearing the same logo as the blue jerseys of the victorious GDR team, namely Picasso's dove of peace, a huge new victory was won. [...]

At 139 kilometres, the final stage from ŁódĐ to Warsaw was the shortest of the race. It was already three o'clock when the thirty-eight riders began their lap of honour, and the image before them will remain unforgettable not only to them, but to all of those who witnessed it. In Stalinogrod* we had been of the opinion that the hundreds of thousands present could never be equalled. Here, in the city of textile workers, we went one better.

In the neutralised zone only a narrow corridor remained for the riders to navigate through. Behind the police cordons and tensioned cables, on every roof, ledge and balcony railing, the tens of thousands crowded.

There was probably not an inch of the city which didn't resonate with joyful acclamation of Królak and Wilczewski, or for the GDR team wearing, for the first time, the blue jerseys at the head of the peloton. Thousands of flowers, from simple bouquets to precious roses, were thrown to the race convoy on the streets of ŁódĐ. There was no trace of the suffering that the people of this city had endured at the hands of the fascist occupiers. 'Best wishes to you participants of the 1953 Peace Race' and other slogans, written in the German language, were stretched across the road. [...]

Reprinted from 'They won the greatest sporting success in the history of our republic', 16 May 1953

---

* Katowice. Stalin had died on 5 March, and two days later they renamed the town Stalinogrod.

DIETER

They were trying to build a national identity for the GDR, and in that respect the blue jersey was extremely important. It was the first time a GDR sporting team had been successful on the international stage, and they saw the effect it had on the people. It confirmed the power of sport as a unifying force, and it started to dawn on them that it was much more persuasive than political rhetoric. GDR athletes who won big events could be useful in engendering patriotism at home, and esteem abroad. Success in sport provided the kind of international recognition that their diplomacy couldn't.

People loved the race regardless of whether they were interested in sport, because it was a big social event. I doubt there was anything like it anywhere else in the world, and I doubt that there ever will be again. Millions watched by the roadside, and the stages always finished in vast stadiums. They would always be full of people because it was such a big celebration.

Then again you need to bear in mind that quite a lot of what you saw was orchestrated. You had a civic responsibility to support it because it was part of the apparatus of the state, and so local politicians competed to put on the best show. They tried to muster as many spectators as they could, so schools and factories would close when the race came by.

It wasn't a 'day off' in the traditional sense, no. You had a civic and social responsibility to contribute to the spectacle, because that's why you'd been given the time off in the first place. That was the way socialism functioned; it tried to organise your leisure time as well as your work time because everything was geared around building a new society. So by attending you were seen to be demonstrating support for your town, and the ideals of socialism as a whole. In reality, though, you probably had very little choice. Everyone loved the race, but if you didn't show up your bosses would take a dim view of it.

SYLVIA

Life got better as the economy improved. We weren't wealthy by any means, but nor were we poor. I'd say we were just a normal family.

Our first car was a little Borgward, but as time went by my dad would buy bigger and better ones. Eventually he got a beautiful BMW, and he'd drive us to the Rhineland on holiday. Sometimes we went to Koblenz, or to the mountains, and later we even started going to Italy.

DIETER

A car? Are you crazy? My family cycled everywhere, just like everyone else!

My dad was mad about cycling, and he was a good mechanic. He fixed bikes up for other people in his spare time, and that was his great passion. As far as I know he didn't ask for money, but people would pay him in kind. He'd get eggs, fruit, bits and pieces of whatever there was.

There were always bikes around, but you needed money to buy one and there was very little of it about. A month after the GDR team won the blue jersey it was my twelfth birthday and I finally got one.

DIETER

On the day I got my bike there was an uprising in Berlin, and it spread all over the GDR.* Everything was being sovietised, and it was obvious that we weren't independent at all. Towns were being renamed, churches closed down, and people who protested were being thrown in prison.

Farmers were losing their land because all the farms were being

---

* It's not clear how many were killed in Berlin during the uprising, though estimates vary from 50 to over 600. There remains speculation that Russian soldiers who refused to shoot protestors were executed. Some estimates have it that up to one million GDR citizens demonstrated, in one form or another, across the country.

collectivised,* and everything was focused on heavy industry. They were building munitions, but food production was down and families were going short. There seemed to be less and less in the shops.

Everyone could see that they were better off in the west, and thousands were emigrating there every month,† then in June they extended work quotas and increased prices, and that was the final straw. It started out as a general strike, and then it became a demonstration. That was when the Russians sent the tanks into Berlin.

So the people *were* coming together, but not as the politicians had hoped. They were uniting in defiance of the party, and in defiance of Moscow. The Hitler years had left them with an ingrained distrust of politicians, and the more they lied the more the people turned against them. They wanted food, housing and a decent standard of living, and they wanted to be rewarded for what they did. I think most people thought that socialism was all well and good in principle, but principle doesn't put food on the table, does it? Communism wasn't working, and the reality was that the GDR, our brave new world, was a puppet state for Russia.

DIETER

It wasn't a racing bike, but that didn't stop me from pretending.

I'd always played football, but I was becoming obsessed with cycling. One of my favourite things was a little book about the Tour de France, and I studied it over and over. I learned everything I could about great champions like Coppi and Bobet, then Hugo Koblet and Ferdi Kübler.

---

* The collectivisation programme began in earnest in 1952. Landowners, perceived as bourgeois, were systematically driven out of business. Their holdings were passed to *Landwirtschaftliche Produktionsgenossenschaft* ('Agricultural Production Co-operatives'), or *LPG*.

† More than 58,000 emigrated during the first three months of 1953.

The book described the great mountains; the Alps and Pyrenees. It seemed like a mystical world to me, and so it became my most treasured possession. I knew it was something I could only ever dream about, and so that's what I did – when I was on my bike I used to daydream that I was riding the Tour de France.

At first a group of us used to go out and ride, but I was much better than the others. After a while they stopped coming with me because they couldn't keep up and they said I was a maniac. I would ride as fast as I could for as long as I could, and I didn't seem to be able to stop myself. Pretty soon I only had myself to ride against, so I started timing myself. I decided I wanted to start racing when I was fourteen, so I only had two years to get ready.

DIETER

My mum's sister had married an American soldier. She was living in New York and she sent parcels. When the Russians sent the tanks in my mum decided she'd had enough. She wanted to go to America, and my aunt had told her she'd pay our airfare. My dad didn't want anything to do with it, though. He said he was nearly fifty, and he wasn't about to be uprooted to the other side of the world. He said he'd been born in Flöha, and he would die in Flöha. That's the kind of man he was.

SYLVIA

We used to send parcels to a place called Flöha. My Great-Aunt Gertrud and Uncle Herbert lived there, and my grandmother told me that they couldn't get a lot of the things we had.

We would send coffee, chocolate, things like that, and one of the things we sent most often was cigars. Uncle Herbert loved to smoke them, but he couldn't get them over there. They were precious for him, and when he got them he'd write back thanking us. When we saw that there was a letter from Herbert Diersche we'd sit down as a family and read it all together. He'd describe the taste of the coffee, the smell of the cigars, the joy of smoking them. He wrote beautifully, and you almost felt like you were there in the room with him.

DIETER

The 1954 race was important for all sorts of reasons. The Russians were there for the first time, but they also invited the first non-European team. They were from India,* and there was a huge amount of attention around them. Most people had never seen an Indian before, so it was another big statement of global fellowship. One guy, a Sikh named Dhana Singh, became the symbol of the whole race. The Indians were hopeless as cyclists, but the rest of the peloton made it their business to try to help them get round.

Obviously we'd won the previous year, so the anticipation was greater than ever. We didn't win a single stage, though, and didn't even have a rider in the top ten. It was a big letdown.

Then, of course, the FRG went and won the football World Cup in 1954, with the entire world watching.

---

*   Peace Race legend has it that the Indian team had been told they were to participate in a 'cycling exhibition', as distinct from a gruelling 2,000-kilometre stage race. One of them, Supravat Chakravati, somehow made it all the way to Prague. The time gaps at the Peace Race were often abyssal, but he contrived to lose over nineteen hours in thirteen stages. The following year Dhana Singh would cement his position as the darling of the Peace Race. He came eightieth and last, his deficit over twenty-eight hours.

In Italy, the staunchly anti-communist government of Mario Scelba refused to issue travel permits to their riders. On the eve of the race *Neues Deutschland* explicitly linked their absence to the 'Montesi Affair'. The previous year Wilma Montesi, a twenty-one-year-old would-be actress, had been found dead on a beach near Rome. It sparked allegations that drugs and sex parties were rampant not only among Rome's socialites, but also her politicians.

NEUES DEUTSCHLAND
ORGAN DES ZENTRALKOMITEES DER SOZIALISTISCHEN EINHEITSPARTEI DEUTSCHLANDS

It was a game that interested the whole world, drew millions of spectators. As the aged Honorary President of FIFA Jules Rimet presented the trophy to the West German captain Fritz Walter, so concluded a World Cup which had moved hearts as never before. The trophy will remain in West Germany for the next four years, before the question will once more be asked in 1958. Fritz Walter took the prized trophy not only as captain, but having played the game of his life in the decisive encounter. The other members of the team coached by Sepp Herberger were scarcely less convincing.

The West German team are world champions. However it's necessary to pay attention to the well-wishers, because among them there are suspicious names which strike an unpleasant chord. This narrow victory was stamped with 'German character', a character the world knows, and has had cause to recover from more than

once. One needs a finely tuned ear to distinguish between the honest joy of sporting success, and the rantings of people who discover sport in their hearts only when that it enables them to play their 'Deutschland, Deutschland Über Alles' records at full blast.

People such as Adenauer, whose telegram also arrived in Switzerland. So far his state budget has provided no money for the promotion of West German sport, and nor has he given any thought to trying to prevent the pressganging of young athletes into the Foreign Legion. Now, though, he seeks to take advantage of the performance of eleven West German footballers for his American propaganda. [...]

This is the Adenauer who, forty-eight hours before the game, threatened the French people with fascist impudence. Among neighbouring populations who couldn't fail to hear Sunday night's caterwauling of 'Deutschland, Deutschland Über Alles', there will be a similar reaction to the Paris speech. Inevitably then, it follows that the sporting performance of the West German team is pushed into the background by this chauvinistic tone. These chauvinistic plans, however, will lead to another war. Two World Cups, as well as thousands of outstanding athletes from all nations, fell victim to the last war.

Fritz Walter wore the uniform of a lance corporal in Hitler's Wehrmacht. Luckily for him his war ended early, and he became a Soviet prisoner of war. Other German internationals, such as the unforgettable Urban and the rapier-quick winger Klingler, were killed. Why recall them now? Because the policies of the Adenauer government set the same course as that which sent Urban, Klingler and many others to their deaths, and because they use the victory of Fritz Walter in Bern as an opportunity to create the atmosphere they need for a new military rampage.

They write: 'Everywhere German hearts beat, they felt this was a German triumph, a triumph of Germanness'. What they actually mean is, 'If we are world champions in football, we'll soon be armed for other actions. We are strengthening!'

Fritz Walter celebrated the greatest day of his life on the football pitch. We are happy for him, but at this time we can't help but commemorate great athletes like Urban and Klingler ...

Reprinted from 'Once again the football World Cup', 6 June 1954

DIETER

The issue was that there was a sporting cold war going on as well as a political one. Sport was absolute, and it was all about winners and losers. People were more interested in sport than in politics, and that's why it started to become the big ideological battleground.

NEUES DEUTSCHLAND

ORGAN DES ZENTRALKOMITEES DER SOZIALISTISCHEN EINHEITSPARTEI DEUTSCHLANDS

The German Democratic Republic Cycling Federation has received the following letter:

Dear friends!

When first we met with sporting people from the GDR, we had so many questions from our sports fans that they didn't know which one to answer first. However, they went to great lengths to explain about life in the GDR, and that of an athlete in particular. We want to be honest: at first we were very sceptical. We could hardly believe the care your government takes of its athletes. The difference between your ways and those of the FRG couldn't be bigger.

Again and again, when we got together with athletes from the GDR we were full of questions, and again and again we received the same answer: 'Yes, really, we have no worries. We get all our equipment from our BSG, they give us every conceivable opportunity to train, and take care of our professional development. If we want we can even study at our universities and colleges free from all material worries.'

However, when we see how many are unemployed in the FRG, and when we note that our government's only interest in sport is to develop us for their army, then we understand in which part of Germany sport has a future. Neither of us want to be soldiers in a new fascist army, but to develop our sporting skills. We don't want to die in another war, but to create a happy and peaceful future. That's why we ask to live and work in the GDR, and that you accept us as members of the democratic sports movement.

Emil Reinecke & Wolfgang Grupe

Reprinted from 'Reinecke and Grupe come to the GDR', 8 February 1955

EMIL

The president of the GDR Cycling Federation, Werner Scharch, asked me whether I was interested in taking part in a Peace Race training camp. They invited me and two other West German riders, Wolfgang Grupe and Hennes Junkermann, to a cross-country skiing training camp in Thüringen. I was asked whether I wanted to ride the Peace Race for the GDR, and naturally I was!

I suppose that they were looking for successful riders who had already ridden for the national team and had international experience; riders they could count on to support their team. It was an easy decision for me to make. In the west I had no professional contract and no offers. I didn't earn enough, couldn't live on the prize money and had to work all day. In the GDR I had no financial worries and far better training opportunities.

The FRG federation wasn't happy about it, but I was young and fearless. I wanted to succeed and to try to take advantage of my opportunity.

Before I went I made it clear to them that I wasn't going to be involved in politics, so I didn't have to take part in any special training or suchlike. They suggested that I join the SED, but I refused and they accepted that.[*]

---

[*] Reprinted from *Friedensfahrt und Tour de France – Emil Reinecke,* by Peter Zetzsche

NEUES DEUTSCHLAND

ORGAN DES ZENTRALKOMITEES DER SOZIALISTISCHEN EINHEITSPARTEI DEUTSCHLANDS

It's just like a scene from a long-forgotten film, where bells ring, foaming breakers race across the deck of a ship shaken by the storm, and hoarse throats call 'Man overboard!' [...]

First, the facts: a bricklayer and a labourer, both of whom previously lived in the FRG, had been unemployed for a year and a day. This may be commonplace in the FRG, but Wolfgang Grupe and Emil Reinecke – enthusiastic and talented cyclists both – were disillusioned with the situation. The idea of years spent unemployed is as anachronistic as the plagues of the Middle Ages.

They therefore took a good look at the GDR, and carefully studied the facilities for the promotion and development of sport. These include the most modern sports university in Europe, and they learned that at DHfK, the new German College for Physical Culture and Sports, the students receive a satisfactory scholarship. Since both are good Germans, they saw nothing untoward in saying goodbye to the FRG and coming over to settle in the GDR, as have hundreds before them. [...]

But those screaming themselves hoarse with 'Man overboard!' will ultimately come to the realisation that the problem is greater than the curses of sailors. A man overboard is painful, but a leaky, sinking ship is far more dangerous.

Reprinted from 'Man overboard!', 12 February 1955

EMIL

We were supposed to complete studies at DHfK* in Leipzig, but I never attended a single lecture. When we first arrived there was a reception for us there; all very ostentatious with speeches and gifts. There was a five-year study plan, but due to the volume of training there was no time for lectures.

The conditions were perfect. There was comprehensive medical care and physiotherapy, and a perfectly developed training plan. We concentrated exclusively on cycling, and we had excellent equipment.[†]

DIETER

The object of the exercise was to prove that our system was better than theirs.

DHfK was the only dedicated sports university in the world at the time. It was in Leipzig, and the whole purpose was to showcase GDR excellence in sport. That meant winning world and European championships and Olympic medals, so it hand-picked the most talented athletes from all over the country. If they fitted the model and they were ideologically sound they were enrolled there and lived on the campus. In a traditional university you'd need three or four years to complete a sports doctorate, but they would be there for up to twelve. That more or less equated to the duration of an athlete's career, because they wanted to keep them in the system for as long as they delivered results.

Ostensibly they were studying sports science, physiology and suchlike, but in reality their job was to deliver results. In cycling that meant winning at the Peace Race and world championships. They were the events the public was interested in, and everything was engineered around them.

---

*   *Deutsche Hochschule für Körperkultur.*

†   Reprinted from *Friedensfahrt und Tour de France – Emil Reinecke*, by Peter Zetzsche

The DHfK athletes were portrayed as shining examples of the sports programme. When they won it proved that socialism was working, so they were treated extremely well compared to the rest. They were given everything they needed to succeed, and those who won big events got huge bursaries compared to normal students. It therefore followed that they would be present at all the big championships, because that was the premise on which it had been created in the first place.

EMIL

I couldn't tell you about daily life in the GDR. We were almost always in training camp, and had very little contact with normal people. We trained and we were on the road. I never met a family, but I know that a normal worker was earning maybe 300–400 marks a month. We got 1,000, with free board and lodging, and in addition to that there were the bonuses. I was able to send my parents 400 Deutschmarks a month.[*]

---

[*] Reprinted from *Friedensfahrt und Tour de France – Emil Reinecke*, by Peter Zetzsche

NEUES DEUTSCHLAND

ORGAN DES ZENTRALKOMITEES DER SOZIALISTISCHEN EINHEITSPARTEI DEUTSCHLANDS

In the early morning hours of Thursday, this year's Peace Race Team flew from the German capital to Bucharest, to complete one final stage race in preparation. On Wednesday evening Manfred Ewald, the president of the State Committee for Physical Culture and Sports, had taken the opportunity to say goodbye at the airport Hotel Schönefeld, and to wish them all the best.

How's the team looking?

Since our team won't be back on German soil until 7 May, cycling fans are asking themselves, 'How are we likely to do after last season's disappointing performance?' It's a question, it transpires, which isn't so easy to answer. Of the sextet from the seventh Peace Race, only the duo of Schur and Funda remain, and the latter's form is under close scrutiny following his surprising abandon last Sunday.

The ranks of the democratic sporting movement are swollen by Grupe and Reinecke, two whizz-kids who have already demonstrated their strength in West Germany. They have the requisite international experience for the Peace Race, the world's most demanding and important stage race. Bernhard Trefflich and Lothar Meister – two longstanding Peace Race participants – were also invited into the circle of candidates for the GDR team. However, both rejected the chance to participate, with flimsy justifications.

The presidium of the Wismut cycling section requested an explanation for this unusual step, but only months later did they receive an answer. Now, just a few weeks before the Peace Race, the two of them are ready to take up systematic training. Following the bad training experiences of previous years, this offer could only be rejected. […]

Reprinted from 'The GDR Peace Race riders set off yesterday', 22 April 1955

DIETER

Each year there was a big build-up to the Peace Race, and they used to run miniature versions for kids up and down the country. So on 1 May 1955 I entered my first event, a fifteen-kilometre scratch event for boys aged fourteen to eighteen. To be honest I shouldn't have been riding because I was still six weeks short of my birthday. I only had the touring bike I'd been given for my birthday two years previously, but they let me ride anyway. And I won.

DIETER

The following weekend the race started, and they left out Bernhard Trefflich and Lothar Meister, two champions from Chemnitz. They chose the West German guys* instead, but Meister had been runner-up at the 1951 Peace Race and national road race champion in 1952. He was still only twenty-five, and he was a brilliant bike rider. Trefflich had finished fourth at the Peace Race in 1953, and then won the national championship. He was a convenient scapegoat for them because he came from an 'old' German background. He was from Weimar, and his family were Protestants who owned a shop.

As far as the party was concerned, people like them, small businessmen and Christians, were the worst kind of bourgeoisie. They had them down as enemies of socialism, and they discriminated against them. I had a friend who couldn't go to high school because his father was a pastor.

---

* Before his death in 2011, Trefflich claimed that his problems with the federation had had nothing to do with his failure to follow the training programme. He added that his career finished when he refused to allow his daughter to undertake *Jugendweihe*.

Conceived to replace confirmation, *Jugendweihe* was the induction ceremony of the *Freie Deutsche Jugend* (FDJ). It was initiated after the Berlin uprising of 1953, and rolled out nationally two years later. FDJ members were aged fourteen to twenty-five, and most graduated from the Young Pioneers. Based on the Kinder Scout movement, this was where six-to fourteen-year-old GDR children began to learn socialist doctrine.

EMIL

The enthusiasm of the people for the Peace Race was enormous. The side of the road would be full of people whether we were in the GDR, Czechoslovakia or Poland. Children had the day off school, and after the race we'd go and talk to them. They'd be spellbound by what we said, and I must say that made a real impression on me. Every day I got a huge pile of mail from kids, from girls, the whole population. People congratulated us and wished us well. It was all very exciting.*

DIETER

A DHfK guy named Gustav-Adolf Schur became the first GDR rider to win the Peace Race.

His nickname was 'Täve', and you couldn't help but like him. He was funny, handsome and charismatic. He was popular with sports fans because he was such a great rider, and he was also a pin-up boy for the girls. The politicians loved him because he was a true believer in socialism, and they used his success as a metaphor for the GDR as a whole. Täve was the biggest star in GDR, as simple as that.

---

* Reprinted from *Friedensfahrt und Tour de France – Emil Reinecke*, by Peter Zetzsche

NEUES DEUTSCHLAND

ORGAN DES ZENTRALKOMITEES DER SOZIALISTISCHEN EINHEITSPARTEI DEUTSCHLANDS

On Saturday morning thousands gathered in front of Berlin's Ostbanhof station. They were there to greet the GDR Peace Race team on their return from Warsaw, with a tumultuous reception. The chairman of the State Committee for Physical Culture and Sport, Manfred Ewald, greeted the riders with their captain, Gustav-Adolf Schur, on the crowded platform. In the afternoon the team was invited by Walter Ulbricht's deputy to the GDR government guest house in Thälmannplatz.

Walter Ulbricht was introduced to the members of the German team and awarded Gustav-Adolf Schur the title 'Honoured Master of Sports'. Benno Funda, Lothar Meister,* Detlef Zabel, Emil Reinecke and Wolfgang Grupe were each presented with the title 'Master of Sports'.

[…]

Reprinted from 'GDR Peace Race team honoured by Walter Ulbricht',
22 May 1955

---

* There were two GDR riders named Lothar Meister. The one who rode the 1955 Peace Race was commonly known as Lothar Meister II.

TÄVE

Winning the Peace Race changed my life for ever. Thousands of people started writing to me, and there were 500 girls camped outside the dormitory. I realised that millions were supporting me. The point is that everybody was part of the success, and everybody *felt* part of it. Technically I was representing the state, but there was no distinction between the people and the state. In the GDR the people *were* the state.

In capitalism everybody just did their own thing. A professional cyclist could always say, 'OK, today I don't have the legs. I have enough money, and so it doesn't matter if I don't race today.' It wasn't like that for me. I was never ambitious for money or fame, but I understood that every time I raced I was defending the values of my country and my society.

EMIL

The prizes – and after the Peace Race they included a sailing boat – were sold, the proceeds put into a pot and shared out. Then Täve Schur divided every last mark up between us.

We had more money in our pockets than we knew what to do with, and through sport we were already privileged. When my girlfriend came to visit me in Leipzig I wanted a room at the Hotel Astoria. When they heard my name they gave me one immediately. If I needed a suit I'd just go to the tailor and he'd make one for me. The tailor knew who I was, and I had anything I wanted. I always had the best place in the restaurant.[*]

TÄVE

At first I was uncomfortable with it, but I had to get used to it. The pressure was enormous, but I had to do my duty and so I learned a new way to live.

---

[*]   Reprinted from *Friedensfahrt und Tour de France – Emil Reinecke*, by Peter Zetzsche

It wasn't always enjoyable – in fact it could be extremely heavy at times – but I understood that I had a responsibility to set a good example.

So in essence that's what I tried to do. I didn't see myself as being different from other people, and nor did they. Everybody was equal in our society, and that was maybe part of the reason it became such a big thing. For some reason people I didn't know would use the informal *Du* to address me, not the formal *Sie*. That was something you never did with people you didn't know, but I didn't mind it.

MfS383/65 bd1, BSTU0018

Mid-term Appraisal

Flöha Primary school

Dieter Wiedemann

Born 17.6.1941 in Flöha

Class 8b

Student: 1947/1955

Behaviour: Good

Comments: He is good in the lessons. He tries hard to meet the required standard. His behaviour is impeccable.

German	3
Geography	2
Mathematics	2
Biology	3
History	2
Physics	3
Attendance	2
Chemistry	3
Russian	2
Sports	2
Music	3
Drawing	3

Flöha, 2.3.1955
Class leader

DIETER

My dad built me a real racing bike for my fourteenth birthday, a 1936 Diamant.

The Diamant factory was in Chemnitz, and it was a VEB,* a publicly owned company. The VEBs had to be protected, so the federation introduced a new rule. It stipulated that if you wanted to race in the GDR you had to do it on a Diamant frame, which meant that the private framebuilders were driven out of business.

My dad was working for a private firm at the time, so his monthly wage was only about 200 marks. A new Diamant racing bike would have cost about 850 marks, and there was no way he could afford that. I think that the bike cost about 200 marks, because he knew a lot of cycling people and he'd have got it for a good price.

The bike wasn't particularly flash, but it was good enough for me. I won all the races I entered that year. Bear in mind that I'd been training seriously for two years to get ready, so I was already pretty good at it.

DIETER

I started work six weeks after my birthday, on 1 September. It was a two-year apprenticeship and I was a lathe operator at a VEB in Einsiedel, south of Chemnitz.

The problem was that there were too few machines and too many people. They didn't have the money to invest in new machinery, so instead everyone worked shifts. They thought it was better than sending people to work in private enterprises, and the whole point was that there was full employment. For a fourteen-year-old boy it was tough. I'd leave

---

* An abbreviation of *Volkseigene Betrieb*. At the cessation, Diamant was one of 850 or so Soviet Zone factories earmarked to be dismantled and shipped to Moscow as part of German reparations. Ultimately, however, around 200 of them were spared. The plant remained intact, albeit under Soviet ownership. In 1952 it was transferred back to GDR public ownership (VEB), and by now was producing over 250,000 bikes a year.

home at 11 p.m. and get home at eleven the next morning, so they were long days.

I suppose I could have looked for a job in a private firm like my dad, but I'd have got much less money.

TÄVE

When I left school I'd started an apprenticeship as a mechanical engineer. It had dawned on me that the boss was earning his money through my work and through the work of my colleagues. He was getting all this money but he just wasted it; he spent it on drink.

I thought that was wrong, so I started to ask myself, 'Why is he using *me* to earn so much money for *himself*?'

DIETER

Pretty soon I was being paid more than my dad, and he'd been working all his adult life. I tried to reason with him to change, and so did my mum. He wouldn't have it, though. He didn't like politicians, and he always said, 'Politics is the biggest whore.' He said most of them were the same people who had followed Hitler.*

TÄVE

I was born in 1931, so I grew up in Hitler's Germany. It was a very authoritarian, very patriarchal society, and it was for ever reinforcing the idea of duty. We didn't wear soldiers' uniforms because we were just kids, but ideas about the state and communal responsibility were instilled into us from a very young age.

---

* In 1954, internal SED party analysis calculated that 25.8 per cent of the membership were former Nazis, though the number is somewhat illusory. Many among the pre-war political classes joined the party, so among the apparatchiks the ratio was much higher.

DIETER

At work you had to join the FDGB,* the trade union, and I had to pay 16 marks for the blue FDJ†shirt. There would be an assembly in the factory, a sort of call to arms. Everyone would put the shirt on, and then somebody would stand up and give a sort of lecture. It would be about Karl Marx, communist theory, fellowship with the Russians or some such, and if memory serves we'd have to sing the FDJ anthem as well. I reckon the whole thing would normally last about fifteen minutes, and then you'd go back to your work.

The GDR was building socialism, and being in the FDJ signified that you were part of that process. The idea was that you were being 'prepared to work and defend the homeland', and so from time to time you'd have lessons in using a firearm. The first time I did that I nearly shot the instructor, so after that I tended to be ill when they did it.

In theory you weren't obliged to be in the FDJ, but it was becoming more and more difficult not to. I'd managed to avoid it because *Jugendweihe* was only just starting in 1955, but there were twelve people in my work group and all of the others were FDJ members. I know a few people refused to join on religious or ideological grounds, but it was ruinous for them. They weren't able to carry on with their studies, and so they never got a good job or a decent place to live.

I had to go to see the section leader and he said, 'I don't see any reason for you not to be a member.' I told him I didn't want to, so he said, 'All right, but at least get yourself a blue shirt and play along with it.' So my wearing the shirt meant that they left me in peace. I put it on

---

*   *Freier Deutscher Gewerkschaftsbund.*

†   FDJ membership was already about 1.2 million in 1955, nearly 50 per cent of the total youth population. From 1956 it was to all intents and purposes mandatory. By the fall of the Berlin Wall in 1989 there were an estimated 2.3 million members.

the same as everyone else, because if I hadn't I'd have been an enemy of socialism and they wouldn't have let me race my bike.

TÄVE

When I was kid there was a tank factory around the corner from us. They hid the tanks in the woods behind our house so that the Allies wouldn't see them. One of my childhood memories is a bombing raid in 1941. I remember being unable to hear for three days after it, and being traumatised by this absolute and total devastation.

Then I started to grow up, and to understand what it had all been about. And what had it all been about? Nothing! Nothing whatsoever except for greed and power! Just bullshit! So when you're confronted by something like that you have to think seriously about it. You have a responsibility to try to find a different way, and to not repeat the same mistakes over and over again. You need to start building a better future, and I think that was what people of my generation started to do.

EMIL

I'd always planned to do just one season in the GDR anyway, but then the payments were discontinued. There was no more western money, and that was the point at which I drew a line. I insisted the GDR Cycling Federation adhered to our agreement, and president Scharch came to the Swiss border in person. He paid me every last pfenning and asked me for a signature confirming that I had no further demands of the GDR. Then he signed to confirm I hadn't taken any GDR property, patted me on the shoulder and said, 'You've done it right.'

So it was a perfectly normal departure with transit to the west, but then later I found out from the press that I'd defected. They revoked the

Master of Sports honour I'd earned at the Peace Race.[*][†]

DIETER

My life was pretty simple. When I wasn't working or sleeping I was on my bike.

I was becoming a pretty decent rider, so I joined the cycling section of the BSG,[‡] the company sports association. Everyone in the GDR was

---

[*]   Reprinted from *Friedensfahrt und Tour de France – Emil Reinecke*, by Peter Zetzsche

[†]   Emil Reinecke finished the Peace Race twentieth, and fourth of the GDR sextet. He signed a professional contract immediately upon his return. He would complete the 1960 Tour de France for the FRG, and became an accomplished six-day rider. He died in 2011.

   Wolfgang Grupe was twenty-fifth. He stayed in the GDR until 1957, but his return to the FRG is shrouded in mystery. His obituary states, somewhat obliquely, that he went back 'under cover of darkness', and he, too, had his Master of Sports award revoked. He died of leukaemia in 1971, aged forty.

[‡] The BSG (*Betriebssportgemeinschaft*) were sports organisations funded by trade union contributions and organised, broadly speaking, according to employment sector and geography. Sixteen were operative, and their management and promotion was invariably delegated to large employers (*Trägerbetriebe*).

   In the mid-fifties new, elite sport clubs were formed, and they appropriated most of the GDR's international class athletes. Eighteen sport clubs were created between 1953 and 1956, sixteen of them 'civilian'. Many had regional branches, and each was focused on producing world-class athletes in targeted sporting disciplines. In addition there were two non-civilian clubs, each with affiliates the length and breadth.

   The principal security agencies in the GDR were grouped together. The sports association under which employees of MfS (Stasi), the Police (*Volkspolizei*) and the customs and border control (*Zollverwaltung*) practised sport was Dynamo. At its heart was Dynamo Berlin, the MfS sport club. It was the biggest single sport club in the GDR, and it covered most Olympic disciplines. Elsewhere the police and customs clubs targeted excellence in specific areas. Dynamo Dresden, a police club, was football-orientated; Dynamo Weisswasser specialised in ice hockey, and so on.

   Vorwärts was the umbrella association of the sport clubs of the *Volksarmee* and other armed forces. In addition to Berlin it had branches in large towns such as Cottbus, Erfurt and Leipzig; wherever there was a military presence. Here again the branches specialised. Oberhof, for example, was a centre for winter sports, while Rostock excelled in rowing and wrestling.

   DHfK aside, Wismut, Dynamo Berlin and ASK Vorwärts Leipzig were among the more successful clubs in road cycling. Track cycling was also extremely popular in the GDR, and here SC Einheit Berlin (later TSC Berlin) was pre-eminent.

encouraged to participate in sports, and the way to do that was through a BSG. So in my section there would have been about twenty cyclists, then there were the footballers, gymnasts, athletes and all the rest. They gave me a jersey and paid my travelling expenses to and from the races, and I did well.

The problem with the BSGs was that they were open to everyone. They were extremely successful in incentivising people to take part in sports, but they weren't designed to create the elite athletes the politicians wanted. They needed a better way to identify the most talented athletes and coaches, and so they started creating new sport clubs. They took the very best athletes out of the BSGs and put them into the sport clubs, with a view to them representing the GDR in international competitions. The better they were the more the state contributed to their earnings, and the best ones were fully funded, full-time athletes. The BSGs were left to concentrate on non-competitive sports, and local level competitions. Hardly any BSG members participated in international events.

Chemnitz was a big uranium mining area and the mining company, SDAG Wismut, ran a BSG. In 1954 they'd been tasked with creating a sport club, and had transferred all the best cyclists out of the BSG and into it.

MfS435/71 BSTU0024

Karl-Marx-Stadt 19.12.55

Commitment

I, Heinz Friedel, born 18.6.1928 in Chemnitz, residing in Schulstrasse, Karl-Marx-Stadt, commit myself to work with the representatives of the MfS, whereby I will report with impartiality to the representatives of the MfS in writing all hostile activities which are made known to me. These include espionage, sabotage, subversion, wrecking tactics as well as agitation towards all the peoples' democratic countries.

I am aware that this commitment requires me to maintain absolute silence, even to my immediate family. I am aware that if I break this commitment I will be punished under GDR law § 959C.

For reasons of vigilance I will submit my reports to the representatives of the MfS under the alias 'Ursel'.

I will at all times and regularly keep to agreed meetings and will carry out the missions assigned to me to the very best of my abilities.

Heinz Friedel

MfS435/71 BSTU0037

Unofficial Informant 'Ursel'
  Case officer: Second Lieutenant Kälber
  Recruited: 19.12.55

Personal:
Heinz FRIEDEL, born 18.6.28 in Chemnitz

Resident: Schulstrasse, Karl-Marx-Stadt

Works: Fitter; Object 37, SDAG Wismut

Password: 'Hello, I'm here about the motor bike.'

'I guess my brother-in-law sent you.'

Meeting place: Conspiratorial dwelling 'Hansi',
Inselstrasse 2, Karl-Marx-Stadt

DIETER

Then in 1956 Motor, another BSG in Chemnitz, was converted to a sport club as well. The cycling coach was a guy called Werner Richter, and he came to our house. He told us that he had been charged with getting the best young cyclists into the club, that he wanted me to join, and that if I did I would get everything I needed. They would sort out the travel, get me a new bike and see to it that I had two afternoons a week off to train. My dad knew him from way back and said he was a good man. I joined straight away, and I started riding quite a lot with Werner's son, Udo.

UDO

My dad had already been quite successful before Dieter and I started riding there.

He was a single-minded person, and he was an optimist. So after he'd finished his own career his goal was to try to make a contribution to building the sports enterprises. As it happened they were looking for a cycling coach, and he decided it would be an interesting job. He wanted to introduce young people to cycling, and to inspire them through it.

MfS383/65 bd1, BSTU0020

BETRIEBSBERUFFSCHULE VEB
GROSSDREHMASCHINENBAU '8 MAI'

WALDSTRASSE 3, EINSIEDEL, KARL-MARX-STADT

27.6.57

Appraisal

Dieter Wiedemann, apprentice lathe operator

Wiedemann has not achieved the required output
quota. He lacks self-belief and applies himself to
cycling more than is healthy.

Initially timid, recently he has become more open
and talkative.

He gets on well with the others socially.

Schubert (acting director)

DIETER

The better I got the less I had to work, and the less I worked the more I was able to train. Berlin was reimbursing the company for the hours I missed, and I got a bit of cash when I won. For a win I'd get about 30 marks, and maybe 20 if I got second, and there were other prizes here and there. I suppose in that sense it was no different from junior racing in the west.

I finished my apprenticeship in August 1957.

MfS383/65 bd1, BSTU0021

Contract of employment

This contract of employment is between:

Dieter Wiedemann, R. Breitscheid Strasse 51, Flöha

and

VEB GROSSDREHMASCHINENBAU '8 MAI', Karl-Marx-Stadt W 30

This is a contract of employment for a publically owned and founded enterprise. This enterprise is based upon relationships of comradely cooperation and socialist mutual assistance of all working people, free from exploitative practices.

This contract of employment provides the following rights and obligations:

§1

Mr. Dieter Wiedemann effective from 1.9.57

§2

The obligation to comply with socialist labour discipline including:

(a) Punctual appearance for work, and full utilisation of the working day

b) Scrupulous adherence to the instructions given by the company's management or their representatives

(c) Punctual and careful implementation of tasks

(d) Protection of socialist property

(e) Compliance with the safety instructions, operating hygiene and fire prevention

(f) Compliance with the provisions of the work order

§3

The activity of the apprentice is

Lathe operator

The contract of employment provides a working salary amounting to 1.66 per hour

§4

The annual paid vacation entitlement is 12 days

(...)

Karl-Marx-Stadt, 31.8.57

NEUES DEUTSCHLAND

ORGAN DES ZENTRALKOMITEES DER SOZIALISTISCHEN EINHEITSPARTEI DEUTSCHLANDS

The Press Office of the Prime Minister announces:

For health reasons the Minister of State Security, Ernst Wollweber, has asked to be relieved of his duties. Prime Minister Grotewohl has accepted his request and has appointed Erich Mielke, the former Deputy Minister for State Security, to replace him from 1 November.

Reprinted from 'Erich Mielke Minister for State Security', 1 November 1957

MfS8963/69 BSTU0017

Flöha, 3.6.58

Zi/Ri

Flöha District Service Unit
  Line VII

Investigation Report

Pawlowski,	(nee Markert),Frieda
Born:	26.8.1897 in Schnellenberg, Flöha District
Resident:	Rudolf-Breitscheid-Strasse, Flöha
Profession:	None
Current:	Housewife
Marital status:	Married
Religion:	Evangalist-Lutherian?
Nationality:	German
Previous convictions:	None

P. comes from master tailor's family and
attended elementary school for 8 years. From 1912-
1914 she worked as a maid. From 1914-1918 she worked
as a cook in Buchholz. From 1919-1923 she was a
seamstress at Salzmann and Co. in Oederan. She
worked at the Gückelsberg cotton mill from 1927-
1933. Between 1944 and 1945 she was employed as a
quality controller at AEG Gückelsberg. She hasn't
been employed since late 1945, and has worked as a
housewife.

On 12.11.1921 she married her present husband,
Edward Pawlowski. Through his political work
she found her way into the Communist Party of
Germany in 1932. Previously, from 1919 she was a
member of the Worker's Samaritan Federation and
the Red Sports Society, and she joined the Workers
Choral Society in 1931.

Through the illegal work of her husband,
she was a fellow advocate of the cause of the

working class. Despite the arrest of her husband, she herself took part in illegal work. In 1933 she was sentenced to three months in jail due to complicity in illegal weapon ownership, but received immunity because of the Hindenburg Amnesty. Even the imprisonment of her husband in 1933 and 1944 did not soften her resolve, and she has remained faithful to the cause of the working class. After the collapse of the fascist regime, she rejoined the Communist Party of Germany, and with the merger of the two parties joined the SED. Furthermore she is a member of the Democratic Women's League of Germany, the Society for German-Soviet Friendship, the Consumer Association and the Union of Persons Persecuted by the Nazi Regime.

Insofar as she is physically able, she is active socially. Amongst others she has held the position of chairperson of the Second Social Commission since 1946. As regards her marriage, a child named (?) was born in 1923. He can be said to have grown into a loyal state functionary.

The Character of P. is friendly, honest and open. Her life experience, acquired as a result of the struggle, helped her develop into a conscious fighter. Her reputation in the town is good. On western travel and western contacts nothing was found.

Second Lieutenant Zimmermann

MfS8963/69 BSTU0038/0039

Flöha, 17.6.58

Zi/Ri

Flöha District Service Unit
  Line VII

Recruitment Report

Between 9.45 and 11.00 on 17.06.1958, a further discussion
was held at the home of the P. family in regard to
their recruitment for a conspiratorial dwelling. In
addition to the undersigned, comrade Lieutenant Bergt
was present.

At the beginning the discussion with P. was on
general issues. Amongst other things he spoke about his
health, his gardening culture, etc. The conversation was
steered towards political events and in this respect
it was clear that he assessed the current political
situation correctly. It was here that the fascist period
1933-1945 was mentioned. He told of his political life
during that era, and described his activity following
the collapse of 1945 as a responsible comrade within
the apparatus of the state. The conversation was
directed by us towards persons (?), (?) and (?), and in
their regard he expressed a view similar to ours. He
correctly stated that they were no longer comrades.
They see only their own personal interests and their
views aren't consistent with the cause of our workers
and farmers state. He himself has had no links to these
people for several years. He got to know them only
through his work after 1945, when they were installed
as functionaries in the state apparatus. However, it
became apparent later on that they do not justify the
confidence of our workers and farmers state.

Throughout the entire conversation it could be
determined that P. expressed his opinion honestly. In
light of this, our intentions for the missions were
confided to him. After the political value of our work

with the MfS was explained to him again, he realised
that the MfS wished to create a closer cooperation
with him. We then submitted our plan to use his
home for the purposes of creating a conspiratorial
dwelling. He readily gave his consent to this, and then
consulted with his wife in regard to the organisational
matters. A discussion followed between ourselves and
the P. family in respect to all of the organisational
matters pertaining to the creation of a conspiratorial
dwelling, and agreement was reached. During a further
conversation, the extreme confidentiality of the
work was made clear to him. In order to establish the
certainty of total confidentiality, the family P. was
ordered to write a vow of silence, which they hand-
wrote according to the rules. All the issues contained
within the vow of silence were properly explained to
them in order to eliminate ambiguity.

The P. family chose the alias 'Kaufmann' for
their conspiratorial cooperation with us, so the
conspiratorial dwelling, as well as any reports
compiled for us, will be signed thus.

Only the study is available as a conspiratorial room,
as already outlined in the diagram.

The P. family have been informed that for their
courtesy in providing the room they will receive 15DM
monthly. No difficulties were mentioned on the part of
the P. family in respect of the recruitment.

It was pointed out that from 1.7.-15.7.58 they will be
away at the Baltic Sea, so during this period the house
may not be used.

After all related issues regarding the use of the
room as a conspiratorial dwelling were clarified, we
said goodbye to the P. family without further incident.

Lieutenant Bergt   Sub-Lieutenant Zimmermann

DIETER

Then in 1958 Motor sacked Richter, the coach. I couldn't understand it because he was a good man and a good coach. He knew cycling, but apparently his methods were old-fashioned. There was a meeting and I got up and said, 'I don't understand why he's being fired. Everyone knows he's a good coach!' One of the officials said, 'That's such a naïve question that it could only have come from somebody very young.' I didn't really know what he meant by that, but I was told that it had to do with his politics. The state was paying his wages, but he wasn't following the party line.

UDO

The issue was that my dad wanted cycling competition between east and west to be revived. He made no secret of the fact, and he expressed his opinion quite openly. He read an article in *Radsport-Woche*, the cycling magazine, and it stated that sporting contacts with 'capitalist countries' were a betrayal of the socialist ideal. He wrote to the editors about it, and was critical of their stance. They replied using quite harsh words.

That was probably why they dismissed him from the club, because that way he wouldn't be able to influence young people's perceptions of socialism.

DIETER

The guy who replaced Richter was called Helmut Wechsler. He'd never ridden, but he was just about as red as they come. He was one of 'them', and I didn't like him and didn't trust him.

WALTER ULBRICHT; FIRST SECRETARY, SOCIALIST UNITY PARTY

'Comrades, the ten commandments for socialist morality and ethics are these:

1. Thou shalt always defend the international solidarity of the working class as well as the unbreakable bonds that unite all socialist countries.

2. Thou shalt love thy Fatherland and always be ready to defend worker and farmer power with all thy strength and capacity.

3. Thou shalt help to eliminate the exploitation of humans by one another.

4. Thou shalt perform good deeds for socialism, since socialism produces a better life for all working people.

5. Thou shalt act in the spirit of mutual support and comradely cooperation during the construction of socialism, respect the collective, and take its criticisms to heart.

6. Thou shalt protect and increase the property of the people.

7. Thou shalt always pursue ways to improve thy performance, be thrifty, and strengthen socialist work discipline.

8. Thou shalt rear thy children in the spirit of peace and socialism to become citizens who are well-educated, strong in character, and physically healthy.

9. Thou shalt live a clean and decent life and respect thy family.

10. Thou shalt exhibit solidarity with all those people who are fighting for national liberation and defending their independence.[...][*]

---

[*] Fifth SED Party Congress, June 1958

MfS697/69 BSTU0017

Karl-Marx-Stadt, 5.9.58

Re: Informant 'Fritzsche'

Final Report

In 1954 the informant was removed from the
archive by department VIII, and collaboration
restored. (...)

The informant 'Fritzsche' has worked for the
City Committee for Physical Culture and Sports
since 4.1.55. At that time his prospects were
limited to the sphere of information. Here he
did not disappoint, though he delivered little
material of value.

Today he works as a full-time coach at the
cycling section of SC Motor.

He loses his values as an informant department
VIII, and it is proposed he be deployed in a
different department.

He has shown himself to be honest and willing
to work in the interests of the party.

Second Lieutenant Freier

MfS697/69 BSTU0020

Karl-Marx-Stadt, 15.10.1959

Karl-Marx-Stadt Area Command
Department V/6

Assessment
Re: Unofficial informant 'Fritzsche' reg. no. 187/55

The informant was recruited in 1951 by the then
Chemnitz Department as an informant on Line III.
Later he was used by Department VIII. There he
was charged only with personal characterisation.
The informant is a comrade and proved in the
previous collaboration that he is class-conscious
and party-connected.

In March 1959, contact was resumed with him
after it had lain fallow for many years with
Department VIII. He works as a trainer (cycling)
at SC Motor Karl-Marx-Stadt.

In this function he travels a lot with
cyclists from the clubs, and our collaboration is
compromised somewhat by this.

Where possible, he has kept to the designated
get-togethers/meetings, otherwise he has notified
the employee.

Apart from his work with Department VIII,
the informant has not been given missions of a
personal nature.

The informant is married, lives in a stable
relationship, and his moral conduct is impeccable.

First Lieutenant Neubert

DIETER

I decided I wanted to leave Motor, but it didn't work like that in GDR sport. I could have requested a transfer, but I couldn't afford for them to think I was siding with Richter. Then in mid-season a directive arrived from Berlin. They were reviewing the structure of the sport clubs again, and Motor was to become a track club. Wismut would focus on the road, and the two disciplines would be separated off. I'd been earmarked as a road cyclist, so in effect I was delegated to Wismut after all.

I was already a pretty good climber and time trialist, but a very ordinary sprinter. I knew that I had to improve on that, and for that to happen I needed to spend time at the track. The problem was that their splitting the two codes meant that I was effectively barred from riding it, so it made no sense whatsoever. It actually had quite a negative impact on my riding, but the people making these decisions were party functionaries, not bike riders. They didn't actually know the first thing about cycling, but as they saw it they were subsidising our careers. That gave them the right to decide things like that, and there was nothing you could do about it.

My dad was a really good mechanic, and Wismut offered him a full-time job. It was a dream for him. He loved the work, he was passionate about cycling and he enjoyed travelling to the races. My little brother started coming along as well.

DIETER

Eberhard started to race, and he was very good. Some of the coaches thought he was even more talented than me.

If you ask me about his character I'd say he and I were very different. I tended to be quite introspective, but Eberhard much more open. He was interested in clothes and I wasn't, he liked to be in a crowd and I didn't. So I was more reserved like our dad, and I guess he was more expressive.

There were four years between us, so we didn't spend that much time together socially. He joined the youth club as I left it, and of course we had different sets of friends. The thing we had in common was cycling. It was what we talked about when we were at home together, and I guess I'd look out for him just like any brothers would.

EBERHARD

My brother was my idol when I was a child. I used to clean his bike, and I cleaned his cycling shoes. I wanted to be a racer like him, and as soon as I began I started to do well. Dieter's success inspired me, and I wanted to prove that I could do it, too.

MfS4458/69 BSTU0028/0029

Berlin, 18.12.1959.

Main department VII/1/A

Appraisal

The informant 'Radler' was enlisted by Karl-Marx-Stadt Department VII in 1952. The handler with whom he worked at the time considered him a good informant who went to great pains to fulfil the set missions. Judging by the reports he made, he also did a good job.

In 1954 the connection with the informant 'Radler' was broken off, since he was transferred to a job as a trainer at SV Dynamo.

On 1.11.58 the collaboration with the informant was resumed by Captain Stenzel. It appears from the file that the cooperation was irregular.

Up till the acquisition of the informant by the undersigned on 4.6.59, three meetings were conducted.

Since the acquisition of the informant there was just one meeting which was very long and detailed, but thereafter the informant failed to turn up to any further meetings. Failure to attend a meeting has to be attributed to the fault of the undersigned (e.g. business trip). Although 'Radler' was in possession of the telephone number 63 34 44 and was explicitly asked to call the number if he was unable to attend and arrange a new meeting, he hasn't yet called. All attempts to reach the informant by 'phone in Wandlitz or in person at home have so far failed.

The informant must be regarded as a comrade who is a trainer through and through. He is one of the few coaches who concerns himself not only with the sports education of his protégés, but also their political and moral education.

He enjoys the confidence of all trainers and comrades of the sport club Dynamo due to his open, honest character. He behaves very critically in all respects, and his criticism is always considered very helpful.

He carries out his sports work tirelessly and has enjoyed great successes. In track cycling, the four-man Dynamo selection prepared by him for the Olympic Games recently broke the world record. At meetings with him he is open, and readily provides information to the MfS. Under specific guidance he is able to deliver good operational analysis reports.

His non-attendance at the meeting reveals that he is not bound closely enough to the MfS and probably underestimates the importance of the collaboration. It is imperative that closer bonds be formed between the informant and the MfS in the coming quarter.

The task is to establish a good network of unofficial staff with a view to securing the delegation for the forthcoming Olympic team in Rome. As the trainer of our world record team, the informant will be in Rome.

Second Lieutenant Jurmann

DIETER

1959 had been a really good year. I'd won a lot, and I was starting to become quite well known around Chemnitz. With the extra money I made we lived pretty well, and we were lucky. They abolished rationing that year, and a lot of people went hungry.

By now cycling was more popular than ever. Täve had won his second Peace Race,[*] and then he'd gone to Holland and won another world championship. It was his second in succession, and he became even more famous. He was on the front page of the papers, and he was always being portrayed as the model socialist. He'd come from peasant stock, but through hard work and sacrifice he'd reached the top. They'd even elected him to the People's Chamber,[†] the parliament.

DIETER

In January 1960 they drew up the provisional list for the 1964 Olympics in Tokyo, and I was on it.

I went on a winter training camp with Täve and the rest of the elites, doing cyclo-cross and cross-country skiing. I enjoyed it and it went well. It was a sort of carrot; they were letting me know that if I progressed and toed the line I'd soon be able to join them, with all the privileges that implied. I'd still be an 'amateur' cyclist, but in reality I'd be a full-time one. They placed a lot of emphasis on sport, so the status of full-time athletes was extremely high.

---

[*]   Prior to the 1959 Peace Race the first and last stages – and with them the huge opening and closing ceremonies – had always been in Warsaw and Prague. The GDR had hosted the middle four stages, usually in Görlitz, Berlin, Leipzig and Karl-Marx-Stadt. Now, however, it was agreed that the route would rotate annually. As such the race started in Berlin, and would conclude there the following year. In effect it was now on an equal footing with Prague and Warsaw.

[†]   Täve had been voted into the *Volkskammer* in 1958. It was unprecedented that a sportsman might be elected, but by then his fame and influence was boundless.

MfS383/65 bd1, BSTU0025

SPORT-CLUB WISMUT

FOOTBALL - SWIMMING - TRACK AND FIELD - CYCLING -
ICE HOCKEY - SPEED SKATING - JUDO - GYMNASTICS

KARL-MARX-STADT W33

17.2.1960

Appraisal

Sportsfriend Dieter Wiedemann
Born: 17.6.1941
Profession: Lathe operator
Workplace: VEB 8 Mai
Resident: Wiesenstrasse 15, Flöha
Organizations: FDGB, DS, FDJ

Sportsfriend Wiedemann joined our club in November
1958. He is an exceptionally talented cyclist, one of the
best in the republic. In 1958/59 he won nearly all of
the races he took part in.

He comes from a workers' family. His father, Karl
Wiedemann, is a mechanic at our club.

By profession he is a lathe operator, and he takes his
work at VEB 8 Mai extremely seriously. The assessment
of the club leaders is very positive, as sportsfriend
Wiedemann is extremely determined and serious about his
efforts.

His wish is that, in addition to achieving great
things in sport, he can become a master lathe operator.

His character is very open-minded, and he fits very
well into the collective. At the outset it was noted that
he seemed to be an outsider, but with time he appears to
have overcome that. He is very open, and speaks his mind
at meetings and discussions.

Sportsfriend Wiedemann is an Olympic candidate, and
his standpoint is that he wants to qualify for the 1964
games. His focus is entirely dedicated to that objective,
and we fully support him.

Secretariat, Sport-Club Wismut, Karl-Marx-Stadt

DIETER

So I started the season well, and in May I got a letter. It said that I was to stop working altogether during the season, and to focus exclusively on cycling. The state would fund my career from here on in, and I would be exempted from military service because I was a sportsman.

I would say that there would have been about 120 full-time road cyclists in the country, and I'm pretty sure I was the youngest. Obviously I wasn't ready for the Peace Race yet, but I'd been identified as a candidate for later on. The GDR sent teams to amateur stage races all over East Europe and North Africa, and I was better suited to them than to single-day races. Like everyone else I wanted to travel, and I knew that if I got good results I might eventually qualify for the Peace Race and the World Championships. Of course the biggest dream of all was to compete at the Olympics, and now that I was full-time it was something I could genuinely aspire to.

DIETER

One of my Wismut team-mates, Johannes Schober, was selected to ride the Peace Race, but we'd expected a guy named Manfred Weissleder to make it as well. He was an excellent sprinter, and his results were exceptional. However it was starting to dawn on me that things were becoming more complicated among the seniors.

Ours was a provincial club and it wasn't political at all. Others were, though, and they had much more influence than us.

The most powerful of all was DHfK. I'd been invited to enrol there the previous year, but I'd turned it down. I hadn't wanted to move to Leipzig. I was worried there would be Stasi there, and I'm not a herd animal anyway.

We were ostensibly amateurs, so we had to have an occupation outside of cycling. Obviously you couldn't do a job, so you became a student. I was on a teacher training course at a polytechnic in Chemnitz, working towards a teaching degree. There were about eight of us cyclists. We studied on site during the off-season, and did the rest as a correspondence course. In principle the DHfK guys were also studying, but in reality only the guys lower down the scale did, not the elites. In that sense we were at a disadvantage, but the real problem was that all the national team coaches and selectors worked at DHfK. To do that you had to be a party member and a good socialist, and obviously they looked after their own.

DHfK was the seat of power in GDR sport, and cycling was an extremely popular sport. The riders there were the chosen ones, and when they selected the Peace Race team there were four from DHfK. Then you had Schober from Wismut, and a guy called Egon Adler. He was from Leipzig as well, but he wasn't enrolled at DHfK. He rode for Rotation, another sport club in Leipzig, but he was so good that it was inconceivable they might leave him out.

A few days before the race Günter Lörke, one of the DHfK riders, fell ill. So they called Weissleder up after all, and he won four stages.

It turned out to be one of the greatest races of all time. The last stage was Magdeburg to Berlin. The GDR team had the blue jerseys, and Adler the yellow one. Then a DHfK guy named Erich Hagen was second at thirty-eight seconds, a Belgian guy named Claes third at one minute and another Belgian fourth. It was a flat stage, but at the Peace Race the stage winner got a one-minute time bonus, the runner-up thirty seconds and the third fifteen. That meant that, come what may, the Peace Race would be decided at the stadium.

Claes wasn't a sprinter, but Adler crashed after twenty kilometres and the Belgians saw their chance to eliminate him. The GDR team decided to have Täve and Weissleder wait, to try to tow Adler back on. They were the strongest time trialists, and the three of them were effectively riding a team pursuit to try to bridge across to the peloton. The problem was the Belgians were too strong, and after eighty kilometres they were cooked. That left Hagen, Schober and another DHfK guy named Eckstein fighting against the whole Belgian team. The first three from each team counted towards the team prize, and the Belgians knew that if they dropped one of the remaining GDR riders they could win it. So a mechanical problem or puncture would be disastrous for the team competition, and if something happened to Hagen we'd lose everything.

Luckily they didn't have any mechanicals, and they managed to chase everything down. That still left the sprint at the stadium, and there were 70,000 people there to watch it. They all knew exactly what was happening, and so did everyone else because the entire country was listening on the radio. Weissleder would probably have won the sprint had he been there, and Täve was pretty fast, too. As it was, both of them were back down the road with Adler, and it was clear they'd made a big mistake in having them wait for him. Neither Eckstein nor Schober were sprinters, and if Claes beat Hagen and finished first or second he'd win the Peace Race. Hagen was a decent sprinter, but he was totally exposed. There were often crashes because it was a cinder track, and if one of the Belgians brought him off that would be that.

In the event Hagen won the stage and the yellow jersey, and the GDR team held on to the blue ones. It was probably the most dramatic Peace Race finale in history, and an unprecedented success for the GDR.

WALTER ULBRICHT; FIRST SECRETARY, SOCIALIST UNITY PARTY

We are thrilled that the most important amateur road race in the world enjoyed its highpoint and conclusion in Berlin. We are pleased that, in conjunction with world of cycling, the capital of the GDR was able to host athletes from twenty European countries. I want to thank them for their sporting success, but also to state our appreciation and gratitude for the service they have rendered to the pursuit of friendship and cooperation between their peoples. All the riders, and the millions of peace-loving people who cheered them, have demonstrated for total and universal disarmament, for the settlement of all disputes, and for understanding between nations on the basis of the United Nations charter.

The condemnation of the espionage and diversionary acts undertaken by the rulers of USA and West Germany is a prerequisite for ensuring peace. Only by strict respect for the United Nations charter can respect for the sovereignty of peaceful states be secured. Im sure youll understand the particular joy for the GDR team. I congratulate Schur, Hagen, Adler, Weissleder, Eckstein and Schober for their excellent collective and individual performances. [...]

We are certain that the massive interest of the populations of Czechoslovakia, Poland and the GDR is a reaction to the basic idea of athletic competition in close correlation with the journey towards peace and friendship. Millions have cheered them, in recognition and appreciation of their wonderful demonstration against war and ethnic hatred.

We believe that the future of humanity is better served when the youth of the sporting world competes across national boundaries. Meanwhile the US government continues along the path of espionage as it seeks to create the conditions for war. Mr Eisenhower has received a million simple ripostes: the voices of a million envoys of peace, cheering for friendship, were more than loud enough to put the American provocateurs in their place [...]*

* Cited in *Neues Deutschland*, 18 May 1960

MANFRED

Everyone had the same objective. You wanted to do well at the Peace Race and the Olympics, then to turn pro' and ride with a sponsor's name on your jersey. You didn't articulate that to the coaches, though, because you risked being turfed out straight away.

I'd won four stages, and between me, Schur, Adler and Hagen we'd had the yellow jersey from beginning to end. After the Peace Race I was offered contracts by professional teams from France, West Germany and Belgium. I thought about it a lot, but in the end I decided against going. On a sporting level I was tempted, but I wanted to ride in the Olympics in Rome, and I didn't want to leave my family.

They didn't select me for Rome,[*] so they basically threw away a gold medal in the team time trial.

---

[*] The GDR quartet for the 100-kilometre team time trial was Schur, Hagen and Lörke (all DHfK) and Adler (Rotation Leipzig). On a blistering hot Rome morning they finished second, two minutes behind the Italians. A Danish rider, twenty-two-year-old Knud Enemark Jensen, died shortly after the race. He was later discovered to have taken both a vasodilator and amphetamine. The following year an Italian professional, Bruno Busso, died under similar circumstances at the Tour of Piedmont.

MfS4458/69 BSTU0038

Berlin, 30.5.60

Strictly Confidential!

Government of the German Democratic Republic
Ministry of the Interior
Ministry for State Security
Main department VII/1/A

Order
Redeployment of Informant

Alias: 'Radler'   Reg.no. 2163/58

From Informant to Main Informant

Grounds for redeployment:

The informant is a politically good and
consistent comrade, who has worked for many years
as a trainer at SV Dynamo. As such he knows the
situation at both the central office and the sport
club very well. He has a very good reputation as a
trainer.

The informant has worked for the MfS since
1952, and has proved to be worthy of great
confidence. He completes his tasks punctually and
conscientiously through his work, enjoys great
confidence within the MfS and punctually and
faithfully complies with any task.

Approved: 3.6.60

DIETER

I'd been training with Weissleder and Schober, and so their performances at the Peace Race gave me a barometer of my progress. I had
my nineteenth birthday the following month, and I knew that with each
passing week I was getting closer to their level. I lived and breathed
cycling, and I was working my way up the pecking order at Wismut. I
was focused on trying to qualify for the national team time trial championships in August, and I trained like fury to get there. Weissleder,
Schober and a guy called Härtel pretty much selected themselves, so my
big objective was to be chosen for the final spot.

And then, of course, you know what happened in July.

SYLVIA

Remember the aunt and uncle I told you about, the ones with the cigars
in Flöha? My grandmother said she wanted to visit them during the
summer holidays, to see her sister again. She asked me if I wanted to go
with her, and I said I did. I'd never met them before, and I'd always liked
the letters Uncle Herbert had sent. So I wanted to meet them and I guess
it was a kind of adventure for me as well.

My aunt and uncle were very nice, but they were quite poor compared
to us. I was surprised because they didn't have a lot of the things we took
for granted, but they were very nice and they did their best to give us the
best of the things they did. I was fine there, but I remember thinking, 'It's
OK because I don't have to stay very long, and then I'll go back to my
own world.'

The problem was that they only had a tiny flat, and they didn't have
anywhere for me to sleep. A divorced woman lived upstairs from them,
though, and her name was Annemarie Müller. She was a lovely person,
and she had two sons called Rainer and Stephan. Rainer was away with
the army, so I slept in his bed.

DIETER

I had an old school friend who lived on the next street to us, about 100 metres away. His name was Rainer Müller, and I used to pass his flat on the way to get the milk from the farmer each morning.

RAINER

Dieter and I had been best friends at school, but we pretty much went our separate ways after that. I remember his getting his racing bike for his fourteenth birthday, and after that he was focused on his cycling. I was more interested in football, and then of course we'd both started work. We'd still chat when we bumped into each other, but not often because I went off to the army and he was always off somewhere racing.

SYLVIA

One morning I was up in the bedroom doing nothing much. I was just gazing out of the window, and I saw a guy walk past. He glanced up at the window, so I said hello.

DIETER

One day as I was walking down Rainer's street I saw his girlfriend, Brigitte, leaning out of his bedroom window. I was surprised because he was away on military service, but I didn't think much of it.

As I passed underneath the flat she shouted, 'Grüss Gott', but that was a southern German greeting. People from Flöha never used it because we said 'Guten Tag'. So I knew it couldn't have been Brigitte, so I did a double take and I realised that it wasn't. There was a girl in Rainer's bedroom who looked almost identical to Brigitte, but it was somebody else. I thought, 'That's really strange! Who's that girl in Rainer's bedroom?'

DIETER

Two days later I went down to the river with a cycling friend of mine. Rainer's little brother was there with the girl from the bedroom window.

SYLVIA

It was hot when Stephan and I went down to the river. I had my swimming costume on, and we just stood there paddling in the water, playing with stones and suchlike. Then the boy I'd seen passing the window appeared, and he was with another boy. The other one started joking around, like boys will. He pinched my shoe and made it float on the river, just to make fun of me. He was a bit full of himself, and in the end I got a bit fed up with it.

Anyway, he gave me my shoe back eventually, and we started talking. I wasn't sure about the mouthy one to be honest, but the boy I'd seen passing the flat was nice. He didn't say very much, but he was courteous and I could tell he was quite shy. Before they left he asked me if I wanted to play badminton with him some time, and I said I would. He seemed like a kind person, and he was very handsome. I liked him, and I was bored of spending all my time with Stephan and the old people.

DIETER

We played around for a while, and then we started chatting. I could tell that she was from the west straight away. She had a yellow bikini on, and then there were her shoes. I'd been to the west in 1957 and I'd seen shoes like that. They were made by Salamander, and you couldn't get them in the GDR. The colours were different, the style was different, and the quality was totally different.

To be honest I didn't know anything about girls, and if I'd been alone I wouldn't have had the courage to speak with her.

SYLVIA

When I went back to my great-aunt's house they asked what I'd been doing, and I told them about the boys we'd met. Annemarie said, 'Oh that's Dieter, Rainer's friend! Yes, he's a very nice boy ...'

Later in the week he called round and asked if I wanted to play badminton with him. I said yes, and we played in the street in front of the house. He paid me a compliment, and I could tell that it took a lot of courage for him. When you're that age you don't really know who you are, so little things like that are really important, you know?

Anyway, he was very nice, and we had fun playing badminton. Before I went home I said to my great-uncle, 'If he asks you for my address you can give it to him!'

RAINER

I came home at the weekend, but I couldn't sleep in my room because there was a girl there!

SYLVIA

I was sure I'd be getting a letter. Absolutely sure of it.

DIETER

Normal families didn't have telephones back then, no. Businesses had them, but the joke went that if you had access to a phone you were probably Stasi. So when Sylvia went home I went to see her uncle and asked for her address. If I'd known she was only fourteen I wouldn't have asked, but she looked older, sixteen or something.

SYLVIA

I got home from school one day and my mum said, 'You've got a letter with a GDR postmark!' I wasn't used to getting letters, and I knew straight away it would be from Dieter. I ran straight up to my room and read it on my bed.

Flöha, 28 August 1960

Dear Sylvia,

Today is 28 August, and finally I have some time to write to you.

I've been very busy cycling, more or less all of August. Now that I have the time I wanted to tell you that it's a real pity that we didn't see each other the evening before you departed. I would have liked to say goodbye to you, but unfortunately we didn't have the chance. I'd wanted to ask you for your address, and whether it would be alright for me to write to you.

Anyway you left a note with your aunt. She told me that you would be very pleased for me to write, so she gave me your address.

It's a pity that we met so late. It would have been much nicer if we'd had more time to spend together. I would have liked to play more badminton with you, and to have had the chance to talk more.

Dear Sylvia, please let me know where Mitterteich is, and which is the nearest big city. I looked on the map but I didn't manage to find it, so I guess it's probably a very small town.

I'm interested to know how old you are, and when your birthday is – please let me know in due course. Your aunt told me that you'd like to have a picture of me. I'll send one with my next letter because I don't have a nice one. I need to go and see the photographer, and then I'll let you have a very nice picture of myself! I'd also like a photo' of you, and I'll keep it with me as a lucky charm.

I need to tell you that I'm very busy with cycling. I race more or less every Sunday, so I don't have much free time.

What are you going to do next year during the holidays? Do you have any plans, or do you intend to come back to Flöha? Please let me know about your interests, and what you do during your free time.

Today I did some training, about 150 kilometres, so I'm very tired. So I'll end now, and I'll hope to receive a letter from you soon.

Yours,

Dieter

DIETER

It wasn't because I thought we would eventually be together, nothing like that. You don't think like that at nineteen, but I'd enjoyed spending time with her. I'd never really spent time alone with a girl before, and I liked it. I liked her as well, so I just decided to write.

DIETER

The GDR hosted the Cycling World Championships that summer. The idea was to celebrate Täve, and they knew that if he won a third rainbow jersey at home it would be a great coup.

They wanted to have the Worlds, but you couldn't have the amateur race without the professional one. The problem was that communist doctrine was against professional sport, but for that week they set aside their ideological opposition and welcomed the professionals with open arms. They said they wanted to demonstrate the beauty of the country and the ideals of socialism to the world but in reality it was all about using sport – and specifically Täve's fame – for propaganda purposes at home. It was classic GDR.

The race was the Sachsenring motor racing circuit, and of course the whole country wanted to see him win. On Friday I went to have a look with a friend of mine who had lived in the west, and I saw a big advertising hoarding for Torpedo, a West German 'pro team from Schweinfurt. My friend knew some of the riders from his time there, and we got talking to their mechanic. He gave me a Torpedo cap and *bidon*, and I was really proud of them. You couldn't get things like that in the GDR, so to have them was really special.

The weather was awful the following day, but the crowds were massive. It seemed like the whole country had come to watch Täve.

DIETER

It was the most famous race in the history of GDR cycling, and one of the most important sporting moments. What happened was that a Belgian named Willy Vandenberghen broke away. Täve was the strongest in the race, and on the final lap he bridged across with another GDR rider, Bernhard Eckstein. When they reached Vandenberghen, Eckstein attacked to try to force him to chase. The idea was that Vandenberghen would wear himself out getting back on, and Täve would be able to ride away and win another rainbow jersey.

It all seemed simple, but when Eckstein attacked Vandenberghen just sat up. He knew that if he chased he would be beaten anyway, and so he played the only card he had. He called Täve's bluff because he reasoned there was a chance that Täve's ambition would get the better of him. If he did he might just chase Eckstein down himself, because everything was geared around him winning a third world championship. He was the team captain, and Vandenberghen reasoned that the idea had probably been for Eckstein to sacrifice himself for *him*. Vandenberghen figured that if he did nothing then Täve might be tempted to chase Eckstein down, and that if he did he'd be able to sit on his wheel and follow. That would have left him the freshest, and besides it was the only chance he had to win.

However, Täve knew that if he dragged Vandenberghen across the GDR risked getting nothing, so they both just watched Eckstein ride away. The upshot of it all was that Eckstein won the world championship unopposed, and Täve beat Vandenberghen in the sprint for silver.

Eckstein was the champion, but the way the race had played itself out made Täve even more popular. The media portrayed it as an act of extreme altruism on his part. It's true that Täve was a good sportsman, but it's also true that it was a pretty standard bike racing decision. There was nothing wrong in that, but Täve hadn't set out to sacrifice himself for Eckstein. It had been a win-win situation for the team, and as it turned out it favoured Eckstein instead of Täve.

NEUES DEUTSCHLAND
ORGAN DES ZENTRALKOMITEES DER SOZIALISTISCHEN EINHEITSPARTEI DEUTSCHLANDS

[...]

Up front Willy Vandenberghen, a world-class rider, was fighting for the victory. At first glance the mighty Belgian seemed to hold all the cards. However, he was trumped because somebody else, namely our Täve, had the better hand. It was that of the stronger team and the better collective. In the final analysis two boys, each clad in the white jersey with the black and red rings, came out on top.

When Willy Vandenberghen saw the two white jerseys at his side, he knew the game was up, and even his desperate sprint for second place failed. Thanks to Eckstein and Schur, the amateur title went to the GDR for the third time in succession. Thanks also to Günter Lörke, Erich Hagen, Lothar Höhne and Egon Adler, who selflessly helped to prepare the triumph of all triumphs.

Over the past three days, West German journalists, visiting the GDR as guests of the World Cycling Championships, tried to launch a major offensive against the sporting movement of our republic. On Saturday Axel Springer's tabloid *Bild-Zeitung* even raged that this was the last World Championship which would take place in the GDR.

Such hopes can only be described as wishful thinking. Now, as the GDR celebrates its triumph, we can only pity the West German journalists. Their attack has ground to a halt in the volley of a new triumph of the socialist sports movement.

Reprinted from 'Triumph of triumphs', 14 August 1960

DIETER

The issue was that the journalists – who were all party members – turned it completely on its head. *Neues Deutschland* used it as an example of the moral virtue of socialism, but it wasn't at all. It was just a bike race, and one of ours had won it fair and square. Nobody gave Eckstein much credit for it, because it was all about Täve and the glory of socialism. That wasn't Täve's fault, but I was starting to understand that everything was a propaganda exercise.

KLAUS

It's true that there was no sports journalist in the world whose work was as politicised as the GDR sports journalist. We didn't choose for it to be like that, but you have to understand what was happening. The FRG and its journalists had ambitions to be the only legitimate German state, and that's the way they portrayed themselves. Obviously our party had to fight against that, and so that's what we did.

It was a political fight. It was about our fight for international recognition, and part of that was having our own sports teams.

DIETER

I thought my new Torpedo cap was cool, so I wore it for training. They told me I had to take it off, because it was contrary to socialist principles. I thought, 'That doesn't make sense! You welcome the professionals when it suits you, but now you're getting stroppy with me because I'm wearing one of their caps!'

In September I rode the national team time trial championship with Wismut, and we won it. Suddenly everything seemed to be going well. I was nineteen, I was already riding with the champions, and I was earning 350 marks a month plus my prizes. People like Täve and Eckstein were getting much more, but that was normal because they were the best.

And besides, normal working people were getting paid 1.30 marks an hour, about 250 marks a month.

MfS383/65 bd1, BSTU0024

BETRIEBSBERUFFSCHULE VEB GROSSDREHMASCHINENBAU '8 MAI'

WALDSTRASSE 3, EISENDEL, KARL-MARX-STADT
KARL-MARX-STADT 20.9.60

APPRAISAL

Dieter Wiedemann, born 17.6.41 in Flöha

Resident in R. Breitscheid-Strasse 51, Flöha

Colleague Wiedemann carried out his apprenticeship 1.9.55-31.8.57. Upon completion he began working as a qualified lathe operator from 1.5.57.

Initially he worked very slowly, but progressively he worked faster. This led to him accomplishing tasks of moderate difficulty and an improvement in his output.

Colleague Wiedemann belongs to the elite cycling group of the GDR, and was recently added to the list of Olympic candidates. Therefore he trained a lot, and hasn't worked for a long time. Given the generous support our company offers Wiedemann, he should have more appreciation of the social system.

Colleague Wiedemann has a shy and reserved character and he needs to be harder temperamentally due to the rigorous nature of his sports training.

Bischoff

Work Group Instructor

Flöha, 21 September 1960

Dear Sylvia,

I was very happy to get your letter yesterday. Thank you very much for the two photographs, which are really nice.

When I went to a race in Stuttgart earlier this year we passed through Hof, which I now know is close to where you live in Mitterteich.

To be honest I'd never have thought you were so young. I'd guessed at around 15 or 16 years old. Anyway, I would be very happy if you come back to visit your aunt again next year during the holidays. The problem is all that bureaucratic stuff that you have to go through to get a travel permit. It would be much easier if there was a united Germany, as opposed to East and West.

I have a brother who's 15, and he started his apprenticeship on 1 September. During my free time I read and listen to the radio, and I record the best songs. I listen to BAYERN 1, BAYERN 2, Hessischer Rundfunk and so on.

Dear Sylvia, although you're still so young I'd like to continue to write and to be pen-friends, and I hope you'd like that too. I love writing, and because my life is so busy with cycling I don't go dancing. Nor do I drink alcohol or smoke, because I have to be in good shape for my sport.

You asked me if I have a girlfriend, and I don't. I was born on 17 June 1941. For sure you will be surprised at that, but as you see I'm only five years older than you.

I'm an amateur cyclist. I work 12-16 hours a week during the off-season but I spend the rest of my time training, which is paid for by the company. We ride 15-18,000 kilometres a year and we do 30-40 races, usually at weekends.

On 18 September we won a race. I was riding for my club, SC Wismut, and with my team mates Weissleder, Schober and Härtel we became national champions in the 100 kilometre team time trial. Our time was 2.16.56. I enclose a picture from the local newspaper; it's not very nice but maybe you will like it.

Say hello to your parents and your brother. Hoping to hear from you very soon.

Yours,
Dieter.

SYLVIA

At first we'd write about every two weeks, and the letters were very innocent. We'd write about music, the books we liked reading, I'd ask him about his cycling and so on. I had a much busier social life than him, with more friends and more things to do. He was busy training, and he was a shy person anyway. He wrote that he wasn't one for going out dancing, going to bars, those things.

At first I had to show my parents the letters, but that was fine. They didn't have any problems with the fact that we were writing, and nor with the fact that he was five years older than me. After all he lived in a different country, so it wasn't as if I was going to come to any harm.

DIETER

Thousands were leaving every day now, and the population just seemed to be dwindling all the time. Everyone either had a relative or a friend who had gone.

You had the sensation that something had to happen because otherwise there would be nothing left. It seemed like there was just less and less of everything. There were fewer people, and those that were left seemed more and more disillusioned.

NEUES DEUTSCHLAND

ORGAN DES ZENTRALKOMITEES DER SOZIALISTISCHEN EINHEITSPARTEI DEUTSCHLANDS

As communicated by the General Secretariat of the German Cycling Federation, former president Werner Scharch, has defected. He has abandoned his wife and children, betrayed the Republic and is currently seeking asylum in Austria. The reasons for his humanly indecent and politically treacherous act are to be found in his profound moral decay.

Recently Scharch had been consuming more and more alcohol, and had sought relationships with dubious women. This led to irreconcilable differences between him and the athletes and coaches during the Olympic Games in Rome, and they demanded his immediate resignation. Instead of embarking upon a detoxification programme as was suggested to him, he continued to entertain relations with dubious West German women, who played him into the hands of agents of the Bonn government.

Reprinted from 'Scharch betrayed the Republic', 16 October 1960

WERNER

I don't intend to give all the reasons for my having defected from the GDR. They are of a personal nature, but one of them must be revealed. It concerns the status of our sportsmen, and it brought me face-to-face with a serious case of conscience.

The Olympic charter provides a clear definition of the amateur status of sportsmen. In order to establish who may participate at the games, the International Cycling Union instituted three categories: amateurs, independents and professionals. The status of each is unequivocally defined, but in recent years the states of the east have created an entirely new category of their own: the state professional. I mention this because in these countries amateurs are treated as professionals. They receive a fee for their performances, and this represents a flagrant transgression of their amateur status.

In point of fact, it is on account of these problems that I resigned my post. It is imperative that a solution be found for, in the long run, the position of athletes in the countries of the east will become intolerable to integral amateur status.

On a strictly sporting basis the situation has already become untenable. In the present conditions amateurs riding for countries where professionalism exists are competing against racers from the east who are in fact professionals. Schur, for example, could compete on equal terms with the greatest champions among the professionals, and has no difficulty in beating young competitors who are still genuine amateurs. Obviously this situation is inadmissible.

In western countries, professional riders belong to a company, represent a brand or a group of ultra-trained sportsmen. They are paid according to what they yield, or to their standing. In the GDR the racers belong to a club which pays them a fee. Schur, Hagen and Eckstein earn 600 to 1,200 marks per month, a large sum of money by our standards.

What is more their housing is provided and they are paid bonuses. These can reach up to 7,000 marks when they win an international title. The fact that some of them — Schur, for example – carry out very serious studies makes no difference, since the rules state that student scholarships must not exceed 300 marks a month.

I raise no objection to the fact that they receive money, but they ought to be classed with, and compete against, the professional riders of other countries. Besides, this would be in their own interests.[*]

---

[*]   Reprinted from 'Ex-leader Scharch interviewed', *L'Équipe*, October 1960

NEUES DEUTSCHLAND

ORGAN DES ZENTRALKOMITEES DER SOZIALISTISCHEN EINHEITSPARTEI DEUTSCHLANDS

The best of our republic's road cyclists, recently returned from China and including twice world champion Täve Schur and current world champion Bernard Eckstein, have issued the following statement from the presidium of the GDR Cycling Federation in respect to the betrayal of the former president of the Federation.

The statement, signed by coach Werner Schiffner, Peace Race winner Erich Hagen, Günter Lörke, Egon Adler and also Schur and Eckstein, states: 'A traitor cannot stop the development of our sport. Through extensive training and continued high performance, we want to continue the development of socialist physical culture in our country.'

The cycling presidium states the following in respect to the dubious lifestyle of Scharch:

'Because of his immoral attitude, Scharch was relieved of his position as president of the federation. He then showed his true character by betraying the socialist sports movement and our workers and farmers' state. His untruthful statements in the West German media and that of other countries, serve exclusively to further his own possibilities and to enable him to continue his unsound moral conduct. The presidium maintains that our association has at all times respected and adhered to the statutes of the UCI, and will continue to do so.' [...]

Reprinted from 'A traitor cannot stop us', 31 October 1960

HEINZ SCHÖBEL; PRESIDENT,
GDR NATIONAL OLYMPIC COMMITTEE

After contacting the leaders of the German
Cycling Federation, I can assure you that
the allegations brought forward by Mr
Scharch are utterly devoid of foundation and
have been conceived by Mr Scharch and his
supporters solely with one purpose, namely
that of stirring trouble and disturbing the
collaboration existing between the sportsmen
of the two different German States and of
spoiling the friendly relations among the
sportsmen throughout the world. Previous to
receiving your two letters, I was informed by
the leaders of the German Cycling Federation
that Scharch, who left the Democratic German
Republic (East), is spreading most shocking
lies about the cyclists of our country, in West
Germany and abroad.

The German Cycling Federation begged me
to emphasise the fact that the federation
is determined to implement at all times the
rules and principles laid down by the IOC
and the UCI.*

---

* *Reprinted from 'The Olympic committee of the German Democratic Republic replies to*
Mr Scharch's allegations – Letter of 15 November 1960', IOC Bulletin no. 73

NEUE ZEIT

Berlin (ADN). The General Public Prosecutor of Berlin announces that, according to an investigation initiated because of continued misappropriation and fraud, an arrest warrant has been issued against the former president of the GDR Cycling Federation, Werner Scharch. In his capacity as president of the GDR Cycling Federation, Scharch embezzled funds entrusted to him, and spent them for personal purposes. Search measures have been initiated against the defector.

Reprinted from 'Proceedings against Scharch', 15 November 1960[*]

---

[*]   *Neue Zeit* was the daily paper of the CDU, one of the GDR bloc parties. It ceased publication in 1994.

DIETER

1960 had been the best year of my life. I had been the youngest in the group, so I'd had no pressure and I'd improved a lot. Then our team had won the Peace Race and the World Championship, and I'd been to the Sachsenring as a guest. I'd also won the national championship with Wismut and met Sylvia. Life was fun, and looking back now I honestly don't think I've ever been happier.

I wasn't ready for the Peace Race, but I started the new year with another big objective. It was the Tour of Egypt, a twelve-day stage race in January.

Egypt was prestigious because it confirmed that they thought I was one of the most promising young riders in the GDR, a potential Peace Race candidate. What's more, it was a chance to fly, and to experience a part of the world that normal people could never dream of seeing. I was still only nineteen, so it was a huge step in my career and a big moment in my life. It was my first time outside of Germany, and my first time on an aeroplane.

We set off in the middle of January, because it started on the 26th, the last Thursday of the month. We stopped off in Prague, then the plane failed in Budapest so we had an overnight stay there. Then we went on to Bucharest, and there was another three-day stopover in Tirana because of fog. We'd set off ten days early to acclimatise, but by the time we got there we'd been travelling for a week. Even when we reached Cairo we still had to take a train to Luxor. It was 850 kilometres, and it was 30°.

The flights were terrifying, but being in Egypt was magical. There were sights and sounds I could never have dreamed of: the Pyramids, Cairo, the food.

Flöha, 19.3.1961

Dear Sylvia,

Thanks for your letter dated 11 February. It was a real pleasure to receive it as always, and thanks also for the chewing gum.

You ask whether it would be worth going back to Egypt and yes, it would be a marvellous place for a wedding one day. I had never dreamed of being able to go, and I'm sorry you couldn't come with me.

You read correctly that I'd like to be a sports teacher one day. I'll start studying this year but it takes four years because it's interrupted by a lot of training.

The girls over here are very vain, and for some of them the only important thing is to have a famous boyfriend. However they don't realise that the boyfriend would be training very hard and travelling a lot, and that they would be alone a lot. But now I'm going to tell you more about Egypt.

We started on 23 January, and we flew with a Russian TU104 from Tirana to Cairo. The weather was very nice, and the height was 5000 metres. You could still see the ships in the Mediterranean, but they were very small.

We arrived in Cairo at 3 o'clock in the afternoon and the airport was in the middle of the desert. They took us to the hotel, and we saw the traffic jams in Cairo. There are cars everywhere! They were driving on the left, on the right and in the middle! They have all the newest cars, like the Opel P4 and Fords. On 24 January we went by train to Luxor. The train was extremely dirty and the seats very narrow. Looking out of the window we saw orange and mandarin trees, and also eucalyptus trees, which I'd never even heard of before. Then there were also all the different types of palms.

We arrived after a 14-hour train journey, and we stayed at the Hotel Luxor. We trained in the morning, and in the afternoon we went sightseeing at the Valley of the Kings. There we had our first sight of the art and architecture of ancient Egypt. You can't imagine the beauty of it, and I'm not even able to put it into words. I'm still so astonished by it that I don't know what to say. So many years ago they built these beautiful statues. There is a lot of gold, but you also see lots of very poor people. Then on the other hand you have a lot of tourists from all over the world, and the hotels are extremely luxurious.

On 26 January we had a 220 kilometre stage through the desert. The roads were very sandy, it was extremely hot, and the last 80 kilometres were along the Nile. When we got back after seven hours we were absolutely filthy. (…)

The seventh stage was 175 kilometres, with 80 along the Suez Canal. We had a wonderful hotel with a view of the Mediterranean. It would be a great place to have a holiday. It's just a pity I don't have a camera, because I'd have liked to have taken a picture.

The closer you get to the Nile Delta the greener the landscape becomes. We had dinner in a German restaurant, and I wasn't expecting that in Egypt! We talked to the owner, and he was so happy to see some Germans that he gave us some stickers for our suitcases and a copy of the menu as a souvenir. We ate different soups, some cheese I've never had before, butter, roulade and black bread. I also had fresh fish! I'd never eaten it before, but it was delicious! Then there were also fruits I'd never had before like oranges, mandarins and bananas. I was eating about five bananas a day because at home we can't buy them.

We went shopping in Cairo, but you need much longer because there are no fixed prices. It's a big market, and sometimes I had to spend two or three hours in one shop just to get a good price! We stayed in the Hilton Hotel, and one night there costs the same as a doctor's salary for a month! (…)

It was very nice to be a tourist there, but GDR salaries are like those in Egypt. So our money doesn't go very far, and things seem really expensive. We were lucky that all our expenses were paid, and
I bought you a bag because leather goods are really special and not very expensive. Egyptian women are very pretty, but you don't see too much because most of their face is covered.

Enough for today.

Regards and best wishes,
Dieter.

DIETER

Egypt had been twelve stages and 1,800 kilometres in ferocious heat. I'd finished seventh on GC and we'd won the team prize, so it was a big success. The problem was that I already had 5,000 kilometres in my legs, and they put me straight back on the same training programme as the others. My body wasn't ready for that kind of workload, and I needed two or three weeks of low-intensity riding to recover.

They said I had to stick to the training plan but by the time the domestic races started I was exhausted. In the first race I was out the back after 80 kilometres, then 60 kilometres the following week. By April I was in a terrible state.

I went to see the doctor and he told me I needed to take four weeks off. I read, wrote to Sylvia, walked in the forest and just did light exercises. Then, in May, I followed the Peace Race on the radio and in the papers.

MANFRED

I'd won four stages at the 1960 Peace Race, but everyone remembers me for a stage I didn't win, in 1961. If I run into somebody round town they don't say, 'You're Weissleder! You had the yellow jersey and won all those stages!' Instead they say, 'You're Weissleder! I remember you! You hit that Russian guy with your pump!'

It happened in the stadium at Poznań. I was already well known because I'd won in Poznań the previous year, but now there was a group of seven of us coming into the stadium. Two of them were Russians, Pietrow and Melichow, the yellow jersey. They knew I was the fastest, so Melichow just grabbed hold of my jersey. That enabled Pietrow to win the stage, but I wasn't having it because it was unsporting. I whacked Melichow with my pump, and at that moment I became a big hero for the Polish people.*

Bernhard Trefflich had told me that there was hostility to the GDR riders in Poland, but he'd ridden in the early 1950s. By the time we came along the Russians were the common enemy, and the Polish fans hated them. I wasn't interested in politics, and I didn't view it in ideological terms. For me it was just a bike race, but when I hit Melichow they said that I'd 'violated German–Soviet friendship'.

Then again everyone in the stadium – and everyone at home – had thought that what I'd done was correct. They still thank me for it today, but it had serious repercussions for my cycling career.

DIETER

I hadn't touched the bike for a month, but when the Peace Race finished I started training again. I felt better, and I wanted to be ready for the Tour of the GDR in August.

DIETER

Politics weren't something that interested me, and I certainly wouldn't describe myself as a dissident or anything like that. I suppose you could say that I'd managed to avoid it until that point, but that all changed on Sunday 13 August 1961.†

---

* The incident mirrored Królak's in 1956, and provoked outrage in the stadium. The jury, fearing a riot, demoted Melichow but not Weissleder. It made no difference, though, as the Russian went on to claim the USSR's first Peace Race win, by eleven minutes. In general terms Soviet success met with polite indifference in 'little brother' GDR. In Poland and Czechoslovakia, however, the crowds were known to be openly hostile. When Melichow clinched both stage and GC on Prague, they set fire to seats and newspapers, and apparently hurled bottles.

† The construction of what would become the Berlin Wall began in the early hours of Sunday 13 August. Approximately thirty-thousand had defected in July alone, half of them under the age of twenty-five. The GDR had lost 2.7 million citizens in just thirteen years, and thus Moscow had reluctantly acquiesced.

WALTER ULBRICHT; FIRST SECRETARY,
SOCIALIST UNITY PARTY:

'The builders of our capital are fully
engaged in residential construction, and
its labor force is deployed for that.
Nobody has any intention of building a
wall.' *

† Press conference, 15 June 1961

NEUES DEUTSCHLAND
ORGAN DES ZENTRALKOMITEES DER SOZIALISTISCHEN EINHEITSPARTEI DEUTSCHLANDS

The traditional Berlin–Lübben–Berlin race, 160 kilometres, was won yesterday by Barleben (SC Einheit Berlin) in 3.50.40. [...] The group from West Berlin was unable to contest any of the leading positions.

Reprinted from 'Berlin–Lübben–Berlin for Barleben', 14 August 1961

DIETER

You assumed that it was a temporary thing, and I don't think anybody really understood the full implications of it. The feeling was that the politicians would sort it out somehow, and that things would just go back to normal.

My first direct encounter with it was on 17 August, four days later. I went to Berlin to ride the Tour of the GDR, and normally the race started in the centre, on Alexanderplatz or at the Brandenburg Gate. There were tanks there, though, so we had to start somewhere else.* Even the Berlin riders didn't really know what was going on. They started telling us about friends who had gone to work in West Berlin, in restaurants and suchlike, and hadn't been able to get home. That's how the reality of what they'd done began to sink in.

---

* The opening stage began on Stalinallee (later renamed Karl-Marx-Allee).

NEUES DEUTSCHLAND

ORGAN DES ZENTRALKOMITEES DER SOZIALISTISCHEN EINHEITSPARTEI DEUTSCHLANDS

At the Park Hotel in Düsseldorf – site last year of the meeting between the two German Olympic committees prior to the Rome games – members of the FRG Olympic Committee and the executive board of the FRG Sports Confederation bowed to the command of the Bonn extremists on Wednesday: sporting relations between the two German states were to be terminated, and negotiations with FRG sports associations prohibited!

The step will be met with dismay not only in Germany, but across the world. Early opinion suggests that international sporting federations are absolutely unwilling to follow this path.

The general secretary of the European Swimming Union, the Swede Bertil Sällfors, emphatically declared that the European

Swimming Championships of 1962 will go ahead in Leipzig; 'We are very pleased with the preparations, and see no reason to change our decision.' Within the last few days representatives of other sports federations have made similar statements.

Eyewitnesses in Düsseldorf assure us that Willi Daume, president of the FRG Olympic Committee, had great difficulty in enforcing the demand – made *inter alia* by Willy Brandt – to terminate sporting relations. The conference was scheduled to finish at 10 p.m., but lasted ten hours and finished at midnight. [...]*

The measures of the GDR government were implemented in the small hours of Sunday morning. Later that morning the capital hosted the start of

---

* Willy Brandt was mayor of West Berlin in 1961. He would later become chancellor of the FDR. He resigned in 1974 when it was revealed that Günter Guillaume, one of his closest aides, was a Stasi agent.

the Berlin–Lübben–Berlin bike race. At the start thirty-five West Berlin amateurs were present, and almost to a man they'd arrived that very morning. The race therefore disproved for ever the assertion that the GDR has impeded sporting relations anywhere. [...]

Daume is a well-known member of the International Olympic Committee. In reference to its members, the IOC statutes expressly specify that: 'The IOC chooses its members as lifelong agents for work in the country concerned. They must be independent, and may not accept orders from local state or sporting authorities.'

And yet there is proof that the termination of sporting relations was in fact just such an order. It was first reported in *Bild-Zeitüng* on Monday, while the bourgeois *Welt* underlined it on Tuesday. On Wednesday the failure, Willy Brandt, simply used it to appease his disillusioned followers.

That ten hours were necessary speaks volumes for the fact that it was extremely difficult to silence the voice of reason. Daume, however, followed the orders of the extremists in Bonn and West Berlin. One thinks: the politician Kennedy saw no reason to instigate 'measures', while the supposedly apolitical Daume was obliged so to do. By whom? That question has answered itself [...]

At almost precisely the same time that the decision to boycott the GDR was made, the International Archery Federation (FITA) in Oslo recognised the GDR as a full and equal member!

Reprinted from 'Bonn orders: Terminate!', 18 August 1961

NEUES DEUTSCHLAND

ORGAN DES ZENTRALKOMITEES DER SOZIALISTISCHEN EINHEITSPARTEI DEUTSCHLANDS

Dessau, 24 August. On Wednesday morning, long before the Tour of the GDR family woke, a famous racing cyclist-turned-coach drove to the train station in Nordhausen. Alongside Otto Busse sat a cyclist who has ridden for GDR many times, and who in 1960 won the biggest prize of all, the Peace Race. His name: Erich Hagen.

Few words were exchanged as the Leipziger took his leave. Hagen was bidding farewell not only to this year's tour, but also to the group seeking to earn selection for the world championships. He had punctured, fallen behind and had apparently taken umbrage at the comments of some ill-informed fans. His answer had consisted of raising the white flag and putting his bike into the sag-wagon long before Nordhausen. With this attitude, he did no favours to either his team or the event, but more importantly it seems to us that this affair should be seen an altogether different light […]

In reference to Gorki's famous 'universities', someone once called our tour the primary school of GDR cycling. Since even the aces are present every year, it proves just how difficult it is to graduate from this primary school. Young, enthusiastic riders afford the famous riders no privileges, and don't give them an inch without a fight. Year after year each of them must demonstrate his ability anew. No factory team helps him, but he and his team is all that exists.

Those who are not prepared – and this applies both to body and nerve – will not pass the examination. Even if, like Erich Hagen, they can point to great victories, they will find themselves driving, silent and unnoticed, to the train station in the early morning,. That's not to say that Erich won't be awarded a very good mark at the next exam […]

Reprinted from 'The hard exam', 25 August 1961

DIETER

I don't know exactly what Hagen said, but I know that he expressed some sort of anti-wall sentiment. He was thrown out of DHfK, sent back to work and back to his BSG.* Hagen was a champion, and so they were sending out a pretty clear warning. They were saying that if you criticised them in any way they would make you pay, irrespective of who you were.

On a personal level the race was a success. I won the time trial to Kyffhäuser and finished third on GC behind Täve and Klaus Ampler.

---

* Erich Hagen built himself a bike and continued to ride for Motor Schkeuditz, a BSG in Leipzig. In December 1961 he stated that he agreed with the 'education' measures. He said that the western press had fabricated stories about him having been suspended for speaking his mind. He was readmitted to DHfK in 1963, and rode the Tour of the GDR. His career finished when, aged just twenty-seven, he failed to qualify for the Olympics the following year. He died in a traffic accident in 1978.

NEUES DEUTSCHLAND

ORGAN DES ZENTRALKOMITEES DER SOZIALISTISCHEN EINHEITSPARTEI DEUTSCHLANDS

Forty-eight hours ago the West Berlin police built a camp at the border. Their tents contain a list with the names of ninety persons who, in the humble opinion of interior minister Lipschitz, are considered 'undesirable'. Among them is the name of Gustav-Adolf Schur, a man who can claim, uniquely, to have won the rainbow jerseys of the world amateur champion twice in succession. This is doubtless an invitation for satirists, because who would be inclined to take this 'blacklist' at all seriously? Täve Schur, who two days ago won his fourth Tour of the GDR, is celebrated in Australia as well as in Italy, France, Holland and Sweden. He has won the Tour of Dortmund and the Conti-Pris in Hannover, and is a byword for fair, honest athletes not just in the GDR. In the desk of his apartment in Leipzig's Ebertallee the invitations stack up from any number of countries and cities. Lipschitz may be sure that this latest initiative is guaranteed to flop.

Reprinted from 'Lipschitz blacklists Täve', 27 August 1961

DIETER

When people talk about the border closure they tend to focus on the fact that you could no longer travel. That was a big problem for border communities, people who worked in West Berlin and people with family in the west. The majority of the GDR people, however, didn't live near the border, and couldn't afford to buy anything in the west anyway.

Prior to the wall most people had tolerated the shortages and the propaganda, even if they didn't believe in it. Most people weren't interested in politics, and just wanted to be left alone. My dad would be an example of that. He thought all the sloganeering was nonsense, but he put up with it because he didn't want to uproot his family.

For most people the bigger problem was that day-to-day life started to become more oppressive once it was built. Previously they'd been trying to dissuade people from defecting, but now there was no way for them to leave.

So they didn't need to pretend any more, and the political rhetoric started to become even more aggressive. Then it seemed like there were more and more people who just didn't contribute. The army, the police, the Stasi … It was bad enough that none of them were producing anything, but they seemed intent on interfering in other people's lives as well. The climate changed almost overnight, and I'd say that it became a climate of fear. You were in a trap, but you'd no choice but to conform if you didn't want to be singled out.

People would rush to the polling booths early in the morning. They were trying to demonstrate that they were committed socialists, but in reality it was all about being seen to be. That was the way you got a decent job, a decent home and an education for your kids. So you had to vote just to get along, but in themselves the elections were a pointless exercise.[*]

---

[*] In the GDR the list of candidates was pre-selected by the National Front, and you voted either 'Yes' or 'No'. Those who chose the latter course did so in a separate booth, with no anonymity. At the 1958 elections the official list received 99.9 per cent of the vote. The turnout was recorded as 99.2 per cent.

RAINER

If you didn't vote you got a knock on the door, so you just played the game. You voted.

DIETER

My being a cyclist indemnified me to a degree, but it also meant that I saw both sides of it. I was privileged and well paid, and I got everything I needed to do my job. Then again I knew that I was very much the exception. I knew that there was progressively less in the shops, because my mum spent all week running around trying to get things. At the same time there was an elite class consuming things which ordinary people couldn't buy in the shops. They had been chosen because they were politicians, sportsmen and suchlike, but there was no way for normal working people even to aspire to those things. They kept telling us that capitalism was terrible, but this was the opposite of communism.

Millions of people in the GDR had grown up under fascism, and then they'd lived through the war. Many of them had never travelled, didn't know any other way of living, and didn't know what was going on in the west. It was quite easy to convince them that the GDR was better, and that's what the party tried to do. They told them that thanks to Moscow they were living in a haven of peace and fellowship, while Bonn and Washington were full of criminals, hooligans and warmongers. People read *Neues Deutschland* every day, absorbed the propaganda on the radio and got on with it as best they could. After a while they stopped questioning what was happening to their country, I guess because they'd nothing better to compare it with.

Anyway the wall was built now, and it was clear that it was here to stay. The Americans hadn't done anything, and there was nothing anybody else could do.

SYLVIA

Gradually we started to write more frequently. Sometimes I wouldn't have time, and he'd become frustrated if I didn't write.

Everyone thought I was a bit odd. My mum and dad couldn't understand it, but my grandfather was the worst. He said, 'Why do you want to carry on writing to this sports kid from the GDR, when there's a wall between you and him? It'll never work! You're a dreamer, and so is he!'

I started working in a department store, doing merchandising and window dressing. My boss said there were lots of boys I could have gone out with in Mitterteich, instead of wasting my time with one I could never hope to be with. There was a guy who used to drive past the shop every day, and when he saw me in the window he'd wave and sound his horn. He liked me, and so did the butcher's son. He was always asking me out, but I wasn't in the least bit interested. I was just a typical teenager I guess, and the more they told me it was stupid the more determined I was to carry on. Everything was against us, but that's part of being a teenager, isn't it? I suppose Dieter and I were building our own secret world. We were building a fence around ourselves, and nobody else was allowed in.

I was growing up now, and gradually the substance of the letters started to change. We became braver in what we wrote, and they became more and more personal. We were discovering who we were, and I guess you could say that slowly they were starting to become love letters.

Flöha, 7 December 1961

Dear Sylvia,

I got your letter 24 November. Thank you very much especially for the chewing gum, which as you know isn't available here.

Sorry not to have answered earlier, but I've been really busy. I've been studying and training a lot, both of which are exhausting for me. Then there are invitations to sports parties, and last Sunday we played football with the cyclists from DHfK. On 20 December we'll have the sport club party, so I haven't had much time.

You misunderstood what I wrote in my last letter about dancing. I love dancing, but only if I'm invited. I don't go out dancing, so there's no reason for you to be jealous. (...)

The important thing for me is that you want to continue to write, because I'm always pleased when your letters arrive. As I've already told you, I don't have any other girlfriends. I'm only interested in cycling and in writing to you.

I really hope that you will be able to come to Flöha, and that we'll have the chance to see each other again. What's the weather like there? How is your job? Have you bought any new records? Have you been to the cinema recently? Did you see any interesting films? Have you been out dancing again? I saw an Agatha Christie film at the cinema. It made me laugh, and I liked it a lot.

From the start of January I will be travelling a lot, so I won't be home much. I've been selected for the Peace Race next year, so from 4–16 January I'll go to Schreckenstein to do winter sports. Then from 22 January to 7 February we'll be in Carlsbad training, from 11 February to 9 March training in Leipzig, and on 12 March we'll go to Bulgaria for four weeks to train for the Peace Race.

Well now I don't know what else to write! Say hello to your parents and to your brother, and I hope you write back very soon.

Lots of love,
Dieter

UDO

I hadn't been planning on changing my circumstances, but that changed suddenly. They'd sealed off the border completely on 13 August 1961, and now they were introducing conscription.[*]

We'd always been taught that the GDR was a peaceful country, and that no citizen would ever have to take up arms again after the terrible events of the war. Now I understood that we'd been lied to, and I didn't want to stay in that country.

My training partner was a guy named Peter Warzeschka. He and I spent a lot of time together, and he was the one friend I had absolute trust in. It seemed to us that the only sensible way to get out was across the Baltic Sea, to Denmark.

We decided it would be better not to mention it to friends or relatives, or even our parents. My father probably suspected something though, because we started preparing a folding kayak in his workshop.

---

[*] According to official SED data, 9,968 fifteen–eighteen-year-olds defected illegally in 1960. Among eighteen–twenty-five-year-olds the number was recorded at 24,248. One of the principal reasons given was pressure for eighteen–twenty-two-year-olds to enlist for military service in the *Volksarmee*. Though not technically mandatory (the *Volksarmee* was ostensibly a volunteer force), failure to do so implied opposition to the state, and could have damaging social and economic consequences. Young men weaned on the idea that the GDR was a peaceable country were thus placed in an invidious position: take up arms, risk being ostracised or leave their homeland. This gave rise to a virulent conscientious objector movement, but once the wall was built there was no way out. As such the party no longer felt the need to pretend, and conscription was enacted on 24 January 1962.

In 1964 the GDR would introduce, uniquely in the Eastern Bloc, an alternative to armed military service. The so-called 'spade soldier' (*Bausoldat*) would be deployed in civilian works, usually construction. Here again, however, a raft of empirical evidence suggests that his training and employment opportunities were restricted as a consequence.

MfS383/65 bd2, BSTU0055/0056

Ministry for State Security

Service unit...............V/6/1

Berlin, 12.3.62

Registration no. XV/1593/62

Strictly confidential!

Order

For the creation / addition of ....
UNOFFICIAL INFORMANT

Intended category:.........UNOFFICIAL INFORMANT

Candidate's physical address: Flöha, Rudolf-
Breitscheid-Strasse 51

Grounds for the creation / addition

The cycling section of SC Wismut Karl-Marx-Stadt
is a priority, and should be safeguarded by the
recruitment of an informant.

In addition, it is envisaged that the candidate
will become a main informant group leader.

Staff...............................Bergmann

Approved.....................Berlin, 12.3.1962

MfS8963/69 BSTU0021/0022

Ministry for State Security

Service unit...............V/6/1

Berlin, 12.3.62

Registration no. XV/1607/62

Strictly confidential!

Order

For the creation / addition of ....
UNOFFICIAL INFORMANT

Intended category:..................UNOFFICIAL INFORMANT

Candidate's physical address: Berlin -
Hohenschönhausen (?)

Grounds for the creation / addition

The cycling section of SC Dynamo Berlin is
a priority, and should be safeguarded by the
recruitment of an unofficial informant.

Furthermore the candidate is often in capitalist
countries, and so may be used to secure the entire
team.

Staff.............................Bergmann

Approved.....................Berlin, 13.3.1962

MfS383/65 bd1, BSTU0026

Karl-Marx-Stadt 29.3.1962

Subject: Wiedemann, Dieter

I have known Dieter Wiedemann since 1960, as a cyclist from SC Wismut.

As I understand it Wiedemann works in Object 37. He comes from a working-class family. His father works as a cycling mechanic at SC Wismut, but is not a party member.

From a young age Wiedemann developed into a very good cyclist. He had good results (third place at the Tour of the GDR, winner of the 1961 team time trial, a good performance at the Tour of Egypt).

His individual results are very good, but he also works well as part of the collective.

The problem as I see it is that when he fails (e.g. early season 1961) he needs a long time to recover, and loses discipline as regards the training plan.

In this respect he was also negatively affected by his parents. It needs stronger arguments with them to bring him into line. Politically he is totally disinterested, and of course he's not a party member. However he appreciates and is thankful to the Wismut company, which supports him in his training. He's grateful for that, though he doesn't support GDR ideology.

He's extremely shy and doesn't talk about himself. He spends time with friends from the sport club. He doesn't discuss his aims or his feelings, but I think he has a good character and with the influence of the sport club he could achieve good results in the Peace Race.

On western contacts I have nothing to declare. In moral terms I can't say anything derogatory about him.

'Siegfried Wenzel'

MfS383/65 bd1, BSTU0028/0029/0030

Karl-Marx-Stadt, 12.5.62

Intelligence Report

WIEDEMANN, Dieter
Born 17.6.1941 in Flöha
Resident: Wiesenstrasse 15, Flöha
Employment: VEB '8 Mai', Karl-Marx-Stadt, lathe operator

Wiedemann is from a working-class family. His father, Karl Wiedemann, is a metal worker and a mechanic at SC Wismut. He attended school in Flöha from 1947–1955, but chose an apprenticeship instead of continuing on to High School. (...)

He is positive about our state, but should be forthcoming as regards attending and contributing to meetings and discussions.

He acknowledges that athletic development isn't possible without the support of our state, but has little understanding of social issues. He knows that his politics must be strengthened significantly.

This is in large measure a result of the abstract treatment of political problems by the sports functionaries. They do not know how to combine the interest of the athlete with theoretical political issues. (...)

He has no contact with West Berlin, with West Germany or any other capitalist countries. We have discovered that he has an aunt living in USA, but he has no contact with her.

Wiedemann is not married. He lives with his parents and younger brother, who is also doing an apprenticeship. As far as we know he has no further relatives.

He has good relationships with other cyclists, with Olympic candidates and sports functionaries. There is no contact with work colleagues. We raise no objections to his being permitted to travel abroad.

Sub-lieutenant Reichenbach

MANFRED

They became even more paranoid after the wall. It wasn't about performance any more, just whether or not you toed the line. My problem was
the fact that I was just too outspoken.

They tried to make you join the party when you became famous,
because that was worth a lot more to them than when a normal person
joined. They tried with me for years, but I wouldn't join and I knew they
couldn't force me. I said I was a Christian, and my final argument was
that Yuri Gagarin hadn't had to join the party, and he was a cosmonaut.
They didn't like that one little bit, especially after what had happened
with Melichow. I got away with it, though, because my results spoke for
themselves. It was a game, and while I was winning on the bike I was
always one step ahead.

They started going round everybody asking whether I could be trusted
to travel, and I was left out of the 1962 Peace Race. I was good enough to
have been in the team, absolutely, but there had been the incident with
Melichow and I was critical of the way they trained. They'd been looking
for an excuse to lever me out, and they said I hadn't followed the training
plan.

DIETER

I was a candidate for the 1962 Peace Race, and this time I got in. It was a
new team, and four of us were riding it for the first time. We didn't have
a proven sprinter because Weissleder was left out, then Adler was ill and
for the first time in ten years there was no Täve.

The first five stages were in the GDR – Berlin, Leipzig, Erfurt, a time
trial to Jena and then Chemnitz. At the Peace Race it was important that
you won your home stages at the very least, but you could tell straight
away that the Russians were going to be too powerful. You could see
that they would dominate the race, and no matter how hard we tried

we didn't stand a chance against them. By the rest day in Chemnitz we hadn't even had anyone on the podium.

That morning I went for a ride to Flöha with two of my team-mates. When we got back the head coach told us that the riders, trainers and mechanics had to meet in the hotel conference room at four o'clock. So we all waited there, and in walked Ewald, the sports minister. He said, 'You have let down the entire republic, and you should be ashamed of yourselves.' He carried on like that for ten minutes, ranting and raving like a lunatic, and then he just upped and went. We couldn't believe what was happening. Everybody was left feeling totally demoralised.

I managed to work my way into the top ten, but then I had a mechanical on the stage to Poznań and lost twelve minutes. In the end I finished seventeenth on GC, but all things considered it wasn't too bad for me personally. I was still only twenty, the youngest in the group, but I realised that I was capable of riding at that level.

The problem was that collectively we just hadn't been good enough. We didn't win a single stage, didn't have anybody on the podium, and only managed third in the team prize. We did what we could, but we were a young team which wasn't ready to win.

After the race we flew from Warsaw to Berlin, and there was a reception for us as per Peace Race tradition. Ewald and his cronies 'congratulated' us for finishing third in the team prize. They put us in limousines to take us home, but it was all false. In the papers they made out that everything was fine because ours was a new team, but in reality they were livid.

DIETER

Flöha was a different story. To have a twenty-year-old local finish the Peace Race was a very big thing, and there was a big civic reception for me. You're talking about a small provincial town, and talented athletes or artists from places like that normally moved to Berlin or Leipzig. I was quite happy at home, though, and didn't want to move. Riding the Peace Race had made me a hero there, and almost the whole town turned out to welcome me home. I think there were probably more people than for the May Day parade to be honest.

Afterwards the mayor came to see me, a guy called Siegfried Hense. He started addressing me using the informal *du*, and to be extremely friendly. He said, 'Look, Dieter, you have to understand that you've bestowed great prestige upon our community. You're an important person now, and so if there's anything I can do for you all you need do is ask. Anything at all, you come and see me and I'll see what I can do …'

I don't think he was doing it for altruistic reasons, not at all. He contacted the press and had them write a story about it, because it was good for his own political aspirations. I was the local hero and he needed to be seen to be taking care of me.

I didn't much like all the fuss to be honest. I didn't need anything from him and I'd have been ashamed to ask. The problem was that things would turn up at home anyway. I'd get home and there would be a radio waiting for me, stuff like that.

DIETER

A week or so after the Peace Race I was out on my bike and a big EMW* car came by me as I was climbing a hill. It braked suddenly and five blokes in leather coats jumped out. They told me they needed to talk with me and that they'd follow me home. I was very scared, as you can imagine, because I knew instantly that they were Stasi. I told them there

---

* Before the war BMW had a factory in Eisenach. When the country was partitioned after the war the plant, now under Soviet ownership, carried on regardless. A lawsuit in 1952 compelled it to desist from using the BMW brand name, so they rebranded the cars EMW. The company logotype was very similar to that of BMW, but red and white instead of blue and white. Later it became a VEB, and from 1955 the cars manufactured there carried the Wartburg brand name.

was nobody at home and that I didn't have a key. It wasn't true, but I didn't want people to see them coming to my house. I met them at a restaurant nearby instead.

I was convinced they were going to quiz me about the letters to Sylvia. Instead they started by asking me whether there had been differences of political opinion within the Peace Race team. I told them there hadn't, because there hadn't *been* any political opinion – we were a bunch of cyclists doing a bike race. They were wanting to know why the results hadn't been good enough, and I said that we were a new team and that the Russians had just been stronger than us. They made a big thing of whether the coaches had stuck to the training plan.

It lasted about forty-five minutes but it seemed like an eternity. You could probably describe it as an interrogation, yes, and it was certainly a harrowing experience. To the best of my knowledge it was the one and only time in my life I had a direct conversation with the Stasi, but I could be wrong.

MfS383/65 bd2, BSTU0081/0082/0083

Main Department V/6/I

Berlin, 12.6.62

Contact with: Dieter Wiedemann

On the 7.6.1962, an interview was conducted with W. The responsible member of staff present was Comrade Reichenbach.

Comrade Reichenbach and I introduced ourselves as MfS employees and explained our interest in interviewing him.

W. explained his views on the Peace Race to us, as well as the preparations for the race, in order for us to draw the appropriate conclusions.

W. announced that in the first instance he was happy to be able to take part at all. He said in this context that his good fortune was the misfortune of athlete (?), who hadn't been able to race because of illness.

W. said that the Peace Race had been a big event for him, and that he had only positive impressions. (...)

W. stated only positive thoughts as regards the organisation, both as regards food and transport. He noticed no difference in this regards between the three countries.

As regards the question of preparation, W. stated that in his opinion (?) was the strongest rider in the GDR. In his opinion(?) had been left out incorrectly. W. then explained that the training plans were drawn up without taking into account the individual characteristics of the riders.

He said that he personally has to cope with too large a training schedule, only half of which he needed. The fact that he completed it risked compromising his performance in the competition.

This was why (?) had been accused of indiscipline and not nominated for the Peace Race. In this respect W. estimated that (?) hadn't been right in the way he'd handled things. If he was opposed to the training plan he should have gone about his complaint in a different way, for example with the cycling federation. Beyond that he believed the team selection had been correct.

Asked about his sporting perspective, he offered that he hoped to earn selection for the 100-kilometre team time trial at the 1964 Olympics. He also stated that he hoped his first Peace Race wouldn't be his last. Asked about his relationship with the leadership of SC Wismut, W. stated that it was thanks to their commitment that he'd become a good cyclist.

He was then informed that in sport, and specifically in cycling, an increase in performance is required in view of the Olympic qualification events to be held against the FRG. With this in mind bad organisation, improper training schedules, methodology or management could have a serious effect in respect to the standing of the GDR.

This is the reason why MfS is concerned with sporting issues, the result of which is personal conversations with athletes considered by us to be reliable and very positive. Who, if not the athletes themselves, can offer us a better overview? This was why we had wanted to meet with him, and why it would be appropriate to him to continue the conversation which had been started. Asked for his opinion, he expressed his agreement and said that if his training plan permitted he would be open to further discussions, though he's often away for several weeks at a time.

No concrete date has been agreed at this point. It was therefore agreed that comrade Reichenbach would make an appointment with him personally, and then advise.

Further, it was communicated to W. that he should refrain from mentioning our interview to anybody. It would be inappropriate if his sports colleagues were to hear about it, because one doesn't know how they might feel about it. Further it wouldn't be helpful if rumours were to spread that MfS is interested in sport. W. agreed, and considered this to be a matter of course.

Assessment:

W. was initially very reluctant. As time went by he became slightly more talkative. However he pondered the questions before responding, and was careful in what he said. The answers he gave portrayed the situation more positively than the reality.

First and foremost, all his remarks were absolutely positive as regards SC Wismut, even his opinion of the trainer (?)

The formal interview took place at the end of his training ride, and he wanted to go home immediately. He had been stopped suddenly, and had expressed beforehand that he was not interested in a longer discussion. This is a result of the fact that the interview had not been previously arranged with him.

Under these circumstances the conclusion is that the discussion was positive.

MfS8963/69BSTU0103/0104/0105/0106

Berlin, 30.6.1962

Application Report

Comrade Elste was approached at the sports
school of SC Dynamo Berlin at 13.00 on 19.6.1962.
This meeting had already been agreed with him.
Department leader SALATSKI took part in this
interview.

At the start of the interview the training
preparation of the four-man team was discussed
for the World Championships. Comrade Elste stated
that he thought he knew the training methods of
the Soviet friends, and is now using these with
the team at Dynamo. He is trying them out before
officially announcing them to the functionaries
of the cycling federation, because he knows that
they won't believe him. He knows from experience
that approval only comes through practical
success.

This was brought home to him during a
conference between 12.6 and 16.6 in Kienbaum,
to evaluate the 1962 Peace Race. During this
conference the finishing position of the GDR team
was presented as having been good. The fact is,
however, that the third place is deceptive. The
team only got up to speed during the second part
of the race, and the fact is that the Soviet and
Polish teams had already built a significant lead
by then. As a result of this the Polish and Soviet
teams were no longer driving the race, but the
GDR team was trying to improve its position. This
wasn't successful, however, because the Poles and
Soviets needed simply to follow the right wheels,
so the GDR riders turned themselves inside out
for no gain.

Comrade (?) is wedded to the training methods he has developed over many years, and which have delivered great success in the past. However he is not prepared to acknowledge or adopt the new developments of our friends, or even to further develop the old methods. Comrade Elste is of the opinion that (?) is a hindrance in the current cycling situation. In practice it seems that many trainers believe that (?) is no longer the right man for the job. However none of them are prepared to say so because they all know that (?) enjoys great support at the German Sports Federation. (...)

The work of the MfS in sport in general, and in particular with regards to the protection of our athletes whilst they are in capitalist countries, was explained to him. It was thereby made clear to him that we are interested in an unofficial collaboration with him.

Comrade Elste saw the necessity of this, and declared himself ready to support the MfS. He stated that he understand cycling very well, comes into personal contact with many functionaries, and as a result is in a good position to discuss many problems. The meaning of the unofficial collaboration was then explained to him, as was the fact that he should not speak with third parties about it.

Comrade Elste confirmed that he is fully understanding of this type of work and that we can have absolute trust in him. It was pointed out to him that a written declaration of commitment is necessary for this type of collaboration, to which he agreed. A written declaration was not made, because at that precise moment the janitor appeared. It was agreed that we would meet again at S-Bahn Station Lichtenburg on 26.6.1962 at ten o'clock in order to continue the conversation.

On 26.6.62 comrade Elste arrived punctually
by car. We proceeded to conspiratorial dwelling
'Fichte' and here the reason for the written
declaration and an alias was once more pointed
out to him. Elste subsequently wrote the
declaration without fuss. As an alias he chose the
name 'Werner Hildebrand'. As passwords, 'rim' and
'gear ratio' were agreed upon.

When taking up contact with a member of the
MfS, the informant will be asked, 'With which
rims did you ride the World Championships, the
German Championships, or this or that Tour?' The
informant will respond, 'We didn't place too much
value on the rims. We were more interested in
gear ratios.'

In written communication a letter will be sent
to the informant's address. The letter will be
signed with the name 'Fred'. The text of the letter
will mention a date and time. The meeting day
will be three days after the date specified in the
letter. The time is the same and the place always
the conspiratorial dwelling 'Fichte'.

From the text of the letter it will seem that a
junior from some sport club or other is applying
to be a member of a club or wants to discuss the
possibility thereof.

The informant further received the MfS
telephone number 557703 ext. 2655 and in
emergencies ext. 2629. Then a few sporting matters
were discussed. During the course of this comrade
Elste said that he has been working very closely
with (?)

(?) is responsible for cycling at SC Dynamo.
He puts everything into his work, and has
developed medical analyses on all the riders.
The two of them are currently working together
on establishing which medicinal substances

might enable the athletes to achieve higher performance. Advanced courses of treatment have already been discussed. (...)

Finally comrade Elste is to keep an eye on (?) in order to discover his political views and to establish possible connections with West Berlin, West Germany or even (?)

Furthermore I asked him to prepare a CV with family connections. The next meeting is 20.7.62, at 10.00 at the conspiratorial dwelling 'Fichte'.

Bergmann

MfS8963/69 BSTU0107

Berlin, 26.6.62

Commitment

I herewith commit myself to work with the MfS (...)

For reasons of vigilance I will use the alias 'Werner Hildebrand'

Roland Elste.

DIETER

Neues Deutschland published almost nothing about the 1962 Tour de France. Two years earlier they'd invited the professionals to the GDR for the Worlds, but now it was as if they didn't exist. It was almost total blackout, like they'd drawn a veil over everything that happened on the other side of the wall.

People had always made comparisons between the Tour and the Peace Race, but in most respects they were worlds apart. The Peace Race had a lot more spectators, and of course there was a lot of symbolism attached to it. It had the best cyclists in the Soviet Bloc, but they were competing against amateurs and under-23 riders from the west. For the Belgians, the Dutch and the French our great race was really just a finishing school. They knew that the Peace Race would be tough, and that if they did well it would go a long way towards earning them a professional contract. So for them it was a means to an end, whether we liked it or not.

The Tour was more important because it had the best riders, the biggest mountains and the most prestige. Everybody knew that it was the ultimate for a bike racer, and yet to articulate that in the GDR was regarded as a heresy. Täve, for example, always maintained that Peace Race was bigger, and you couldn't convince him otherwise. Anyone who knew anything about cycling couldn't fail to see it, and yet everybody was forced to play along with the charade. The evidence was irrefutable, but everybody seemed to be turning into a big lie. Rainer Marks, a famous DHfK rider, was actually thrown out for saying he thought the Tour was more important than the Peace Race.

EBERHARD

When they let me give up my job and ride full-time I was very successful. I won a lot of races, and in 1962 I was part of the Wismut team for the GDR junior team time trial championship. We won it, as had Dieter with the seniors. I won a lot of other races as well, and we won the championship again in 1963.

So, yes, in answer to your question I'd say that I was one of the best juniors in the country.

DIETER

In the GDR they cultivated the idea that the government in Bonn was our enemy, so a party member would never have sent letters to the west unless they were to family. It wasn't *forbidden* to send letters, but it was certainly discouraged. They were of the opinion that too much contact with the western bourgeoisie contaminated socialism.

My writing to Sylvia wasn't a way of rebelling as such, but I was conscious of the fact that I was exercising a basic human right. I hadn't intended it to be like that, but nor had I created the political situation. I figured they were probably being opened, so in some respects it was a bit of a game.

For example, on a Wednesday night Sylvia and I would both listen to the West German hit parade. You could receive it in the GDR, but technically you weren't supposed to listen to it because it was 'western'. Lots of people did, though, and she and I would write about the songs we'd heard. In itself it was something you could get away with. They tolerated it, but only if you were discreet about it and didn't publicise the fact; they didn't want an epidemic of people enjoying themselves, you know?

Anyway, as far as I was concerned I wasn't going to give it up for anybody.

NEUES DEUTSCHLAND

ORGAN DES ZENTRALKOMITEES DER SOZIALISTISCHEN EINHEITSPARTEI DEUTSCHLANDS

On 13 August last year the eyes of the world turned to Berlin. Everyone thought that a decision of far-reaching implications had been made. Few people, however, truly understood. What happened that day was no more or less than the salvation of peace.

Let us remember what went on last summer! The hooligans in Bonn, in their megalomaniac delusion, decided that the time had come to introduce strong-arm politics, and to force the GDR to roll over. On 11 July 1961, Adenauer's CDU government met and proclaimed in a policy statement that the German question need be solved, and the 'zone' integrated into the NATO area. They intensified their agitation against our republic to extreme levels. They spared no effort, and no crime aimed at creating panic and confusion among citizens of the GDR. Thus they attempted to make the GDR ripe for storming. It was thought that this military provocation would be followed by an all-out attack. The autumn of 1961 threatened war. On 13 August the government of the German Democratic Republic, in full accord with the other states of the Warsaw Pact, took the necessary measures. Thus, at a stroke, the diabolical programme concocted by the hooligans themselves was thwarted. Peace was saved not only for our workers and farmers state, but also for West Berliners, West Germans, perhaps for all the world. [...]

Reprinted from 'Here's to 13 August', 13 August 1962

DIETER

The Tour of the GDR began on 14 August, and it was eight days. It was a big race in its own right, but still more so this time. The World Championships were being held in Italy the week after it finished, so in effect it was a qualifier for that. My form was really good, and before the race I was summoned to Berlin to arrange travel permits for Italy. Then I went on to Magdeburg for the opening stage.

After four stages I was lying comfortably second on GC behind Ampler, climbing solidly and recovering really well. I was earning my ticket to Italy, but then at Zschopau an official came up to us and told us we wouldn't be going. Apparently when the federation had applied they'd received a letter back which said, 'Please refer to the NATO agreement to understand why you are unable to participate.'

It was absolutely devastating. You knew that as a GDR amateur you'd never be able to ride the Tour de France, but you wanted the chance to be part of the World Championships. You wanted to see the great Belgians, French and Italian professionals at close quarters, and to ride on the roads they did.

It was the GDR politicians who had built the wall, nobody else. They had turned the country into a prison, but then they were outraged because NATO didn't accept that sportsmen should be treated differently to ordinary people. They said, 'Politics shouldn't interfere with sport', but that was totally disingenuous. The only cyclists precluded from riding were the GDR ones, and it was GDR politics which stopped us from being able to compete.

NEUES DEUTSCHLAND

ORGAN DES ZENTRALKOMITEES DER SOZIALISTISCHEN EINHEITSPARTEI DEUTSCHLANDS

In gross disregard of all sports practices and of the Olympic ideal, the Italian government and the Bonn-influenced Allied Travel Office,* has refused the GDR team entry to the World Cycling Championships in Italy. The refusal of entry for the team built around the two-time world champion Gustav-Adolf Schur is a blatant violation of the recommendations of the International Olympic Committee to hold World and European Championships only in countries which guarantee all participants unrestricted travel.

Reprinted from 'Visa refusal for GDR cyclists', 19 August 1962

---

* The Allied Travel Office was responsible for issuing temporary travel permits to GDR citizens. Athletes, artists and diplomats were almost always refused in the period following the construction of the wall.

DIETER

I just wanted to be able to race my bike, and to feel like I had the same chance as everybody else. Now it really dawned on me that I didn't, and probably never would have. From here on in there'd be no Worlds, and we'd be limited to riding in non-NATO countries. I finished the Tour second behind Ampler, and in some respects that made it even worse. I'd earned the right to go to Italy, but instead I went back to Flöha in a state of shock.

UDO

It had taken us four or five months to prepare everything. We had to paint the kayak black, and then we had to learn how to use it. We also had to learn how to master the water and the waves, so we trained a lot.

In August we took the kayak to a place called Graal Müritz, on the Baltic coast. We set off in the dead of night, rowing towards Gedser.* Of course we were terrified because there were Coastal Defence boats and we could have run into one any time. Eventually we saw a ferry, and we got it to stop by using light signals. We climbed aboard using a rope ladder, and luckily it was headed for Travemünde, in the FRG.

UDO

Warzeschka and I went to Cologne after we'd left the GDR. People were always looking for tradesmen there, so you could find work without any problem.

I had no contact whatsoever with former friends, work colleagues or acquaintances. I had mail contact with my parents, but only very rarely. It was well known that anyone who received mail or calls from the FRG was targeted by the Stasi. My family didn't suffer any visible reprisals

---

* Gedser is Denmark's southernmost point. It's a distance of about forty-five kilometres as the crow flies.

from the defection, but I know that the endless interviews and interrogations were extremely unpleasant for them.

DIETER

That winter was brutally cold. One day it was −20°, but the training plan stipulated that we had to ride sixty kilometres. It made no sense, so we all agreed it would be better if we played ice hockey on the lake instead. That way we figured our hands and feet would be less cold than if we were sat still on our bikes, but suddenly a guy from the federation in Berlin arrived. Me, Weissleder and Immo Rittmeyer, the three Peace Race candidates, were picked out, and summoned to the Kienbaum sports school in Berlin. That was where the teams for the Tours of Tunisia and Morocco were training, the younger guys. We had to stay there for three weeks, and of course that was humiliating both for us and for the club.

So I'd had Ewald's verbal assault at the Peace Race, then the 'meeting' with the Stasi, and finally we'd been refused travel to Italy because of the wall. Allied to all of that you had the fact that the Peace Race – the symbol of global fellowship through sport – now took place in what was effectively a prison. Then just before Christmas I was appointed a 'Master of Sports'. It was one of the highest awards in GDR sports, and I got it for having honoured my country at the Peace Race. It was becoming totally schizophrenic, and I guess it's hard for somebody who never lived in the GDR to understand it. To be honest I struggle to make sense of it myself sometimes, even fifty years later.

Sozialistische Einheitspartei Deutschlands Kreisleitung
Flöha

Herrn

Dieter W i e d e m a n n

F l ö h a
Wiesenstraße

Telefon-Nummer 417/419

Bankkonto:
Deutsche Notenbank, Zweigstelle Flöha
Konto Nr. 8326

Unser Zeichen   Ihr Zeichen

FLÖHA, den   15. 12. 1962

Dear Dieter!

It's with great joy that we received notification of your 'Master of Sports' award.

The leadership of the Flöha district office of the Socialist Unity Party of Germany congratulates you warmly on this great award.

For both the office and the entire population of our district it is both a pleasure and a high honour to have such an outstanding athlete, who through his good performance in 1962 was able to compete in the International Peace Race for the first time.

Furthermore, we hope that you will be one of the strongest 'aces' of the GDR team for 1963. For our people the Peace Race is probably the most significant event in international cycling.

With fingers crossed we wish you further success in your sports career.

Good health and best wishes to you and yours!

SED – Flöha district office
Secretary

DIETER

The pressure to join the party was increasing, but I didn't want to and my dad was dead set against it. So in that respect my family was different, and I suppose I was different. I wasn't political at all, but nor did I want my life to become *politicised*.

NEUES DEUTSCHLAND

ORGAN DES ZENTRALKOMITEES DER SOZIALISTISCHEN EINHEITSPARTEI DEUTSCHLANDS

The Chairman of the State Committee for Physical Culture and Sports, Alfred B. Neumann, awarded medals of merit to four sports officials on behalf of Prime Minister Otto Grotewohl at the hall of ministers in Berlin on Saturday morning. In addition twenty-seven athletes, coaches, officials and the sports editor of *Neues Deutschland*, Klaus-Ullrich Huhn,* received the title 'Honoured Master of Sports'. A further eighty-three athletes were awarded the title 'Master of Sports'. [...]

ROAD CYCLING:

Masters of Sports: Klaus Ampler (DHfK Leipzig), Lothar Appler, Manfred Brüning, Eberhard Butzke, Alexander Fehsler, Siegfried Fehsler (all SC Dynamo Berlin), Günter Lux (DHfK Leipzig), Hans-Dieter Taufmann (SC Dynamo Berlin), Dieter Wiedemann (SC Wismut Karl-Marx-Stadt).

Reprinted from 'High state awards for sportsmen', 16 December 1962

---

* 'Klaus Ullrich' was Klaus Huhn's pen-name.

DIETER

Why so many Dynamo riders? I'll tell you.

The country was getting more and more oppressive. There were more police, more people being arrested, and more Stasi.[*]

Dynamo was the Stasi sport club, and the Stasi boss was Erich Mielke. He was also chairman of the sport club, and he was one of the most callous and powerful men in the GDR. He liked the fact that people were afraid of him, and afraid of the Stasi. If he decided he wanted Dynamo athletes at the big international sporting events he'd have them, come what may. He was much more interested in football than cycling, but that wasn't the point. Mielke was a man who got what he wanted, and he wanted his sport club to be the best.

---

[*] By 1962 the Stasi had over 25,000 full-time employees and 100,000 unofficial informants. These would increase to over 91,000 and 170,000 respectively by 1989.

Flöha, 30 December 1962

My dearest Sylvia,

Before the end of the year I'd like to answer your last letter. Thank you very much; it was an extremely lovely letter, and thanks also for the Christmas card and for the pictures you included. They arrived on 24 December, and so they were a very nice Christmas surprise. I'll keep them with me when I travel, so that you're always close to me. (...)

I haven't been able to train because the temperatures were −10°–18°. We haven't had snow but it's been very cold. I hope you got nice presents. I got a shirt from my parents, socks, sweets and a pullover. I also got a very interesting book, and I've already read it. (...)

You wrote that I could write to you from my bed, but I don't want to. When I'm tired I can't concentrate, and you won't be able to understand my handwriting. It's better to sit at my desk dreaming of you.

I'm not the only one in the GDR who is very pessimistic. There are a lot of other people who feel like I do. Maybe you can understand what I mean. Personally I'm OK, and some people have much worse conditions. (...)

You don't need to panic. Even though I go out I'm not looking at other girls. Do you understand that now? You write that your results are very good and I'm happy about that, and also the fact that you like the same music as me. I like to sit at my desk with a candle and dream about you, and to eat your sweets.

Well that's all for now. Say hello to all of your family. A big hug and a goodnight kiss to you. I wish you a happy new year, and hope you have a lovely new year's eve. I'm thinking of you, and as ever I'm impatient for your next letter to arrive.

Lots of love,

Dieter

SYLVIA

I knew he must have been extremely upset because it was the one and only time he mentioned the situation in the GDR. We had family over there, so we understood that you couldn't write or send anything that might be construed as anti-communist. You couldn't send West German magazines, for example, and even patriotic German folk music was banned.

I remember writing to him when they shot John F. Kennedy in November 1963. It was a really important thing, but he didn't have anything to say about it. He just wrote, 'It's a pity.'

DIETER

She's right that I never mentioned politics, and right about the the killing of JFK. The reason I didn't comment on things like that was because it served no purpose, and it would have been dangerous. By now people who expressed political opinions, however innocuous, were being dragged out of restaurants. You learned to say nothing, because that way they didn't have a reason to come after you.

To you it's all perfectly normal. It looks like a boy and a girl writing letters, but actually you have no idea what it was like to live under those conditions. We're talking about the GDR in the immediate aftermath of the wall. The country was being run by Leninist-Marxist fundamentalists. They were absolutely convinced that capitalism threatened not only their ideology, but their very existence.

They were crazy, and they were convinced that people from the west were their enemies. I was a sportsman being supported by the state, and I was writing letters to a girl from Bavaria. They didn't care about human beings, and they certainly didn't care about bourgeois sentiments like love.

The only thing that mattered to them was winning the war.

DIETER

By 1963 everything seemed to be getting worse, and the cycling was certainly getting worse. I'd been denied the chance to ride the World Championships, and then they told us that the Tours of Egypt and Tunisia were cancelled. That just left Eastern Bloc races, and the Peace Race if you happened to qualify. Even that was a political football, though.

My problems were partly the way I rode, partly my character and mainly political. I couldn't win a sprint, but stage races weren't about winning sprints. I was consistent and I think I was pretty tough, but I didn't care about being interviewed by journalists or talking on the radio. I rode my bike, kept myself to myself and I wasn't bothered about trying to promote myself or the party. Even when I finished second at the Tour of the GDR they never really wrote about me because I was no use to them. I was from the wrong club and the wrong town, and I wasn't interested in being used to promote the ideology.

I'd been runner-up at the Tour of the GDR the previous season, and anyone could see that I was one of the best stage racers in the country. And so of course I wasn't chosen for the Peace Race[*].

What happened was that I had some dental problems, and they said I wasn't sufficiently recovered. I told them that I knew my body, and in training I was one of the strongest. I was ready to ride, but it made no difference. They chose two from Dynamo and three from DHfK, and so that only left one spot for the rest. They chose Weissleder instead of me, so basically they used the thing with my teeth as a mechanism to lever me out.

---

[*] From 1963 the start date was pushed back a week. From here on in the race would begin on or around 8 May, VE Day.

DIETER

All I wanted was that they treated me fairly and let me ride. Now, though, it was increasingly clear that they weren't about to. Anyway, Ampler won the Peace Race and the GDR won the team prize. They got what they wanted, and they got it with DHfK and Dynamo riders. I guess in that sense they were justified in leaving me out after all.

What they did was to select me for the Tour of Lower Austria with Rittmeyer and Lörke. It was a sop to keep me sweet, but also a complete sham. Neither Austria nor Sweden were part of NATO, so technically they were both neutral. However, both had economic and diplomatic links with the NATO countries, and so given that the GDR was a pariah they couldn't be seen to invite us. Equally they couldn't be seen not to, so what they did was to invite small teams of riders on the pretext that they were riding for the same club. The official version was that they were representing the club as distinct to the state, and that's how they got round it.

It was politically expedient to present it that way. *Neues Deutschland* never referenced the fact that we were ostensibly riding for a single club, but referred to us as the 'GDR team'. The inference was that the Swedes and Austrians invited us because they were enlightened, peaceful nations, while the rest didn't because they had caved in to Bonn. That was the level of duplicity.

DIETER

I'd grown up dreaming of the World Championships and the Tour de France, but for my troubles I'd been sent to the Tour of Lower Austria.

While we were there something incredible happened. One of my team-mates came up to me and said, 'Why don't we try to defect while we're here?' It was an absolute bolt from the blue, and I remember it as if it were yesterday because I was so astonished. I thought about it for a second or two, and then just laughed. I just made out I thought he was joking.

DIETER

Why didn't I answer?

In the weeks before the race I'd thought about defecting a lot, but I'd decided I couldn't. I'd only met Sylvia once, she was only seventeen and I didn't know what she really felt. I wasn't sure whether she meant what she wrote, or whether the letters were just a way to pass the time. The other thing was that even if I had wanted to go I couldn't have. My dad was working on the race as a mechanic, and it would have been pretty terrible for him to go home without me.

By now you were living in constant fear of saying the wrong thing. You had to be watchful all the time, because you felt like you were being *watched* all the time. That's why, particularly after 1961, it became almost impossible to build genuine friendships. I liked the guy, and the chances are that he really wanted to go. Equally it was possible he just wanted to know how I'd respond. If I'd said, 'Oh yes, that's a great idea!' he might have gone straight back to the coach, or to the Stasi, or whomever. For all I knew – and for all I know today – he might have been Stasi himself.

You could have a lot of ideas, but it was best not to articulate them. My way of dealing with it was to keep myself to myself and say nothing to anybody. I'm quite a shy person by nature, but the point is that you learned to internalise everything. You had to think about the potential ramifications of everything you said, and the net result was that you had your public self and your private self.

MfSXIV/491/63 BSTU0037/0038

17.5.63

Commitment

I, (?), born 26.3.1941 in Flöha and, residing in
(?), Flöha, herewith commit myself to work with
the representatives of the MfS in line with
my abilities and active possibilities, in the
fight against the enemies of the GDR. In my
collaboration with the MfS I will do my upmost to
fulfil the tasks assigned to me.

(...)

To better guarantee the secrecy of the
collaboration I will use the alias 'Orion'.

(...)
(?)

Resident Flöha (?)

DIETER

You couldn't know, for example, whether your girlfriend's dad might be Stasi. You couldn't know whether your girlfriend *herself* was Stasi. They would send a pretty girl, they'd kid you into thinking they were in love with you, and that would be the end of you. You'd finish up in prison.

DIETER

So I was second again in Lower Austria, and more importantly we won the team prize. I went back in July for the full Tour of Austria. I did a decent ride there as well, without going too deep. I finished tenth, but by the time I got home my form was as good as it had ever been.

NEUES DEUTSCHLAND

ORGAN DES ZENTRALKOMITEES DER SOZIALISTISCHEN EINHEITSPARTEI DEUTSCHLANDS

A hearty encounter between Peace Race winner Klaus Ampler, the Chairman of the Council of Agriculture Georg Ewald, and the crew of a combine harvester. Otto Lipkowski and Walter Götze, from the Görzig LPG, are the current leaders of the harvesting competition. Thursday afternoon's encounter came down to a twenty-seven-hectare barley fight. Beaming with happiness, the two comradely farmers each received a symbolic yellow jersey from Germany's best cyclist. He told them, 'You are the winners of the first stage. Let's hope you're able to defend your yellow jerseys to the end!'

[...]

The heroes of the fields waved the hero of the road off with a firm handshake; 'All the best, and stay at the front!'

Reprinted from 'Yellow jerseys', 26 July 1963

DIETER

The 1963 Tour of the GDR was the last week in July, and I had the form of my life. I fancied myself to win it, but they surpassed themselves this time. I was on the start line ready to go, and a guy from the federation came up to me. He said, 'You're not starting because you have to go to Berlin. You've been selected for the team time trial at the Worlds, and you need to do a training camp with Appler, Brüning and Müller.'

The point is that the championships were in Belgium, and it was clear to everyone that we wouldn't be permitted to travel. Nothing had changed, so their pulling me out of the race was a complete waste of time in that respect.

I was a good time trialist, but my being withdrawn wasn't because of that. The point was that by pulling me out they ensured that Ampler, who was one of the DHfK pin-up boys, would win the Tour of the GDR. There was nothing I could do about it except wait for the official announcement that we wouldn't be travelling to Belgium. Sure enough it arrived four days later and so that was that; another chance missed and another total waste of time.

NEUES DEUTSCHLAND

ORGAN DES ZENTRALKOMITEES DER SOZIALISTISCHEN EINHEITSPARTEI DEUTSCHLANDS

A further page has been added to the NATO authorities' inglorious chapter of discrimination against GDR athletes. This latest Bonn-inspired policy has it that our world-class track and road cyclists are excluded from competing in the World Championships in Belgium, just as they were in Italy last year. [...]

It later transpired that the Belgian government had issued the visas, and the GDR Cycling Federation was even notified of their numbers. Federation president Heinz Przybyl, general secretary Heinz Dietrich, trainer Gallinge and the world-class track foursome Barleben, Köhler, Schmelzer and Kissner, the first part of the GDR team, arrived at Brussels airport on Sunday, the Belgian police forced them to return home immediately.

The GDR Cycling Federation wrote to the UCI congress, due to be held in Liège on 31 July. On behalf of its 16,000 members it issued the sharpest protest against this outrageous act of political interference in matters of international sport. The federation stresses that it has always made every effort in endeavouring to further the development of cycling in the world. It is an equal member of the UCI and has the right to participate both at congress and in the World Championships. The world governing body has a duty to provide protection for its members. [...]

Reprinted from 'GDR cyclists refused entry', 30 July 1963

DIETER

So I'd missed out on both the Peace Race and the Tour of the GDR. I had the feeling that sooner or later there would be nothing left for me to ride but pointless criteriums, races I didn't have a hope of winning. I was like a tree that can't bear fruit, and the only things growing were anger and resentment.

Ampler won the Tour of the GDR, DHfK riders were second and third, and I was delegated to the Tour of Bulgaria. I'd started to hate all the hypocrisy of GDR cycling, and to resent the fact that my career was being hijacked by politicians.

I was becoming fixated on the idea of getting out. All I wanted was to be a proper cyclist and to be free to come and go as I pleased. I'd had enough. My mind was made up.

SYLVIA

A letter arrived from Flöha, but this time it was addressed to my mum and dad.

Flöha, 28 August 1963

Dear Mrs and Mr Hermann,

I am writing to you because I would like to ask for a very big favour regarding Sylvia's vacation. My parents and I would like to invite her to their silver wedding anniversary in October. I would be delighted if she could be present, because it's not every year that we have such a big event.

Sylvia and I have been writing the whole year, and I sincerely hope you will allow her to be present. I would be very, very happy if you could fulfil this one big wish. Obviously in the event that you are free you are also invited to accompany her to the party.

I very much look forward to seeing you, and of course Sylvia, in Flöha.

Yours sincerely,
Dieter Wiedemann

SYLVIA

My mum said she didn't mind me going, but only on condition that she came with me.

Dieter and I had been writing for three years now, and I was always insisting that I would go to live with him when I was twenty-one. I guess she wanted to make sure that he was OK just in case I didn't change my mind. She wrote to my great-uncle in Flöha and asked him to apply for the permits.

The problem was that we weren't immediate family. They were only my mum's aunt and uncle, so the permit was refused. My uncle went to see Dieter to tell him that it was impossible for me to come.

DIETER

The permits were refused, as I'd suspected they would be. I went straight to the town hall and asked to see the mayor. I reminded him that he'd promised me a favour after the Peace Race, and that I'd never taken him up on it. Now I said I wanted to use it, and so he needed to help me.

I told him that I wanted to have 'a girl' sitting next to me for the anniversary party. I explained that because of my cycling commitments I never had time to think about girlfriends, or to go to the kind of places where you might meet one. I said I didn't want the embarrassment of being seated there alone for the big event, but that there was a girl from the west I sometimes exchanged letters with. I explained that she had an aunt and uncle in Flöha that she wanted to visit, and that she'd said she'd be happy to come to the party while she was here. The problem was that she'd been refused a permit, and so if he could help it would be appreciated.

Why didn't I tell him she was a sort of girlfriend? I'll explain as best I can.

I was hedging my bets, but it was based on the assumption that he didn't know the true nature of our relationship. He was the mayor and so he was an important person, but that didn't mean he'd seen the letters. I'd always assumed that the Stasi had been reading them, but unless he was Stasi himself he'd have no access to them and no way of knowing. There was no point in making it any more complicated than needed be, and if I'd said, 'She's my girlfriend and we're in love with one another' he might have turned me down outright.

I knew he wanted to look after me because I was the golden boy, but I also knew that he wouldn't have wanted to compromise his own position. You didn't get to be the mayor unless you were trusted by the party and they – in the guise of the Stasi – had decreed that she couldn't come. The Stasi was their 'shield and sword', and the rules were clear. And yet here I was asking him to appeal to them on her behalf.

I wasn't in the party and I'd never expressed any interest in joining. I wasn't a Täve, so politically the mayor had nothing to gain from Sylvia's coming, but probably quite a bit to lose. In isolation his appealing to the Stasi probably wasn't too damaging, but nor would it have been helpful for his career. The reason she'd been refused a permit was because things like that were considered 'anti-communist'. If, therefore, anything had gone wrong, he'd have been the architect because he'd been the one facil-itating the visit. Then the fact that he'd appealed on my behalf would be recorded in *his* Stasi file, and so in some respects I was asking him to roll the dice.

I knew that had I not been Dieter Wiedemann, Peace Race rider and local hero, there's no way in the world he'd have even considered doing it. He'd promised me a favour, but he could easily have said, 'When I said I could do you a favour I meant that I can get you to the top of the waiting list for a car.' Equally he could have said one thing and done another. He could have gone away and done nothing, then told me that the Stasi had turned him down. I'd have been none the wiser and he wouldn't have had to ask them a favour.

What happened was that he told me to leave it with him for three days and he'd see what he could do. So I was betting on him keeping his word, and on his having friends in high places at the Stasi. I was asking him to sway them into bending their own rules for a nineteen-year-old girl who, according to their doctrine, had no right to travel.

MfS383/65 bd1, BSTU0041

Hermann, Sylvia

Born 4.6.1946 Mitterteich

Single – Apprentice – Private business

Mitterteich Oberflatz, Vörstadt. Kleinsiedlung 37

German – 1946

Meeting with Mr Wiedemann 19.9 – 30.9. 1963

Diersche, Herbert

Conductor – German Railways

XIV 1759728

Flöha, Gartenstrasse 3, Acquaintance – 1960

Flöha, 17.9.1963

According to the applicant she was born in West Germany, and has lived there since 1946. Miss Hermann would like to visit Mr Wiedemann with her mother, Ilse Hermann.

This request is endorsed on the grounds of Mr Wiedemann's service to the German Peace Race team.

Mayor

DIETER

When I went back he said he'd been to see them. They'd told him the permits wouldn't be a problem, and all I had to do was just tell Sylvia's uncle to reapply.

I'd done it, and I headed off to Bulgaria knowing that I'd be seeing her again. It was all arranged.

NEUES DEUTSCHLAND

ORGAN DES ZENTRALKOMITEES DER SOZIALISTISCHEN EINHEITSPARTEI DEUTSCHLANDS

The Karl-Marx-Stadt rider, Dieter Wiedemann, delivered the GDR's first win on the fourth stage of the Tour of Bulgaria. He rode the 28.5-kilometre time trial between Stara Zagora and Nova Zagora in 44.32, beating the second-placed Polish rider, Palka (45:12) [...]

Reprinted from 'Stage winner Wiedemann', 24 September 1963

Marianne Wiedemann with her first-born, Dieter. Flöha, 1941.

Miniature Peace Race, 1952. Number 25 Eberhard Wiedemann (and teddy-bear) leads, his father built the side-car. Dieter (centre, white shirt, shorts and socks) is third wheel.

A life around bikes: Karl Wiedemann in winter training kit.

Golden boy: Mayor Hense (left) holds court for Dieter and Marianne Wiedemann.

Though Karl never competed, cycling was his *raison d'être*.

Above: Club lunch: Karl Wiedemann (seated, left) with little Eberhard and Dieter.

Champion in the making: Eberhard Wiedemann was prodigiously talented.

Flöha Elementary School, c. 1951. Rainer Müller is the blond boy in the middle of the front row; Dieter (in lederhosen) is third from the right on the back row. One of the boys would become 'Orion', a Stasi informant who reported on Dieter.

Promotional poster, 1953 Peace Race. Note the heavy industry (a classic socialist leitmotif), the cheering proletariat, the dove on the blue jersey and the flags of the three hosts.

Ian Steel, winner of the 1952 race. He and his British colleagues were given jerseys without the dove. © *East News/REX*

Above: The GDR team, held over in Tirana in advance of the 1961 Tour of Egypt. Wiedemann is third from the left.

Below: Time trial, 1964 Peace Race. Catching the Russian, Kulibin. Wiedemann would finish the stage sixth and move up to third on GC.

Classic early 1950s Peace Race photo. The billboard behind the peloton reads, 'Praise the Polish miners – heroes of the Socialist labour'.

S.C Wismut, winners of the 1960 GDR team time trial championships. Manfred Weissleder is far right, alongside Wiedemann.

Go east, young man: Marx and Lenin confer their approval upon the Peace Race peloton.

Warsaw, the colossal opening ceremony of the 1952 Peace Race. The banner reads, 'Constitution – the great charter of our nation's victory'. Stalin had just rubberstamped the 'Dictatorship of the Proletariat', enshrining communist rule in Polish law. Here he flanks Bierut, Gottwald and Pieck, party leaders of the three host nations. © *East News/REX*

The final podium of the 1964 Peace Race, Prague. Left to right: Dieter Wiedemann, Jan Smolik, Günter Hoffmann.

The race of millions: note the red kerchiefs and berets of the Young Socialist Movement. © *East News/REX*

Peace Race stage finishes were played out, almost without exception, to vast audiences in huge stadiums. © *East News/REX*

Täve, sporting symbol of socialism's great victory. A pin-up boy for the regime, his popularity knew no bounds. © *Deutsche Fotothek*

Fourteen-year-old Sylvia Hermann at home in Mitterteich, 1960.

Flöha, den 28.8.60

Liebe Sylvia!

Heute am 28.8.60 komme ich endlich dazu
Dir zu schreiben. Ich war fast den ganzen
August durch den Radsport unterwegs. Nun habe
ich endlich wieder etwas Zeit. Schade, daß Du
am letzten Abend vor Deiner Abreise nicht
mehr auf der Straße warst. Ich wollte mich
gerne von Dir verabschieden. Außerdem wollte
ich nach Deiner Adresse fragen u. ob ich Dir
mal schreiben darf. Du hättest aber zu meiner
großen Freude Frau Tursche gesagt; daß ich
Dir mal schreiben könnte." Ebenfalls möchte ich mich
für die Grüße die mir Frau Tursche von Dir aus-
richtete bedanken. Bedauerlich, daß wir erst so spät
ins Gespräch gekommen sind. Ich hätte gerne
noch ein paar Federballturniere mit Dir gespielt.
Liebe Sylvia würdest Du mir bitte mal schreiben wo
Mittweida liegt, bei welcher größeren Stadt. Ich
habe auf dem Atlas nachgesehen, habe es aber nicht

The end of the beginning: Dieter's first letter to Sylvia dated 28 August 1960.
Twelve months later the border was closed.

Left: Sylvia posing with the family car in 1962.

Below: Together at last: Sylvia and Dieter in Flöha, November 1963.

Abschrift!

Lieber Dieter W i e d e m a n n !

wir sind sehr erstaunt über die Handlungsweise unseres Bür-
germstr. Hense und anderen Funktionären, die es fertig gebracht
haben, "geschenkte" Sachen in Deiner elterlichen Wohnung abzuholen! Wir sind der Meinung, daß Du die Sachen ehrlich und wür-
dig verdient hast. Man hält es nicht für möglich, geschenkte
Sachen wieder abzuholen. Wir verwerfen Dies umsomehr, da doch
die Funktionäre gern mit Dir feierten. Ebenso verwerflich ist,
wie sie mit Deinem Vater und Bruder umgegangen sind!-
Du kannst Dir nicht vorstellen, wie viele Bürger Deiner Heimat
und Kreises noch hinter Dir stehen.
Wir wünschen Dir weiterhin noch recht viel Erfolg in Deiner
sportlichen Laufbahn und vorallendingen Gesundheit.
Wir achten Dich heute genau so wie zuvor und verbleiben mit herzl.
Grüßen die Sportanhänger des Kreises und Deiner Heimatstadt
Flöha.

An anonymous letter of support from 'the sporting people of Flöha',
September 1964.

Dieter (right) rode as a professional in West Germany. Here he's preparing to race having completed the Tour of Switzerland the previous day and having driven through the night with just two hours sleep.

It's the rest day of the 1967 Tour de France, at Belfort. The previous day Dieter (third from the left) was acquainted with the brutal climb of the Ballon d'Alsace.

Wiedemann raced for three years as a professional, before the Torpedo team folded.
He never won, but would have become a solid stage racer.

Right: Before the storm:
The Tour de France
peloton during the first
week of the race.
© *Offside / L'Equipe*

Below: Crossing the line
at Ballon d'Alsace. Dieter
lost six minutes to stage
winner Lucien Aimar.
Many conceded over
twenty minutes.

The worst of times: Britain's Tommy Simpson rode himself to death on Mont Ventoux. © *Offside / L'Equipe*

SYLVIA

Dieter went to see my uncle. He told him to reapply, and to request a ten-day permit. The extra days would give my mum a chance to meet his family, and I would be able to spend more time with him. In the event we didn't need the ten days. Dieter was summoned to a training camp, so we had three days less than we'd thought.

My mum was probably hoping that I'd realise that it wasn't such a great idea. Dieter and I might not like each other after all, or I'd see how poor the GDR was and come to my senses.

SYLVIA

Dieter came to meet us on the train, and I knew immediately that it was real. The letters hadn't been an illusion, and that was the most important thing.

He asked my mum if he could take me dancing the following evening, and she said it would be OK as long as he had me back by midnight.

DIETER

I remember the day she came as if it were yesterday. I was excited, but also scared. Aside from my cycling she was the only thing that mattered to me, and so all of a sudden I had everything to lose. It had been three years since I'd seen her, and three years is a very long time. We'd both grown, and I was worried that we might not like each other after all.

I set out for the train station and I was full of doubts. I was thinking, 'Is this really happening? Is she really going to come? What if it's all been a waste of time? What if there's no chemistry between us after all?'

Then immediately she stepped off the train I knew. She was even more beautiful than I'd imagined.

SYLVIA

The following day I had to go to the police station with my mum. We had to sign to confirm that we'd arrived, and to fill in the forms. We had to tell them which train we'd be taking home; things like that. I thought it was all a bit strange, but those were the rules, you know?

That evening I went dancing with Dieter, and I had my first ever glass of champagne. Then we took the train back to Flöha. He walked me back to my aunt's, and that's where he kissed me for the first time.

DIETER

We took the train to Chemnitz on the third day, and went dancing at a hotel. I was careful about what I said, and I avoided talking about the differences between east and west. I was quite well known, and you didn't know who might be listening.

We had a wonderful night together, and I was sure to get her home before midnight. When I went to bed my head was spinning, but I knew that I really was in love with her.

I had to make my mind up quickly. She'd be going back in a few days, so it was now or never. If I didn't do something I might not ever see her again.

SYLVIA

The next evening there was the party for the wedding anniversary at Dieter's house. There weren't many people there, just family and very close friends. I met all of his family and they seemed like nice people. I knew that I was different to them, but I didn't feel ill at ease. They were very kind, and I was comfortable being around new people anyway. It was fun.

I was watching my mum, and I could tell that she liked Dieter. He was courteous and quiet, and she liked the fact that he didn't speak for the sake of it. He didn't smoke or drink, he did sports and he seemed trustworthy.

SYLVIA

The day after the party we went for a walk in the forest. I told him I wanted to come to live with him, but that we'd have to wait until I was twenty-one. He said it was hopeless, and that it would never work. I'd been used to a much higher standard of living in the west, and so the adjustment would be impossible for me. I told him I didn't care about material things, and that my grandfather would make my clothes and then send them. I was very young and naïve, you know? Just a girl.

I was used to saying what I wanted, and to whom I wanted. Dieter said you couldn't do that in the GDR, and that you couldn't trust people the way I was used to. I listened to everything he said and told him I understood, but I didn't really. I was falling in love with him, and I would have done anything to be with him.

Then he told me about Giessen.

DIETER

So we went walking and I couldn't wait any more – I told her that I wanted to be with her. She said she did, too, but that we'd have to wait another couple of years before she could come. I knew we couldn't, and I knew that it would be impossible for her to come east. Then I told her about the qualification races for the Tokyo Olympics.

DIETER

The GDR and FRG used to compete together as a united German team. The way it worked was that each of the sports had to arrange qualifying events, and they had to be fair and equal. In practical terms that meant that there were two qualifiers, one either side of the border.

In cycling the races were scheduled for Giessen in the west, and then Erfurt in the east. The way it worked was that you got points according to your position in each race, and the five riders with the highest aggregate went to the Olympics. The races would be in July, so I told her that if we were careful and I stayed healthy I would be racing in the west, at Giessen. That would be our chance, and if she was sure I'd try to defect while I was there.

I explained that it was important she didn't mention it to anybody for now, though, not even her parents. If everything went according to plan she would be able to tell them later, but for now she mustn't say a word to anybody.

Then I explained that her visiting could have consequences for me. I told her about the Stasi, and that if anybody asked she'd to explain that we were only friends. She was to say that she hadn't even thought about us living together, and that I seemed happy with my life in the GDR. If they pressed her she was to tell them that she wasn't allowed to leave home until she was twenty-one, and that she understood there was no way I would be able to move to the west.

SYLVIA

The days flew by. He showed me around Chemnitz, we walked along the river, sat and read together at his house.

As the time passed I became more worried. Previously we'd been writing, dreaming really. Now it was different because he was real, and I was falling in love with him. He was slipping away from me hour by hour and I remember thinking, 'I don't know how I'm going to be able to cope with this. It's going to be much worse than before.'

DIETER

On the day she left we took the train from Flöha to Chemnitz. We said our goodbyes and got off, and Sylvia and her mum stepped on to the train headed to Hof, across the border.

I didn't go any further because it was the border train and it was full of Stasi. I didn't want to give them any sort of pretext for stopping her, so we said our goodbyes. I got off the train, she got on another one and the Stasi got on with her.

How did I know they were Stasi? Everyone knew they were Stasi! The train was going across the border, and normal people couldn't cross the border. Then you could tell the difference between people from the west and the east, so it wasn't rocket science. The haircuts, the clothes, the way they pretended to do 'normal' things. Just think of every Stasi cliché you've ever heard about. Black leather jacket, drinking a beer alone, pretending to read the paper.

SYLVIA

There were no kisses or anything like that because it was too dangerous. Dieter just said goodbye, and I boarded the train home with my mother.

When we got to Gutenfürst, the last station before the border, they pulled me and my mum aside and we were separated. Then they led me into an office and started checking my bags. I told them that if they didn't hurry up I wouldn't have time to get back on the train, and then I'd have to wait for the next one. They said, 'Well, then you'll have to wait for the next train …'

So they were going through the bags, and then they started interrogating me. They asked me what I'd been doing in the GDR, why I had friends in the east when I was from the west, all those things. They wanted to know about my relationship with Dieter and I told them that we were just friends. I said the main reason for my visit had been my family. They kept pressing me, but Dieter had told me what to say. I told them that I liked him, but that my mother and father wouldn't allow me to come to live with him until I was twenty-one. I said that Dieter had a good job as a cyclist and that he wasn't interested in leaving the GDR.

In the end we were there eleven hours, until midnight. It was horrible, and they treated me like I was some kind of a criminal. They treated me like dirt, but I had to sit there and take it from them. I'd understood that there were differences between east and west, but I hadn't realised that the people there were like that. I remember thinking, 'I love him but there's no way in the world I will ever come back to this awful country!'

Thinking about it now, maybe that was the reason they treated me like that. Maybe they didn't want me to go back there either.

DIETER

After Sylvia had gone home I went to the final training camp in Berlin, and then the assistant trainer of the club came to see me. His nickname was 'The Red Baron,'* and he'd ridden for Dynamo, the Stasi club. Everyone knew he was one of them.

Wismut and Motor were being consolidated into a single sport club, SC Karl-Marx-Stadt. That meant that Helmut Wechsler, the guy who had replaced Werner Richter, was also coming across to our club. I didn't much fancy that, and then the Baron told me that I needed to think about moving into the club dormitory. I said I didn't want to because I was happy at home. I explained that I enjoyed riding the extra few kilometres to and from the club, and that it was pointless for me to change. I could tell he was losing patience, though, and in the end he said, 'Look, it's pretty simple really – if you don't move into the club by 1 November your career will be finished!'

There were about eight or nine other cyclists living at the club, but they were the guys who came from a long way away. It was too far for

---

*   Werner Fritzsche, not to be confused with the informant 'Fritzsche'.

them to travel each day, so it was the only way for them to train. Then you had Weissleder who came from Weimar, 130 kilometres away, but he lived in a flat in town with his coach. The thing was that I lived ten kilometres away, so in a sporting sense there was no value in my moving into the club dormitory. They'd always quite liked the fact that I did a few extra kilometres each day, but apparently they didn't any more. They were making an exception of me, and I think it was their way of letting me know that they were on to me.

The Stasi had files on everybody, and when they told me to move in I assumed they'd got wind of what was going on. I assumed – and I still assume – that the mayor's request for Sylvia to come had set alarm bells ringing.

I therefore had no choice, but I figured that it would only be for two months. I'd be away all of January at winter training camp, then a week of physical testing at DHfK. Then we'd be into serious training, and pretty soon we'd be racing. I'd be able to spend weekends at home before the season started, and anyway it wasn't like he was giving me an option.

I told him that I'd move in, but only on the proviso that they gave me a single room. I told him I snored, but he knew that what I really wanted was to be left alone. He could have challenged me, but it wouldn't have made much sense for him. I was an important rider for the club and it wouldn't have been good for his own career had he lost me. So it was a sort of trade, as everything was in the GDR. It was the best I could hope for in the circumstances, and he got what he wanted. I went to the town hall to register a change of residence, and moved in on 1 November 1963.

MfS8963/69 BSTU0137/0138/0139/0140
Berlin, 6 December 1963

Main Department V/6/I
Meeting report
With: Informant 'Hildebrand'
Time: 4.12.63, 14.00
Location: conspiratorial dwelling 'Vineta'

The informant stated that from 22.3.1964–3.4.1964
the following sportsmen and functionaries would be
designated to the Tour of Tunisia

Leader:	Scholz	German Cycling Federation
Trainer:	Elste	Dynamo Berlin
Team physician:	Dr. Wuscheck	Dynamo Berlin
Masseur:	Horn, Kurt	Dynamo Berlin
Mechanic:	Letz	Dynamo Berlin
Athletes:	Butzke	Dynamo Berlin
	Burho	Dynamo Berlin
	Peschel	Dynamo Berlin
	Krause	DHfK
	Marks	DHfK
	Kaczmierak	ASK
	Kellermann	ASK
	Giese	ASK
	Adler	ASK

For the Tour of Morocco from 15.4–3.5.1964 the
following will be delegated:

Trainer:	Löhse	SC Karl-Marx-Stadt
Team physician:	Dr. Weber	SC Karl-Marx-Stadt
Masseur:	Landrock	SC Karl-Marx-Stadt
Athletes:	Müller	Dynamo Berlin
	Scheibner	Dynamo Berlin
	Peschel	Dynamo Berlin
	Rittmeyer	SC Karl-Marx-Stadt
	Weissleder	SC Karl-Marx-Stadt
	Höhne	ASK
	Lörke	DHfK

For the 1964 Peace Race the following are
candidates:

Brüning	Dynamo Berlin
Appler	Dynamo Berlin
Peschel	Dynamo Berlin
Hoffmann	ASK
Wiedemann	SC Karl-Marx-Stadt
Schur	DHfK
Ampler	DHfK
Lux	DHfK
Eckstein	DHfK
Mickein	DHfK

(...)

During the conversation the informant reported
that a conference on scientific methods took place
in the last week of November 1963 in Karl-Marx-
Stadt. (...)

The informant further alleges that following
negotiations with the west zone about the
Olympic qualifiers, comrade (?) from the cycling
federation reported that western riders are
following a similar training plan to ours.

The informant therefore suspects that there
must be traitors among the cycling functionaries,
who are passing information about our training
methodology and planning to the western cycling
functionaries.

The informant was tasked with submitting an
evaluation on the Olympic cycling candidates (?)
and (?).

Next meeting 24.1.1964, 13.30. Conspiratorial
dwelling 'Vineta'

Lieutenant Müller

DIETER

So I knew that 1964 would be the critical year. I was pretty sure that they knew all about Sylvia, and that they would be watching my every move.

I knew that if I was successful on the bike I could spin the whole thing out a little longer, but time was running out for me and for them. If I rode badly or got injured I wouldn't be on the bus to Giessen, and that would be the end of it.

The whole thing was closing in on me, and I'd used my joker now. I had to keep my head down, and above all to stay fit so that I'd be selected for the Olympic qualifier. There would be more pressure to join the party, but if I knew that if I could just get to Giessen I would at least have a chance.

I was playing a game with them, and I suppose you could say it was the endgame.

SYLVIA

I told my mum and dad about him coming in the spring, and they said they were fine with it as long as I was sure.

My mum had met his family, and she had told my dad that they were nice, simple people. She liked the fact that they kept rabbits and that Dieter's dad tended his smallholding. That they weren't like those crazy GDR people you read about, with guns hidden behind the wardrobe!

We never discussed politics, or the implications of having him come to stay. To be honest I don't even think it crossed their minds, and if it did they never mentioned it to me. As far as my dad was concerned it was just something I dearly wanted, and he thought it would be nice to have a son-in-law.

DIETER

I was one of the candidates for the Peace Race, and I was going well.

A few weeks before the race there was a terrible tragedy. One of the team from the previous year, Manfred Brüning, was hit by a truck in Berlin and killed. Manfred and I were about the same age, and he was a really nice person.

MfS383/65 bd4, BSTU0006

Karl-Marx-Stadt, 24.4.64

Sport Club Karl-Marx-Stadt

Addendum to the assessment of
Sportsfriend Dieter Wiedemann

In addition to the previous assessment, we add
that the sportsfriend has been boarding at our
club, at 485 Zwickauer Strasse, for about half a
year. In a discussion with him he expressed that
he wants a different room. Along the corridor,
where he is currently situated, there is too much
traffic, and as such he doesn't find the necessary
peace. We are aware that sportsfriend Wiedemann
goes to bed very early, so a decision has been made
to resolve this situation upon his return from
the Peace Race.

He is optimistic about fulfilling his
performance target. He was pleased that he was
nominated for the Peace Race squad. He forecasts
so that it will go well, that this year's Peace
Race team will be a good collective, and that
their mutual understanding will be very good. He
is convinced that we will do well.

Sportsfriend Wiedemann has a solid lifestyle.
His whole life is subordinated to his athletic
duties.

The management of the Sport Club Karl-Marx-
Stadt has full confidence in him, and endorses his
deployment in capitalist countries at any time.

Management, Sport Club Karl-Marx-Stadt

DIETER

When they chose the team they always picked a reserve as well, in case someone fell ill or got injured beforehand. This time it was me, Lothar Appler from Dynamo and the usual DHfK cadre. You had Schur, Eckstein, Ampler and a new lad named Dieter Mickein. The reserve was Günter Hoffmann, from ASK Vorwärts.

You couldn't argue with them selecting Ampler, and Mickein was the new star. Täve was thirty-three, but he said he wanted to do one more Peace Race and they needed a road captain. Then when you had Täve you always had Eckstein as well, but it made no sense because Hoffmann had the best form of anyone in the GDR. Anyway, two days before the race there was a meeting and they put him in instead of Eckstein. The trainer, coach, mechanic and masseur were all DHfK.

NEUES DEUTSCHLAND

ORGAN DES ZENTRALKOMITEES DER SOZIALISTISCHEN EINHEITSPARTEI DEUTSCHLANDS

Today sees the start of the seventeenth International Peace Race. It begins with a ninety-four-kilometre criterium, a 'Tour of Warsaw'. Riders from Belgium, Denmark, Czechoslovakia, Hungary, Poland, USSR, Finland, the GDR, England, France, Cuba, Yugoslavia, Romania, Bulgaria and, for the first time, an international team, will take to the road to fight for peace. After the first four stages on Polish territory, the riders will reach the GDR on Thursday 14 May, with the finish in Berlin. They will leave our republic on Wednesday 20 May, from Aue, before the winner is honoured in Prague on 24 May.

The Peace Race has lent her character to an era. When, sixteen years ago, the first edition ran between the rivers Vltava and Vistula, amateur stage racing was almost unknown throughout the world. Conscientiously, through adversity and against all odds, the number of participating countries increased.

Now bright-eyed guests from dozens of countries celebrate May Day.

The athletic idea bore handsome fruit: there are now stage races of prestige and tradition in all socialist countries. England announced its tour, the United Arab Republic directed a stage race in the Nile Delta. Socialist Cuba, Tunisia and Morocco were the final links in the chain of countries providing amateur riders with a new sporting highlight, a Peace Race replica. Even the conservative Tour de France felt compelled to introduce a special amateur race.

Through this example the Peace Race has provided crucial impulse to cycling the world over. And of that the organisers may be justly proud. [...]

Cleverly, the popularity of the race was used to encourage hundreds of thousands to participate in miniature peace races each year. Not only does this help to identify new talent, but first and foremost fulfils the demand within our society to develop well-rounded people who appreciate the joy of movement and competition, and the moral and physical values of sport.

From the outset the Peace Race simply welcomed guests. It knows of no single case of political or racial discrimination, a practice which is unfortunately all too commonplace among the governments of the NATO block. For almost two decades the Peace Race has been providing a compelling example of the Olympic ideal in action, and of the pioneering work of socialist countries in the promotion of physical culture and sport.

The Peace Race is also a valuable contribution in the global effort for peaceful coexistence. Riders from NATO block countries find themselves in the company of those from the socialist camp. Riders from kingdoms strive to win the winning laurel together with riders from states ruled by workers and farmers. They may have the different views, but they are united by the symbols of the turning wheel and Picasso's dove.

In recent days West German newspapers have finally rediscovered their 'love' for the Peace Race, by informing their readers that this year the number of participants is lower than for previous editions,[*] Notwithstanding the fact that this circumstance is due to preparations for the Tokyo Olympics – the reason given by the Dutch for not accepting their invitation – it must be stated that something was finally written in West Germany following a long period of silence about the Peace Race. The revanchist state is the only one which has boycotted the race from the Vistula to the Vltava upon government instructions. The position of Bonn in relation to the Peace Race is clear. The ruling classes over there fear anything which promotes understanding, friendship among young people and peace among men.

To celebrate the Peace Race also means to know both your friends and your foes. This year it has become clear that the number of friends has increased, while the influence of the foes has diminished.

Reprinted from 'Friedensfahrt', 9 May 1964

---

[*] Only fifteen teams were present, four fewer than the previous year. To make up some of the shortfall a 'Three Continents' team was included, and one from Cuba.

DIETER

My previous Peace Race had been a catastrophe for the GDR, but we were much stronger this time.

Dieter Mickein won in Warsaw, and a Czech guy named Jan Smolik was second. Mickein got a minute's time bonus, and Smolik got thirty seconds. So the stage earned Mickein the yellow jersey and the GDR team the blue one.

I came in with the group. I wasn't a sprinter and I wasn't interested in contesting them anyway. The stadiums all had cinder tracks back then, so there tended to be crashes. To win them you needed to be an extremely good bike handler, and you also needed to be brave enough to attack the bends. The sprints at the Peace Race were very difficult to predict for all sorts of reasons. The cinder was treacherous anyway, but the fact that you'd people there who weren't used to it complicated things further. You could be the greatest champion in the world, but if you got brought off by a guy who didn't know how to ride the cinder you were done for. Obviously it was a national teams' event, so people would go there in the hope that one of theirs would win. It was pretty dramatic, and that partly explains why the stadiums were always full. It's also one of the reasons cycling was so popular.

So, all things considered, it was an extremely good day, and the next was the team time trial, eighty-four kilometres to Łódź. It didn't count towards the individual classification, but it was crucial for the blue jersey. We were really strong and we won it easily. Then, because we were the fastest, Hoffmann got the most points and took the violet jersey. Two stages gone and we had all three jerseys.

There was a split the following day, and we all missed it. We only lost about thirty seconds, but Smolik took the jersey from Mickein.

Nothing much happened in Poznań,[*] so I went into the rest day with the same time as the rest of the GDR team, about two minutes down on Smolik.

The race was wide open because we still had the hilly stages and the time trial to come. The only thing that Poland had proved was that the racing was extremely fast, that Ampler wasn't as good as the previous year and that it was going to take a hell of a good rider to beat Smolik.

Everyone came in together in Berlin, so we still had a two minute lead in the team competition. Smolik won the stage, so he got another minute in time bonuses. The Berlin to Leipzig stage was next, and it was always a big event in the Peace Race. Obviously Leipzig was a sports town anyway, but Chemie Leipzig had just won the GDR football championship. The stage was on the Friday, and before it there was a friendly match between Chemie and FC São Paulo. The stadium was full as usual; 100,000 people.[†]

---

[*]   Dieter Mickein crashed near the entrance to the stadium in Poznań, and rode in on a bike borrowed from a spectator.

    Though Jan Veselý and the brilliant Vlastimil Růžička had lit up the early Peace Races, by now the Czechs were much the weakest of the three host nations. Between 1956 and 1963 they had amassed just three stage wins, not a single day in yellow and no podium finishers. However, Smolik, twenty-two, was prodigiously talented. As a sixteen-year-old he'd apparently been given special dispensation to race against the men, and had outsprinted them. All the more impressive when one considers that the runner-up that day, Josef Krivka, had been a Peace Race stage winner in 1955.

[†] Peace Race stage finishes were civic events on a massive scale. As a rule they commenced around midday, five hours or so before the riders appeared. The Berlin stage had begun with a marching parade, followed by music from a 1,500-strong orchestra. Next came gymnastics and athletics displays from both DHfK and SV Dynamo. At two o'clock the GDR national team played Leeds United, just then promoted to the top tier of English football.

The seventh stage was Leipzig to Erfurt.* It was hilly, and quite windy. It was a real battle, and you could tell that it was going to split any minute. I was going really well, and I knew that I had to ride as close to the front as possible so that I'd be OK when it split. Early in the stage there was a really strong crosswind, and it broke up. A group of a dozen or so went away, and I made sure I was in it.

Hoffmann was with me, and then Appler got across. That meant we had the three we needed for the blue jersey. So did the Romanians and Poles, but Smolik was on his own and there were only two Russians. Had we started attacking Smolik one of us would probably have gone clear, but in the Peace Race you always rode for the team first and foremost. So we drove the break instead, and made sure we all came in. It was pointless for Schur, Ampler and Mickein to try to bridge across, because they'd have dragged the Czechs, Russians and Belgians with them and that would have been counterproductive for the blue jersey. Anyway we put five minutes into the peloton, and the upshot was that we increased our lead in the team competition.

Smolik won again, Appler was second and Hoffmann and I came in safely. It was becoming obvious that Smolik was the strongest, but we had three in the top ten now and we'd eliminated everyone but the Poles and Romanians from the team prize. I was tenth at about four minutes, but the three from DHfK were out of the running for the GC. They were all at eight or nine minutes, and there was no way they were going to get that back.

That evening we had dinner, and then went our separate ways. We were staying in some sort of company holiday home, and we were three

---

* After the war, the stadium in Erfurt had been renamed in honour of Georgi Dimitrov, first secretary of the Bulgarian Communist Party. The population of the town was 190,000, and 45,000 of them were present for the sprint.

to a room. I was with Hoffmann and Appler, and the DHfK guys stayed in the other room.

Next was a forty-kilometre time trial to Oberhof, the ski station. Smolik won it, and Täve, me and Ampler were fifth, sixth and seventh. That moved me up to third on GC, behind Smolik and Hoffmann.[*]

The blue jersey was pretty much sewn up, and on the second rest day the coach came to see us. He told us that if we held on to our positions we'd each get half the value of a Trabant as a bonus. That was about 5,000 marks, which was a huge amount of money.

Hoffmann and I were fighting for the podium, but they didn't ride for us. The hierarchy was DHfK, then Dynamo, and then the rest. Appler rode for Dynamo, so instead of looking after us they focused on trying to get him in a position to sprint for the time bonuses. I wasn't one for arguing with my team-mates, but I maintain that, had Ampler and Schur been second and third, as opposed to me and Hoffmann, we'd have been ordered to try to ride Smolik into the ground in the hope that he'd crack. He was the strongest in the race, no question, but his team weren't that good and I still believe that if you're second and third in the Peace Race you deserve some protection. We didn't get any, but at the end of the day I was SC Karl-Marx-Stadt and Hoffmann was ASK Vorwärts. So it wasn't personal, not at all. We got on pretty well individually, but it was what it was.

We held our positions to Prague anyway,[†] and won the blue jersey easily.

---

[*] Smolik led Hoffmann by 7'31", with Wiedemann at 7'41".

[†] The positions remained unchanged. The GDR won the blue jersey by 6'14".

NEUES DEUTSCHLAND

ORGAN DES ZENTRALKOMITEES DER SOZIALISTISCHEN EINHEITSPARTEI DEUTSCHLANDS

This was something completely new for a GDR Peace Race team: coach Weisbrod rarely saw them during the stages. The reason was that they were always at the front of the race, and as such barely visible to the team car. They spared themselves unnecessary pursuits, but rather their almost perfect balance gave them the opportunity to place a 'blue screen' at the head of the peloton. And now here's a short appraisal of the six (in order of their starting numbers):

Klaus Ampler: The radiant winner of last year's race never had a chance to repeat his success. This was clear even from the first stage, when he avoided a time loss thanks only to Schur's help. What was remarkable was the guts and courage he showed by tirelessly fighting for the team. He grew stronger towards the finish, probably due to the improvement in the back injury which had undermined his training and caused his initial difficulties.

Lothar Appler: In many respects the lanky Berliner was unrecognisable from last year. As regards confidence and initiative he was the best in the team. He was always ready to avert danger, and didn't hesitate when important decisions needed to be made.

Günter Hoffmann: The 'substitute' finished second in the Peace Race, and, and for that he deserves a huge round of applause. He never rode among the 'sleepers' (those who sit at the back of the peloton in order to preserve their energy), but was always to be found at the engine of the race.

Dieter Mickein: There wasn't a single metre between Warsaw and Prague in which he played the 'novice'. He was desperately unhappy when he wasn't able to complete the team time trial with the others. He was always in the breakaways, and the opposition knew that with him present their chances of claiming the blue jersey were slim. With a stage victory and two second places, he was the most successful GDR rider.

Gustav-Adolf Schur: A masterful captain, who perhaps hoped for even better. The five minutes he lost for tactical reasons on the road to Leipzig deprived him of the opportunity, and a cold caused further difficulties. He steered his team through the race confidently, and added further still to the laurels he's earned over the course of his career. Those who had written him off need to think again.

Dieter Wiedemann: A road racer of the toughest kind. The sprints aren't his strength, but his rivals learned that he's a relentless fighter who never puts a foot wrong. It's worth noting because he was barely in the headlines, but a third-place finish at the Peace Race speaks for itself.

Reprinted from 'The winning team', 25 May 1964

Prague, 26 May 1964

My dearest Sylvia,

My thoughts are with you, and so I wanted to write to you.
In a few hours we will fly to Berlin, and after that
I'll be back home. I received your two letters just before I left,
but unfortunately I didn't find time to answer them. I'll
answer them as soon as I get back, and I hope that's all
right with you.

I have a problem with my knee, an infection. It hurts, and
I had problems during the stage in Prague. I'm happy with
my results though, so you were a very good talisman!

I'm writing because 5 July is very important, so please
remember it well. I'm looking forward to getting your next
letter, but in the meantime I am missing you so I send hugs
and kisses.

In eternal love,
Dieter

DIETER

When we flew home we had the big welcome party at Schönefeld Airport, and there was a limousine to take me back to Flöha. There were hundreds of people waiting to greet me, and the following afternoon there was a big parade and another reception. Previously I'd been one of the better cyclists, but probably not one of the more famous ones. Now that I was a podium finisher at the Peace Race everybody knew who I was, and I suppose I became quite famous. Half of the town turned out, and it was all over the radio and the local paper. Believe it or not I'm still a hero to some of the people there, even after all these years. Goes to show how big the Peace Race was, I guess.

Mayor Hense told me that they were going to make me a freeman of the town. He said the people of Flöha wanted to award me a television in recognition of what I'd done at the Peace Race. That was a big thing because very few people had a television; you couldn't go to a shop and buy one with GDR wages. He brought it round to our house in person, with one of his staff.

On the Thursday I went back to the sport club for the first time, and the party recruitment officer was waiting for me. He said, 'Well, Dieter, it looks like the time has come for you to join the party!' He said I needed to join because it was important that I be seen to be a member.

I'd come back from Prague with a knee injury though, so I told them I was focused on recovering from that. I said I needed to make sure I was ready for the Olympic trials in July, and that I couldn't think about anything else for now. I said I'd join on Republic Day, 7 October. That way they'd get the publicity value of my doing it on a national holiday, and that's how I managed to put it off.

DIETER

Later I was talking to one of the other Peace Race guys and he said, 'Have you seen the man in black yet?' He was the guy who always delivered the prize money, a tall bloke who carried a black suitcase. He always wore a black suit, black shoes, black tie and black raincoat. We called him the man in black because we had no idea what his name was. I said that he hadn't turned up yet. He said he'd been to see him, but he hadn't given him what we'd been promised. Anyway the man in black came to the club and I went to the secretary's office to meet him. He opened his suitcase and congratulated me. He shook my hand and said, 'Congratulations, you have honoured the GDR.' Then he gave me a brown envelope, and left.

It was 3,000 marks.

DIETER

You ask why I didn't join the party, and if I'm honest it would probably have made my life easier in the short term. It would have tricked them into thinking that I was one of them, and with six weeks till Giessen that would have made sense. I still wasn't going to do it, though, and I'll tell you why.

As I explained to you before, I didn't want to be drawn into their world. I wasn't political, but by now the politics they were practising were so disgusting that I wasn't going to support them in any way. Had I joined I'd have been a hypocrite, and so I was resolved to hold out if I could. Had I actually *won* the Peace Race it would probably have been impossible to avoid, but the focus was more on the team prize than on what Hoffmann and I had done individually.

So the reasons *were* ideological, but I had practical considerations as well.

I'd been brought up in the GDR, so I assumed that the BND[*] would be like the Stasi. If they'd found out that I'd recently joined the party they might have assumed I was a communist, and possibly even a Stasi agent. Then there was the possibility that the Stasi would have fed

***

[*] The FRG intelligence service.

that information to the West German tabloids. I was quite a famous sportsman in the GDR, and if the press had me down as a communist I probably wouldn't be able to get a job because of the negative publicity it might attract. So I didn't know anything about life over there, but I didn't want to risk making it any harder than it already was.

The other thing was that I was about to defect to the Federal Republic of Germany. It was a capitalist country, and there was a war going on. Defection from the GDR was treasonable, and in attempting it I was declaring myself to be an enemy of the state and of socialism. The last thing I wanted to do was to rub their noses in it, or to provoke them any more than was absolutely necessary. I didn't want to run the risk of them coming after me.

DIETER

On my birthday I was at a training camp in Greiz. Dietrich, the general secretary of the federation, called a meeting of the riders and all the staff. It was all about how we should conduct ourselves while we were in the west. He told us what we should do if we were approached by people trying to persuade us to stay.

After he'd finished, Täve, who was the group spokesman, said, 'Hang on, what about the money from the Peace Race?' Dietrich said there was no more money, but Täve told him they'd promised us half a Trabant and that they couldn't play tricks like that. Dietrich grabbed the microphone and shouted, 'Comrade Schur – cease this discussion now! If you don't you'll be thrown out of the party and each of you will pay back the money you've received.' The point is that they were threatening *Täve Schur*, so what hope was there for the likes of me?

The irony was that each time they tried to turn the screw it had completely the reverse effect on me. The more it felt like I was living in a prison the more I was determined to break out of it.

Greiz, 17 June 1964

My dearest Sylvia,

I've been travelling again, and I'm in Greiz. I wanted to use my spare time to write to you on my 23rd birthday, as my thoughts are with you and I miss you a lot.

I've been travelling a lot, and it's been too much. I left on 12 June, home to Flöha. The medical treatment was successful, and I went to race in Erfurt on 13 June. I posted you two postcards from there, and I hope you got them. The race itself was quite good, though I hadn't trained due to the treatment. Afterwards I went home, and the good news is that my knee was fine. The race was tough, but I rode without any problems. It probably helped that you were thinking of me, because you are my talisman.

Yesterday we trained for 150 kilometres, as there will be a race in Chemnitz on Saturday evening. I have one on Sunday as well, so you can see that I'm pretty busy. Today, on my birthday, we trained for eighty kilometres. So I'm not having such a great birthday, as sport is hard and I have to train every day.

We'll have coffee today at 3.30, then play badminton at four o'clock. Later we'll clean our bikes and have dinner around six o'clock.

Thanks for all the kisses you sent me. They make me feel very happy, but it's a pity you're not here and we can't kiss and hug in person. My thoughts are with you the whole day today. My parents bought me flowers for my birthday, and I get a telegram and sweets from them and flowers from my colleagues. It's all like a big dream, but nevertheless I'm thinking about you and feeling very, very lonely. When we trained today we were close to your home town, 100 kilometres away. That's nothing, but the problem is the border.

It's the second time I haven't been at home for my birthday. Birthdays are important for me, and it's a shame that I can't spend the day with my parents, but am alone with my colleagues.

Dear Sylvia you know that you're the only one for me, and I like you so, so much. If I don't get ill, or if nothing goes wrong, I will participate. They told me today that I've been chosen. Understand? If nothing changes they'll confirm it on 28 June, and I'll let you know in due course. OK? In the event that I participate, please come, because then we'll finally have the chance to talk a little. That would be great!

That's all for now. Say hello to your parents, to your grandparents and to Roland. Remember that you are my one and only, and I send you kisses and hugs. I miss you so much.

In eternal love,

Dieter

SYLVIA

We mentioned Giessen in the letters, yes. We were excited, but it was also common sense. It would have seemed a bit strange if we hadn't, because it was logical that I'd be going to watch the race.

He'd send me progress reports on his racing and suchlike, but they were actually written in a sort of code. He would write that he was looking forward to it so much, but he'd also make reference to the chance that he might be able to represent his country in Tokyo. He wrote about my coming back to Flöha as well, so anyone reading the letters would think that Giessen was just another chance for us to see each other. They read like it was a means to an end, but the end was Tokyo, not Mitterteich.

Greiz, 19 June 1964

My dearest Sylvia,

This afternoon I want to write again as I'm thinking of you and missing you very, very much, my love. Yesterday I had a race in Chemnitz and my parents came. They brought a letter from you and I was extremely happy to get it. Thank you for the lovely birthday wishes, and of course for the letter. The parcel arrived yesterday, so thanks very much for that as well. The bananas were great and I really liked them.

Yesterday I was thirteenth of ninety-five, so I did quite a good race. Tomorrow we'll go to Wardenburg, near Dresden, and we'll have two races there.

Thanks very much for the flowers your mum sent; I appreciated them very much. I sent you a very special doll from Poland, and I hope you like it.

Dear Sylvia, believe me that you're not the only one who's lonely. It's very hard for me as well, and I miss you a lot. I can understand your feelings as I have the same ones. Please don't be sad. I'm still thinking of all the things we said, and your words are always on my mind. In a way you're always with me, although we're so far apart. You are my girlfriend, and I'm not interested in anybody else at all. I only think about you, and you are the only one I miss.

I sincerely hope we'll have a chance to talk in more detail when you next come to Flöha. I think it's really important, and it's much easier to talk personally instead of writing letters. Although there is the border, we are all Germans.

I enclose a postcard from Greiz. I wanted to write to you straight away, and so I didn't wait for you to answer my last letter. Don't be sad anymore, as it makes me sad, too. A big hug for your grandmother, for Roland and of course for you. Many, many, many tender kisses for you my dearest Sylvia. I'm thinking about you very, very often, and I miss you a lot.

With love,
Dieter

EBERHARD

The letters were coming all the time, and we all saw the western postmarks. We'd met the girl at the wedding anniversary, and we knew she was important to him. We talked about the possibility of his leaving within the family, but only when he wasn't around.

The contact I had with him was minimal at this point, because we were both busy with our respective training programmes. So our relationship wasn't as close, but obviously I followed his career and I knew he'd be going to Giessen. I wouldn't say I was *expecting* him to defect, no, but I knew him and I thought it was a possibility. As it drew nearer it was just something you kind of waited for.

RAINER

When he went to Giessen I had a feeling he wouldn't come back. Obviously I didn't tell anybody, but I said to myself, 'If Dieter comes back then my name is Maier, not Müller.' They were in love.

DIETER

I thought long and hard about it, and I was resigned to the fact that I may never see my family again. I was leaving everything behind, including friends I'd known since school and from the club.

It was inconceivable I might talk to anybody about it, and it never even crossed my mind. Let's say I spoke to somebody about it in confidence. He might then tell someone else in confidence, and his friend might tell someone else. Somewhere along the line it would have got back to the Stasi, and that would have been me finished. Then even if it went no further I'd have been burdening somebody else with it, and I didn't want to do that.

I was prepared for it intellectually, and as far as I could emotionally, but I couldn't allow myself to dwell on what I was leaving behind.

Regardless, I was focused on my own life, and on what was happening to me.

DIETER

The idea of the Olympic trials was to give both sides an equal chance. So there would be Giessen on 5 July, and the winner would get thirty points. The runner-up would get twenty-six, and so on and so forth. The next week there'd be the decider at Erfurt, and the four with the highest aggregate would qualify, along with a reserve.

I reckoned that if I made it to Japan it would probably be safer. The perfect scenario would have been to walk into the FRG embassy in Tokyo and claim asylum. The problem was the fact that only five would make it, and I didn't fancy my chances. I wasn't a sprinter and I knew the courses wouldn't be selective enough for me to get the points. I knew that Giessen was the best chance I was ever going to have, and probably the only chance.

DIETER

I had an agreement with the bank. I was often away training and racing, and so my mum would go and pick up my wages if I wasn't around at the end of the month. This time it was different, because if everything worked out I was never going to see that money. My mum didn't know that, though, and she went and withdrew the 450 marks as normal.

UDO

Peter and I were still living in Cologne, and we saw in the press that the Olympic qualifiers were in Giessen. We knew a lot of the GDR riders and trainers, so we thought we'd make a weekend of it and drive over there. We thought it would be nice to meet some old cycling friends.

DIETER

On the Thursday morning we packed our bags in Greiz and handed them to the trainers. They put them in the cars and drove them to Erfurt, which was about 120 kilometres. We rode there, showered and had lunch as normal. After that we had free time and so I went straight to the post office. I composed a four-word telegram:

GIESSEN STATION. SATURDAY. TWO O'CLOCK.

I addressed it to 'The Hermann Family' as distinct to Sylvia, because that way it didn't implicate her directly. I was lucky because the clerk at the post office should have insisted on the sender's name but didn't. It meant the telegram was anonymous, just as I'd hoped. It had been sent from a post office in Erfurt, but it could have been sent by anybody.

DIETER

The following morning we had to surrender our ID papers before we got on the bus. They issued us with our travel permits,* but when I looked at mine it said that I was married. I spoke with Günter Hoffmann and Immo Rittmeyer because they were single as well, and theirs also stated that they were married. I couldn't understand it at first, but then it started to dawn on me.

Any GDR citizen could claim asylum in the west, and be granted the same rights as everybody else. However, there was no way I was ever going to be granted a divorce. So in practical terms it meant that I would never be able to marry Sylvia, and we wouldn't be able to get a place together.

I was incensed that they'd do something like that, but it wasn't going to stop me trying. In fact, if anything it just strengthened my resolve.

---

* The temporary ID document was known as a PM12.

When we got on the bus it was already half full. By the time we set off there were probably about fifty people altogether, but only seventeen of us were cyclists. The mechanic, officials and journalists travelled by car, and I'd no idea who the others were. I'd never seen them before in my life, and it wasn't like GDR citizens could just hop on the bus and slip across the border for a weekend.

They weren't cycling people, and they certainly weren't going to Giessen for sightseeing. They were obviously on that bus for a reason, though, so there was only one logical conclusion. We had our seats at the front of the bus, they had theirs behind, and there was no contact between us.

It was common knowledge that they shot people at the wall itself, even though they didn't publish it in the papers. Those people simply 'disappeared', but the Stasi made out that they were traitors who'd escaped and never been heard from again. They had no legal jurisdiction in the west, but you heard all sorts of stories. So I was pretty sure I knew who the people on the bus were, but I didn't know what their orders were or to what lengths they were prepared to go.

DIETER

I can't describe the feeling of release when we crossed the border. I'd felt like I was suffocating, but suddenly I could breathe again. I wasn't euphoric because I knew that I wasn't free yet, but I'd cleared a big hurdle.

I was in the same country as Sylvia, but I wasn't some starry-eyed teenager thinking I'd made it. The situation was still dangerous, and I assumed the people on the bus would be watching our every move. In my mind I'd worked it all out quite methodically, and I was determined to see it through. I reminded myself that I'd to keep my wits about me, and that I still needed to get to the station.

DIETER

As we pulled into the hotel I saw a sign for the station. When we got there I knew it had to be close by because we were staying on the corner of Bahnhofstrasse.

The point about my having specified two o'clock on the telegram was that it was basically an educated guess. On days like these our routine was pretty much set in stone. We would train in the morning, have lunch about one o'clock, and then have a couple of hours free. After that there would be a meeting, dinner, and to bed.

So in the normal course of events two o'clock would have been free time for me, but this was anything but normal. It wasn't every day that you travelled to the west with a bus full of Stasi.

Anyway we went off to our rooms, and again I was sharing with Immo Rittmeyer. That evening we all went to the cinema; the riders, officials and the people on the bus. The following morning we rode the course. I remember thinking that it was a nice rolling circuit, but then realising it made no difference to me because I wouldn't be riding it anyway. When we got back there was a panic because one of the guys had a problem with his bike. They didn't have any replacement parts, so they had to send someone to the border to get some.

DIETER

Giessen is a spa town and it was holiday time, so the hotel reception was always crowded. After lunch we were sitting in the hotel lobby, and the guy at reception asked me if I'd been given my telegram. I said I hadn't, and he said that he'd had to give it to one of the officials because the federation hadn't given the hotel a rooming list. He therefore didn't know which room I was in, so hadn't been able to have it delivered to the room. I spoke with the general secretary about it, a guy named Scholz. He handed me a telegram, but it had been opened. I said, 'Why has it been opened?', but he made light of it and said it wasn't important. I said it was important to *me* that my telegram had been opened. He said, 'Look, it's just a telegram from your parents wishing you luck for the race. There's nothing for you to worry about.'

Later on Täve had a visit from a guy called Horst Gaede. He was from Magdeburg and he'd ridden the Peace Race in 1952, but then he'd gone over to the west before they built the wall. He turned up in a big American car, and you could tell he was trying to impress Täve. When he went everyone started joking that it wasn't his car at all, that he'd just hired it for the day to show off.

DIETER

The officials told us that they had a meeting with the FRG delegation after lunch, and that we'd be free to come and go as we pleased for two hours. So they'd followed protocol, and it dawned on me that if Sylvia turned up I was about to walk out of my life and into a new one.

I didn't doubt for one minute that if she came I was going to go through with it, no. I was sure I was going, but I didn't know whether I'd find Sylvia waiting for me at the station, or the Stasi.

It was hot, and it was about a ten-minute walk to the station. I set off from the hotel and crossed the road, trying to act like a normal person. I stopped to look in shop windows along the way. The problem was that I didn't know whether one or more of the people on the bus were following me, so my heart was racing. In those situations your instinct is to look over your shoulder to check, but I didn't want to seem furtive because that would have given them a sign.

I didn't know for sure that Sylvia would be there, and even if she were I couldn't be sure she was prepared to go through with it. I was thinking, 'This is like a dream', but then I told myself that it wasn't. I was frightened, but I tried to stay as calm as possible and get to the station.

DIETER

When I got there she was waiting with her mum, dad and brother. Their car was parked in front of the station but I told them it was best if we moved away from it. I didn't know what was going to happen, and I wanted to have the station behind me so I could keep my eye on what was happening around me. Then it made sense not to stand next to the car anyway, because I didn't want whoever had followed me to make a note of the registration number.

I'd never met her dad before, so first of all I introduced myself to him. Then I told them that I loved Sylvia, that I wanted to be with her and to stay in the west. She said she wanted to go through with it as well, and we started talking about how we could do it. I asked her dad if it would be possible for me to live at their house until I got a job and a place of my own, and he said it would be fine. In retrospect that was quite a brave thing to do, because none of us had any idea of would happen next.

So everything was agreed, and my mind was made up. Of course with the adrenaline your instinct is to get in the car and get out of there as quickly as possible, but I didn't. What I actually did was to turn round and walk straight back to the hotel.

DIETER

Why did I go back to the hotel? I suppose it might seem strange, but to me it made perfect sense.

I'd had months to think about what would happen, so I'd considered just about every possible scenario. I'd thought about doing the race as normal but riding through the finish line until I saw the car. Then I'd jump into it and we would go. That was just too risky, though, and so I'd scrapped the idea. The second idea had been to climb off during the race itself, and escape. That way I'd have been able to keep my bike, but it was very unlikely that nobody would see me. The other thing was that it would have made a mockery of the race, and I didn't want that. It would have been unfair for the other riders, and it would have created a big story. That was the last thing I needed, so I discounted it.

So I knew I had to go now, but I didn't know whether somebody from the bus was watching me, or whether somebody else from the Stasi was following. Had they been, and had I got in the car there and then, it would have been easy for them to come after us. I couldn't know whether they would, but they'd know exactly what had happened and where to find me.

So the thinking behind going back to the hotel was twofold. First, had the Stasi been watching me, they'd see me go back and assume that everything was in order. I'd simply gone for a walk, chatted to some people and then headed back to the hotel. Therefore logic would have suggested that I'd no interest in defecting – otherwise I'd have done it at the station – so they needn't concern themselves with watching me any more.

The other thing was that I wanted my bike. I had no idea what was waiting for me in the west, and no money to buy a new one. I knew nothing about life over there, but I knew that the bike would give me a chance to race and to make a living. Then I needed to get my travel permit. It had been falsified, but I figured it was better than nothing. At least it had my name on it.

So I told them that I'd be back before three o'clock, but that if I didn't make it they weren't to wait. They should assume something had gone wrong and forget about it.

DIETER

I walked back to the hotel and went up to the room. I assumed that Immo wouldn't be there, because normally when there was free time everyone tended to stay together. Thankfully he wasn't, so I picked up the document and my wallet, and got changed into my cycling shoes and a training jacket. Then I went downstairs to the hotel garage.

The mechanic was there working on the bikes, and he was a good friend of my dad. I told him I wanted to roll around for an hour, just to turn my legs over a bit. He gave me my bike, and I just rode off.

When I got back I climbed off the bike, took the wheels off, and we put it into the boot. They put a hat and sunglasses on me, and we went. I'd made it, and I'd managed to keep hold of my bike. I remember that I felt like I was in a movie.

DIETER

People have subsequently told me that all I needed to do was to ask a policeman. They said I should have just walked up, told him what was happening and asked for help. I'd spent all those hours planning it, thinking about it and worrying about it, and in reality it would have been perfectly simple.

The fact is that asking a policeman hadn't even occurred to me. I'd spent my life in the GDR, and so I was deeply distrustful of them. In fact, a policeman was probably the *last* person I'd have considered asking for help.

SYLVIA

My grandparents lived in Mainzlar, a village ten kilometres from Giessen. We thought it would be a good place to hide Dieter, and so we told them what was happening. We said we didn't want to risk taking Dieter home in case they came after him, but they only had a small house so there wasn't room for everyone. There was also the chance that the Stasi would know where they lived, so we decided that me, my mum and dad would stay there without Dieter. My grandfather told us about a hotel at Lollar, the next town, and so that's where we went. We dropped Dieter and my brother off there, and that's where they spent the night. It was like being in a movie.

DIETER

The hotel in Lollar seemed a good choice for all sorts of reasons. I assumed they knew where Sylvia lived, so it made no sense to go there straight away. Had they done their homework they would have known that she had family in Mainzlar, so they would probably have gone to look there as well. If they found Sylvia there with her parents then so much the better, because it would follow that she was just visiting her grandparents while waiting for the race the following day.

IMMO

Well, he didn't come down for dinner, so it was clear that something had gone wrong. Because he and I roomed together the officials assumed I'd known, and so did Weisbrod, the trainer. They asked me what I knew, but I said we'd gone our separate ways at lunchtime and I hadn't seen him. I didn't know anything, and I didn't ask anything. I always kept my mouth shut because that was the safest thing to do.

They didn't have any cars, so the chaperons borrowed a couple and went looking for him.

MANFRED

When it came to the evening meal and he still hadn't turned up you knew something had happened. Wiedemann was such a quiet guy that he was the last person you'd expect to defect. They might have expected someone like me to do it, someone who was critical, but never him. A load of us went out looking for him on our bikes, but we were assuming something had happened to him, that he'd had an accident.

The initial reaction was one of panic really, but when it became apparent he wasn't coming back it was suppressed. Nobody said, 'This guy has defected', and it was as if they wanted to forget about it and just get the race done. The thinking seemed to be that if they pretended it had never happened it would be less disruptive for the rest of the team, and less embarrassing as regards propaganda. They didn't so much make light of it as wish it away altogether, but you knew there would be consequences later on.

IMMO

The race started very early, because it had to be finished before church. It was pretty disastrous for the team as a whole, but great for me personally. It was windy, and the West Germans formed an echelon. Our guys weren't paying attention and so a gap opened. I was the only GDR rider who saw what was happening, so I was fine. On the last lap a guy named Gottschalk attacked, but I was really strong that day so I went with him. I beat him quite easily in the sprint.

There was no ceremony after the race, so I just rode back to the hotel with Gottschalk. It was implicit that there was to be no contact between ourselves and the FRG riders, but what can you do? I couldn't really tell him to get lost, and anyway it was just chatting away about this and that. Afterwards I got into trouble because I'd broken the rules in speaking with him. They were worried that we'd be coerced into defecting.

DIETER

Lollar was inside the race circuit, and I figured that would be the last place they'd search. So Roland and I stayed in the hotel until after the race finished. The following day Sylvia and her parents came to get us and I went 'home' to Mitterteich with Sylvia and the family.

I wanted to send a telegram to my mum and dad, but we figured it would be best if it didn't come from Mitterteich. We sent it from Tirschenreuth instead, fifteen kilometres away.

MfS383/65 bd1, BStU0077A

Date: 6.7.64 10.18 Nürnberg

Sender: 1984 Tirschenreu th, 9.40

Recipient: Karl Wiedemann, Flöha Wiesenstrasse 15

Text: I'm staying. Don't worry. Letter to follow.
Dieter.

THE SECOND LIFE
OF DIETER WIEDEMANN
(and the Fourth)

MfS383/65 bd2, BSTU0114/0115/0116/0117/0118/0119/0120

Karl-Marx-Stadt 7.7.1964

Department B[*]

Operative Plan

For the operative investigation and processing of the causes and background of the defection of the racing cyclist

Wiedemann, Dieter

Born:	17.6.41 in Flöha
Last address:	Flöha, Wiesenstrasse 15

Defector since: 4.7.64

The objective of the operative reconnaissance process is to check all available, genuine possibilities for repatriating W. to the GDR.

To this end the nature of his relationships to those left behind is to be determined, including possibilities for operative exploitation in order to establish collaborations.

In cooperation with Karl-Marx-Stadt Area Command Department XX, Flöha District Service Unit and Department B of Object Administration 'W', the following measures will be taken:

In the area of Department XX, Karl-Marx-Stadt Area Command:

Compilation of a comprehensive personality profile on Dieter Wiedemann. This is to include a precise investigation into the behaviour and demeanour of W. at Sport Club Karl-Marx-Stadt and in the collective of the German Cycling Federation.

In this the following issues are to be reconnoitred

---

[*] In object administration 'W', department B monitored individuals with western contacts.

His behaviour at the training camp prior to the Peace Race

His demeanour and behaviour, and an evaluation of his performances during the Peace Race

His behaviour after the Peace Race and in the period of preparation for the Olympic qualifiers in West Germany

Due Date: 14.7.1964

Responsibility: Second Lieutenant Süss

Reconnaissance of all of W.'s relatives and contacts as regards the following aspects:

With which citizens of the GDR, West Germany or other countries did W. maintain contact or close friendly ties

What connections or ties are maintained by the parents or the younger brother and what is the nature of these

What relations did W. have among the active sportspersons in the GDR, particularly in the German Cycling Federation. Of particular interest are his connections to trainer (?), also a defector, who tried to make contact with him in Giessen.

What company did W. keep in his former place of work at VEB '8 Mai' and in the dormitory of the sport club Karl-Marx-Stadt

Due Date: 14.7.1964

Responsibility: Second Lieutenant Süss

The informants 'Fritsche' and 'Hammer' of Department XX will be engaged in a comprehensive reconnaissance of the parents' house, and of the role of W.'s mother in his defection.

To do so the informants should introduce a suitable racing cyclist to the mother. Department XX should devise a suitable legend* to facilitate this.

---

* A 'legend' is described in the MfS handbook as a 'plausible pretence used to mislead people about the MfS' true aims or objectives'.

Due Date: 14.7.1964

Responsibility: Second Lieutenant Süss

Control: First Lieutenant Engert

The (?) of the defector W. is to be comprehensively evaluated and reconnoitred at the cycling section of sport club Karl-Marx-Stadt.

W.'s (?)is a supported athlete and belongs to the Olympic squad for 1968. Points of interest:

Performance of (?)

Planned sporting developments

Attitude towards the behaviour of W.

To what extent he may be used operationally for the repatriation of W.

Due Date: 14.7.1964

Responsibility: Second Lieutenant Süss

In the area of the Flöha District Service Unit

Comprehensive reconnaissance of the parents, the brother and their contacts in Flöha.

To be established:

Behaviour to date and how they conduct themselves in society within the neighbourhood

Attitude to the defection of their son

To what extent there are indications that the parents knew about W. Dieter's defection and were involved in the preparation for it

What connections are maintained with capitalist countries and where is the sister of the mother, who allegedly lives in the USA.

To what extent are visits by westerners registered and does the family receive letters, parcels etc. from West Germany, if possible from whom and when

Due Date: 14.7.1964

Responsibility: Captain Liebusch

The five available informants from Flöha District Service Unit, who have the ability to evaluate the W. family through personal contact, are to provide comprehensive personality profiles.

Simultaneously these informants are to unofficially keep tabs on the family in order to monitor people turning up or visitors.

Due Date: ongoing

Responsibility: Captain Liebusch

Utilising the available official sources, establish the possibility of moving a reliable informant into the apartment of W., since the living space exceeds the number of persons.

Due Date: 14.7.1964

Responsibility: Captain Liebusch

Reconnaissance of the (?) family in Flöha, whose son was a footballer and also defected.

Check for personal contact between the (?) family and the W. family

To be ascertained:

How the (?) family behaves in the local neighbourhood

What relationships they maintain

The nature of their relationship with the W. family

Due Date: 14.7.1964

Responsibility: Captain Liebusch

In the area of department B of Object Administration 'W' Karl-Marx-Stadt

Reconnaissance of the behaviour and ongoing connections within SDAG Wismut, Object 37 (workplace)

To be clarified:

What contact did W. have with the company and which persons was he friendly with. Establish the nature of these connections

How W. was evaluated by the company with regards to performance and behaviour in the company

Due Date: 14.7.1964

Responsibility: Second Lieutenant Hörig

Reconnaissance of the (?) of Wiedemann at work, and compilation of a comprehensive personality profile.

Using available unofficial means, check to what extent an informant can be introduced to W. (?) to monitor his reactions and behaviour.

Due Date: 14.7.1964

Responsibility: Second Lieutenant Hörig

Introduction of Measure M and postal monitoring between the parents and the defector as well as other existing connections.

Due Date: 8.7.1964

Responsibility: First Lieutenant Münzner

Reconnaissance of existing known connections

Trainer (?)

Trainer (?) and

Trainer (?)

Of sport club Karl-Marx-Stadt, in the local neighbourhood. Of particular interest here are the ongoing connections of these persons.

Due Date: 14.7.1964

Responsibility: Second Lieutenant Hörig

Leader of Department XX   Leader of Department B

First Lieutenant Engert   First Lieutenant Münzner

Leader of Flöha District Service Unit

Captain Liebusch

IMMO

When we got back to Erfurt there was a press conference. The main thrust of it was the idea that the West German guy had been encouraging me to stay over there. It wasn't true, but that was the message they wanted to portray. As far as I can remember they didn't mention Wiedemann. It was clear there was going to be a kind of media blackout about it, but I've no idea what was going on behind the scenes.

NEUES DEUTSCHLAND

ORGAN DES ZENTRALKOMITEES DER SOZIALISTISCHEN EINHEITSPARTEI DEUTSCHLANDS

This was a defeat that even the most stubborn pessimists had never dared predict. On Sunday morning in Giessen, the complete destruction of the glorious Armada of our road team, for many years one of our blue-ribbon events, was prevented only by the brave Karl-Marx-Stadt rider Immo Rittmeyer. With his victory he accrued thirty Olympic qualification points. However, he was followed by no less than seven West German riders. Thus they have points enough to travel to the second elimination on Sunday in Erfurt in good spirits. [...]

'How could this happen?' will be the question asked, in horror, across the country. In our preview we'd already referenced the fact that this group can't be compared with those of four years ago, and that a carefully prepared opponent lay in wait in Giessen. This was the bitter truth. [...]

The hotels around Giessen were crowded this weekend, every pool filled. Most were honest friends of cycling, but not all. Unfortunately there were also some unscrupulous individuals intent on making money from the conflict. Some met with success when they persuaded Dieter Wiedemann not to return to the GDR. It's not difficult to imagine how the inexplicable actions of Karl-Marx-Stadt rider rocked our team.

Reprinted from 'Rittmeyer wins a consolation prize', 6 July 1964

DIETER

I understand there was very little in the papers about it, but that was pretty much par for the course. Defections to the west sent out a very negative signal, and that's why they reported them in the most cursory way they could. The inference was that I'd been offered money, seduced by unscrupulous capitalists. They did it that way because it suggested I was either weak-minded or opportunistic, and that implied that the GDR would be better off without me.

I heard that some of the people who had been on the bus with us stayed around until the Tuesday, but I don't know whether or not that's true.

To be honest I'll be interested to find out what it says in the file. I'm pretty sure the Stasi was watching me, but it seems that no one *individual* was responsible for watching me. It seems they weren't so bright after all.

EBERHARD

I was racing in Reichenbach the day that Dieter was in Giessen. I won, but the following morning the president of the sport club called me in. He asked me what I'd known about his plans to defect, and I told him I'd known nothing at all. I explained that because we were always training and racing separately I'd hardly seen him, but he suspended me from racing there and then. He said there would be an inquiry, and that I could continue to train until such time as they reached a decision.

MfS383/65 bd1, BSTU0050/0051/0052/0053

Report

Karl-Marx-Stadt, 6 July 1964

On Friday 3 July 1964 the cycling delegation for the Olympic qualifying race with West Germany arrived at the Hotel Kübel in Giessen. The racers arrived from Erfurt by bus, while the trainers and other companions journeyed in the truck or in other cars. The general secretary of the cycling federation had arrived the previous day to organise the provision of the hotel rooms. I was told by some of the riders that the bus ride wasn't very pleasant. It took place on a new bus, and as such they had been obliged to travel at 30kph. Sportsfriend Schur in particular let his feelings be known about this.

Once the riders had bathed or washed, a joint lunch was taken at 15:00. Then the programme was announced, as follows:

After lunch the mechanics worked on the bikes. The riders went to view the race circuit, about ten kilometres from the hotel, and did two to three laps.

At 19:00 we had dinner, after which we went to the cinema. On Saturday we had breakfast at 08:00, then massage, then free time. Lunch was at 12.30, before a final bike check with the mechanics and a brief test.

At 14:00 the officials had a meeting with their West German counterparts, overseen by the race commissar, Mr Stampli from Switzerland. Everyone had dinner together at 18:00.

In the morning, general secretary Werner Scholz had retrieved a telegram from the post office. However, his spectacles were broken and he was unable to read the recipient's name. He therefore assumed it had been addressed to him, and opened it. Then he deciphered the name 'Dieter', and took it to the room of the cyclist (?). However the telegram wasn't for sportsfriend (?), but for sportsfriend Dieter Wiedemann, so (?) gave it to Wiedemann instead.

During lunch, sportsfriend Wiedemann came to the table and asked, in a somewhat irate tone, why his telegram had been opened. Sportsfriend Scholz told him he had got the telegram from the office of the FRG Cycling Federation and had assumed it had been for our federation. Sportsfriend Wiedemann then made some grumpy comments, which I can't recall exactly, and went back to his place.

Then sportsfriend Schur came to the table and asked how it had been allowed to happen. He was told by general secretary Dietrich that it had been an accident, that he would sort it out and that it would not happen again.

At 14:00 I went off for a meeting with the West German Cycling Federation, which lasted until around 17:15. During the meeting I looked into the antechamber of the meeting room, where some riders and press representatives were gathered. A few minutes later sportsfriend (?) walked into the room. He said to me: 'Have you seen the two that defected in the paddleboat, Udo Richter and Warzeschka?' I said that I hadn't because I'd been at the meeting and hadn't seen anybody.

At 18:00 I went for dinner. Sportsfriend (?) approached our table and informed us that Dieter Wiedemann was not there. An inquiry to mechanic (?) revealed that, just like the others, he'd tested his bike between 16.00 and 17.00.

At 19:00 sportsfriend (?) took the motorbike to the race circuit, and searched for Dieter Wiedemann, in case he was still out because his bike had had a defect. Then the trainers went to his room to check whether his personal effects were still there, or were missing. They discovered that only a training jacket and trousers were missing.

At 20:00 (?) came back, but the search had been inconclusive. Therefore the secretary of the GDR Federation, Alfred Heil, instructed to wait until 21.00 and then to have the local police investigate whether a cyclist had been involved in an accident in Giessen or the surrounding area. However, the police didn't find anything, so the president and general secretary of the cycling federation went to a refugee transit camp nearby. This too proved inconclusive.

On Sunday morning I was speaking to the West German sports functionaries, and the race commissar asked me which of the riders had defected. I answered that I knew nothing, that the riders were nothing to do with me, and that I was there only in the capacity of race steward.

During the race (?), a former professional rider from Schweinfurt, came up to me. He said, 'Why do your sportsmen want to come here? He'd have been much better off staying at home, because cycling is much bigger and much better organised than over here.'

Shortly after the race, still on the race circuit, sportsfriend (?) was seen with Richter and Warzeschka, the two defectors. Richter said, 'I don't know anything about a telegram to Wiedemann, it's nothing to do with me.' Afterwards it transpired that sportsfriend (?) had asked Richter and Warzeschka if they had sent the telegram to Dieter Wiedemann. This seems probable because the name Udo appears on the telegram, and Udo is Richter's Christian name.

Throughout the race our riders were subject to defamatory and abusive shouts, in my opinion organised, related to the defection. At the hotel the riders continually met with relatives. I have to mention here that other than the aforementioned Richter and Warzeschka, there were other cases. Sportsfriend Schur, for example, was

visited by a defector with whom he had worked in
Magdeburg. Although sportsfriend Schur said that
he'd just salute the defector, he took him and his
family to his room.

Personally I find Wiedemann's actions
inexplicable. It can only be that persons,
organised in advance, approached him with
promises and lured him away, or that something in
the telegram convinced him to stay.

'Fritzsche'

MfS383/65 bd4, BSTU0029/0030/0031/0032

Berlin 6 July 1964

Operative Information

Cycling Qualifiers in Giessen (West Germany)
On 4.7.64 the GDR Olympic Candidate Wiedemann
defected.

This defection was noticed about 18.30 when
(?) asked, 'Where's Wiedemann?' The trainers
and functionaries began looking for him and
ascertained that he was nowhere to be found in
the hotel.

There were a number of W's personal items in
his room. Just his ID papers and his bicycle were
missing. Upon checking, W. must have defected
between 15.00 and 17.00.

During this time the GDR delegation was in a
meeting with the FRG delegation and only club
trainers were present.

After lunch and midday rest, the trainers
advised the teams that each rider should take his
bike out for a short time to check the set-up etc.
W. disappeared during this time.

The deputy general secretary of the German
Cycling Federation reported thereafter that a
telegram for W. had arrived in the hotel, and he
had handed this over to W. He had indeed opened
the telegram but did not know the contents. He
only knew that it was signed by (?).

Thereupon the Karl-Marx-Stadt club trainer
said 'I know what's going on!' By this he was
referring to the defection of the cyclist Udo
Richter, from Karl-Marx-Stadt, who fled over
the Baltic in 1961. That afternoon R. had been
seen, along with other persons, in the vicinity
of the accommodation of the GDR team. Inquiries
were made with A&E units in Giessen directly
thereafter, to establish whether W. had crashed.

These inquiries were fruitless.

The Cycling Federation lodged a complaint with the West German Cycling Federation.

The following was expressed by the Karl-Marx-Stadt cyclists and functionaries: W. was a mummy's boy. After his success in the 1964 Peace Race, the mother of W. had been interviewed by the Karl-Marx-Stadt newspaper *Volkstimme*. The mother said, 'My son is a good cyclist and is now better than Schur. He's good enough now to ride the Tour de France.' In general it could be ascertained that the active cyclists were very depressed by this news; nobody had expected it.

The informant comments that the defector Richter has also spoken with (?). The content of the conversation was unknown to the informant.

(?) was visited by his brother and family. They stayed until the departure of the GDR team. (?) had stayed away from all social functions and stayed constantly with his brother and family.

A female cousin of (?) was there in a car with registration number (?).

In general it was ascertained that nearly all cyclists (except Schur, Eckstein and Adler) received visits from family and friends. It's worth noting that everywhere our cyclists went, they were spoken to by defectors. These were mostly persons who knew our cyclists from their previous activity in their home towns and regions. So for example the cyclist (?) was spoken to by two persons at the finish line after the race with the intention of persuading him to defect.

The informant estimates that this was not a simple one-off incident but all riders were constantly hassled by two to three persons aged twenty to twenty-five years, sometimes noticeably and sometimes not noticeably.

It was hard to get an exact overview as so many defectors were hanging around the accommodation of the GDR team.

One had the impression that selected persons from the respective home towns or regions were being very skilfully employed as bait by the West German authorities.

Furthermore the defected cyclist and Peace Race participant (?) turned up and tried to speak with Schur. He was dismissed by Schur.

Furthermore, the photographer (?), nicknamed '(?)' was there and he was turned away by the journalists. The journalist from the *Erfurter Bezirkszeitung* was visited by his sister, who is living in West Germany.

The overall conclusion of the informant is that the agreed tactics of our cyclists were wrong. These tactics, which were used to defeat the West German team in 1960, had now been turned against us. There were several situations where our riders had good chances but they were not taken. What could not be understood was the agreement between our cycling federation and the West German federation to select the first three riders to finish from each federation for doping control. For this reason we were under strict orders not to use any stimulants. Obviously this was a smart tactic of the West Germans. After the finish, not one rider from either side was tested.
(...)

First Lieutenant Riedel

MfS8963/69 BSTU0025/0026/0027/0028

Berlin 7.7.1964

Main Department XX/6

Meeting report

Source: Informant 'Hildebrand'

Date 6.7.1964

Location: Breitenbrunn

The informant's mission was to report on the race in Giessen, West Germany. The informant reported the following:

On Saturday afternoon 4.7.64 representative general secretary of the German Cycling Federation, comrade (?) received word from the West German federation in Giessen that there was a telegram for the cyclist Wiedemann.

This telegram was picked up from the West German federation by comrade (?) and handed over to Wiedemann.

This telegram is said to be from Flöha, Wiedemann's home town. The cyclist (?) let it be known to the informant that the contents of the telegram were more or less, 'Wishing you a good race in West Germany'.

According to the informant this telegram carried the signatures of the father, the mother, the brother and either his girlfriend Uta or a certain Udo.

If the signature was of Udo the informant makes the following observations:

There is a former professional cyclist, Werner Richter, living in Karl-Marx-Stadt, whose son, Udo, defected sometime after 13.8.1961 in a folding kayak over the Baltic. The informant is of the opinion that the possible signature of an Udo could have something to do with this Udo Richter.

The cyclists were given the task of checking the bikes once again at around 16.15 by taking them for a quick ride in the vicinity of the hotel. The cyclist Wiedemann from Karl-Marx-Stadt took this opportunity to defect. When W. failed to return from the test ride the first assumptions were that he had been involved in an accident or had got lost, but these were quickly dispelled.

For his defection Wiedemann was dressed only in shirt and trousers. Various other personal items were found at the Hotel Kübel in Giessen. From his personal documents, only the fifteen western marks pocket money and his PM12 were missing.

That same evening there were discussions on the defection with the other riders. They were overwhelmingly of the opinion that they would never have expected such reprehensible behaviour from Wiedemann, and condemned his treason.

The informant goes on to say that even the trainer could have been a contributory factor, possibly unwittingly, because he treated his DHfK people preferentially. (...)

Regarding the race itself, the informant is of the opinion that the athletes were given a preparation in their food which had a negative effect on the course of the race. The riders themselves are of a similar opinion. For example, although the cyclists went to bed in good time, they couldn't get to sleep before 01.00. The next morning they had to get up at 05.00 because the race started at 07.00. Their tiredness was apparent during the race.

The informant, who has been accompanying cyclists to races for many years, said it's the first time he's seen our riders race in such a lacklustre way.

So, for example, the riders Schur and (?) didn't show any sign of influencing the race in any phase. The GDR team doctor couldn't perform any checks in West Germany because he didn't have the wherewithal, so there is no proof for the aforementioned suspicion.

The GDR rider (?) found an empty tube, which had been discarded by a West German rider. He gave the tube to doctor (?). Furthermore the riders claim that during the race the west zone riders started to take tablets from the fourth lap onwards.

On the tactical performance of our team, the informant added that six GDR riders were supposed to have attacked straight from the gun come what may, and drop the whole field. It was apparent, however, that the West German team was ready for this tactic. The informant is of the opinion that this is because the tactic had been leaked to them beforehand by Wiedemann.

To the question why, in light of Wiedemann's defection, we hadn't changed our tactic, the informant couldn't give a clear answer. He simply said that the team leadership and he himself hadn't given it any thought.

(...)

The cyclists (?) and (?) had a conversation with the defector Udo Richter before the start of the race on Sunday 5.7. Richter asked the question, 'Where is Wiedemann then?' During this conversation, Richter said that they were going back to Cologne before the race finished. Richter was in Giessen with a friend whom the informant doesn't know.

Cyclist Schur was in close contact with the defector (?) in Giessen, whom he also took up to his room. This (?) had introduced Schur to cycling in 50/51. The informant can't understand Schur's behaviour because (?) is one of the most pathetic traitors of our republic. Furthermore it's known to the informant that Schur is in continual postal contact with (?) and for this reason a face-to-face meeting was held between comrade (?) and Schur before their departure for West Germany.

During the race (?) tried to provoke our team leadership. He shouted at them in a derogatory way. Among the spectators there were a number of people who tried, in a foul-mouthed way, to undermine our athletes with comments like, 'Communist Pig!' The majority of these persons were defectors. You could tell this from their accents.

Our athletes did not come into contact with the western zone athletes. They saw each other for the first time at the start, and after the race our team went immediately back to the hotel.

It was agreed with the informant that he should keep certain specified persons under control at the qualifier in Erfurt.

The next meeting is scheduled 13.7.1964 15.00 at the conspiratorial dwelling 'Vineta'

Lieutenant Müller

UDO

We had no issues whatsoever about talking with the GDR riders. Unfortunately we couldn't find Dieter Wiedemann, but we had interesting chats with Löhse, the coach, and with Weissleder and Rittmeyer.

MfS383/65 bd1, BSTU0046/0047/0048/0049

Karl-Marx-Stadt 6.7.1964

Section B

Completed discussion with the mother of the
defector Dieter Wiedemann

The investigation by Flöha District Service
Unit has ascertained that the mother of W. stated
that if the MfS try to punish her as a result of
the defection of her son, she will turn on the
gas tap in the family apartment. The visit to
the Wiedemann family was undertaken using the
following legend:

The undersigned passed himself off as a member
of the senior management cadre at SDAG Wismut,
and said that he had been instructed to confiscate
the ID card of her son. This corresponds to an
agreement with the head of Object 37.

The undersigned sought to gain entry into
the Wiedemann apartment using this pretext.
The door was opened by the (?), to whom this was
explained. Only after it had been explained
that the undersigned was a member of the senior
management cadre did the mother appear, and
the undersigned was led into a small living
room in the house. The mother and the (?) looked
for the card in a cupboard in the living room.
After having failed to find it, it was agreed
that the (?) would go to look for the card the
following day, upon his arrival at the dormitory.
On the same day at 13.00 he arrived at the
management offices in room 7 to hand in the
card. An interview then took place with a view to
clarifying the defection.

The mother was informed that a meeting would
take place at her flat concerning the termination
of her son's employment, and she agreed to this.

She stated that, having heard rumours that Dieter
had defected the previous evening, she switched
on the radio at eleven o'clock. Having heard
nothing on the GDR stations, she chanced across
a western FM station, from which all she heard
was: 'Dieter Wiedemann, winning participant of
this year's Peace Race ...' Only later did she hear
confirmation of her son's intentions from the
mayor of Flöha. At midday she received a telegram
confirming her son's intentions. Her son had sent
the telegram to the mayor.

She fails to understand why her son did this,
because he wanted for nothing in the GDR and
had every opportunity for personal development.
Since he was always so quiet and reserved, she
finds it difficult to understand what's going on
inside him. Reading the telegram she could only
deduce that her son was suffering from emotional
problems. This was the only possible explanation.
Dieter has never had a girlfriend, so it can't
be that he was lovesick. (?) also confirmed that
Dieter did not have a girlfriend.

During the search for the ID card, Dieter's
trade union contributions book turned up. The
mother stated that Dieter's contributions had
already been paid for the month of July, and
asked what would happen to the money. It was
explained clearly that the money would not be
reimbursed.

Assessment of the mother

At the beginning of the conversation she cried,
and made a most disturbing spectacle. Only when
the undersigned managed to convince her that he
was from SDAG Wismut did she calm down a little.
Concentrate as she might, she was quite unable
to follow the thread of the conversation. Again
and again she tried to explain that she failed
to understand why Dieter had done this to her,

and that he'd ruined her life and his career. In searching for Dieter's ID card it was clear she was confused. She displayed neither objectivity nor logic.

Assessment of the (?)

From the beginning of the discussion his behaviour was calm and factual. He also expressed that he couldn't understand Dieter's actions and that the personal consequences of this were clear to him. He was impressively honest and open-minded, in contrast to the mother. He promised that the identity card affair would be resolved first thing the following morning, and didn't want the matter to disrupt his training programme. He said that in general he would deal with all operational issues for his (?).

Lieutenant Enzmann

MfS383/65 bd1, BSTU0079/0080/0081

Karl-Marx-Stadt 6.7.64

Department B

Report

Completed discussion with the father of the defected top sportsman Dieter Wiedemann

During the interview Wiedemann's father expressed that he had no prior knowledge of the defection of his son, and that his son had given no indication of his intent.

The first he'd heard about the defection of his son was on Sunday (morning) 5.7.1964 from an acquaintance whose name he apparently doesn't know. This acquaintance had heard via western radio on Saturday that Dieter Wiedemann was staying in West Germany.

The father didn't want to go into the causes and motives for the defection. He explained that his son has no material or financial worries. There was no question of worries about his love life because he doesn't have a steady girlfriend. In his opinion there is only one thing which may be attributable to his defection, and that is that his son had been accused by the leadership of the cycling federation and by some cyclists of not pulling his weight during and after the Peace Race.

Since his son is very sensitive, this attitude towards him had made him ill and worried in the period thereafter.

On the other hand there was a bad or tense atmosphere between the leadership of the cycling federation in Berlin and the functionaries and active cyclists of Karl-Marx-Stadt. The result of this was that the performances of the Karl-Marx-Stadt cyclists at national and international events had always been judged insufficient by comparison to other clubs. This same opinion is held by the cycling functionaries of Karl-Marx-Stadt.

The action of his son to stay in West Germany was unexpected and came as a shock to him and his wife. His wife was completely beside herself and wanted to take her own life. Both he and his wife had been very attached to their son Dieter and could not understand why he had done this to them.

He ruled out the possibility that his son could have been negatively influenced by other persons in this regard because in the past he'd never noticed any signs of such behaviour.

Apart from his aunt in the USA he has no relatives or acquaintances in the west.

At the end of the interview he said that he was waiting impatiently for a letter from Dieter which would explain the reasons for his defection.

Mr Wiedemann promised to drop off all incoming post from his son to the leadership of the sport club without delay, and to keep them informed about telephone calls and visits which might be connected to his son.

Assessment of the father

Mr Wiedemann made a very defeated and depressed impression and you could tell from him that the defection of his son had affected him greatly.

Despite these facts he said that he is distancing himself from the behaviour of his son and that he resolutely disapproves of it.

His whole demeanour leads us to conclude that he is telling the truth and had no prior knowledge of his son's intentions to defect.

First Lieutenant Eichler

MfS383/65 bd1, BSTU0084/0085

7.7.64

Subject: The defection of the cyclist Dieter Wiedemann

Meeting on 7.7.64 with informant 'Siegfried Wenzel', regarding the defection of the cyclist Wiedemann.

The informant reported that he was closer to Karl Wiedemann, due to his function in the cycling association.

The informant estimated that Dieter Wiedemann is easy to influence. If you approach him with any task he carries it out without asking the reasons why. As a consequence it should be easy to entice Wiedemann, and to persuade him to come back to the GDR.

The informant continues to be of the opinion that Wiedemann, as he knows him, will soon regret this ill-considered move. His parents are very attached to their son, and in the opinion of the informant will try anything to have him return to the GDR. Here the mother would play a positive role. The informant illustrated this with the following example:

In the past Wiedemann would ride every day from Flöha to Karl-Marx-Stadt, and back again. The sport club didn't approve of this, because he should have been housed in the dormitory. His mother resisted at first, because she wanted to have her son at home.

This means that, according to the informant, both mother and father have the powers of persuasion to bring him back, since he is so attached to them.

It's important that he be made to understand that he has destroyed the happiness and future of his family. For example, Wiedemann's father, who is a mechanic at SC Karl-Marx-Stadt, would no longer be permitted to take part in races abroad, even though he is loyal towards the GDR.

Wiedemann's (?) is a cyclist in performance category III, and the defection would also inhibit his development. These are all factors that, according to the informant, should lead to Wiedemann's being returned to the GDR.

The informant also stated that in the past he and the section leader of SC Wismut cycling had already headed delegations to the FRG, for example with (?) etc.

The informant is also an honorary member of the board at SC Karl-Marx-Stadt, and a member of the presidium of the cycling federation.

Sub-lieutenant Enskat

MfS383/65 bd1, BSTU0070/0072/0073

Flöha 7.7.64

Transcript:

Information

On the defection of the racing cyclist Wiedemann, Dieter

On 6.7.64, Comrade Police Chief Constable (?) was travelling to work on the 05.20 bus from Augustusburg to Flöha. Several citizens were discussing the fact that the racing cyclist Dieter Wiedemann had scarpered. These unknown persons were of the opinion that he wouldn't be the last not to return from the Olympic qualifiers, nor the Tokyo Olympic Games themselves. The opinion was also expressed that it could be our own fault. Exactly what was meant by this was not explained.

Comrade Staff Sergeant (?) of the Flöha Police Station likewise reported that the railway worker and SED comrade, Gerhard (?), who lives in the same building, had spoken with him on 5.7.64 and had asked if he knew that Wiedemann had absconded. Since this had not been communicated by our broadcasters, it is suspected that (?) had found this out via the western media.

On his patrol, traffic warden comrade (?) expressed the opinion to comrade (?) that Wiedemann's action was a disgrace towards his sporting comrades. He had been given everything in the GDR. (?) judged Wiedemann's betrayal as the absolute worst, and in his view he had lost all respect.

Police Staff Sergeant (?) stated that he had heard from Staff Sergeant (?) of the transport police, that the vast majority of our citizens have condemned Wiedemann's action and are of the opinion that all the gifts he received from our state organs for his sporting successes should be taken away.

From Leubsdorf, (?) said that at the 'Erholung'
pub at about 21.00 on 5.7.64, citizen (?) said that
he had been listening to the West German sports
news (international) at about 19.00. Here it was
reported that the cyclist Wiedemann had not
started the Olympic qualifying race, presumably
because he would be staying in West Germany. (?)
also said that he could not understand this since
our top sportsmen got all the support they needed.
(?) works at the local council building company in
Flöha. Citizen (?), who lives in in (?)and works at
VEB (?), added that Wiedemann's mother in Flöha is
so stuck-up that she doesn't know what to do any
more. She goes everywhere by taxi, no matter how
short the journey, whereas Wiedemann's father has
to cycle to work in Karl-Marx-Stadt every day.

In Niederwiesa, (?) reported that the mother
of top sportsman (?) said the following about
Wiedemann's behaviour. She couldn't understand
why Wiedemann would stay in West Germany
because over here everything is done for talented
sportsmen. She can say this because her son had
received every possible form of support, even
though he is still young. Her son would never
do such a thing. His father (her husband) would
go mad if he heard such a thing. (?) told the
community policeman that Wiedemann is a fool,
and that he'd been given every chance here. He
wouldn't have this in West Germany. When he
finishes cycling over there he'll be finished. Had
it been (?) he wouldn't have been surprised – but
Wiedemann! He also reported that the sport club
should take down Wiedemann's picture from their
hall. After consultation with the mayor, Comrade
Hense, the picture was removed.

At the cotton mill in Flöha the workers (?), (?)
and (?) were told by (?) that Wiedemann's act was
condemned by the vast majority of the workforce.
Among the workforce the opinion was expressed
many times that the gifts which W. had received

from the state organs and companies should be taken back since a traitor like him was not worthy of them.

In Grünhainichen, the office worker (?) from the toy factory said that people like Wiedemann are allowed to travel to West Germany. People like her who originally come from the west aren't allowed to visit their parents over there even though there's no chance of them staying because they have famillies over here. She has no time for this state because her application to visit her parents in West Germany has been turned down.

In Marbach, in conversation with other tractor drivers, tractor driver (?) said that Wiedemann is a bonehead. He'll never get the life he's had here over there, they'll drop him just like they've done with all the other top sportsmen who've trodden the same path. The FRG is only interested in syphoning off our best sportsmen in order to weaken us and to push their sportsmen into the limelight at the Olympics.

Members of the LPG in Leubsdorf expressed the opinion that though Wiedemann is not worthy, he can keep the gift he received at the area delegates' conference in Hohenfichte. All other gifts he received from state organs for his sporting achievements should be taken away.

The population of Erdmannsdorf could not understand that a sportsman who had been given everything he needed here for his sport could exploit the opportunity and trust placed in him to leave his homeland and betray the GDR. It follows that such a betrayal of the GDR should result in the removal of the gifts he has received through his sport.

In Kleinharmannsdorf, citizen (?) let it be known that today a leading functionary in the local council building company had said that various presents like washing machines, televisions and other gifts would be seized this evening.

Citizen (?) said that it's the fault of our state because our sportsmen get sugar blown up their arses. (?) works at (?).

Mill workers in Braunsdorf labelled Wiedemann a traitor; they couldn't imagine that such a thing could happen, since every young sportsperson here has the opportunity to develop and qualify. At the Peace Race he had received high-value prizes in the form of TV sets and the like and this is the thanks we get for it.

At the Gückelsberg cotton mill, (?) said the following in a conversation with police master (?) on 7.7.64:

The previous week, Wiedemann's (?) had told employee (?) that an unmarried person would not be coming back. (?) is of the opinion that this was about a sportsman from our team.

He also said that the great majority of the workforce did not agree with Wiedemann's action and are demanding that the gifts he received for his sporting achievements from our state, organisations and companies be taken away – he is not worthy of them. Comrade (?) told comrade (?) that this information is confidential and for his ears only.

MfS 383/65 bd4, BSTU0060

Berlin 7.7.64

Main Department XX/6

File comments

On 6.7.64 informant 'Hildebrand' made the
following observations on the defection of the
cyclist Wiedemann.

Aside from the reasons we already know, the
informants sees, among other things, the mother
as a driving force for Wiedemann's defection.
According to the informant she is totally obsessed
by money and when her son received 3,000 marks
for this year's Peace Race she is purported to
have said that next year they will be riding for
just 1,000 marks. In 1963 the Peace Race riders had
received a prize of 4,000 marks. The informant
could not say with certainty whether he had
received this information from the cyclist (?) or
(?)

Lieutenant Müller

DIETER

Sylvia's mum took me to the town hall, but there were problems straight away. I was claiming asylum to be with Sylvia, but my papers said that I was married. The woman there knew Sylvia's family and understood that I wasn't lying, but she still couldn't do anything. She said, 'You're telling me that the document is falsified and I believe you, but it makes no difference because I have to record what's written here. You can tell me whatever you want, but you're going to need proof. I'm sorry, but I'm obliged to record what it says on your document.'

I wrote to my mum and asked her to go to the town hall and get a copy of my birth certificate.

MfS383/65 bd1, BSTU0072a

Flöha, 8.7.64

Flöha District Service Unit

Line WKK

Report of meeting with informant 'Nitzsche'

7.7.64

From 17.30 to 18.00

Since conspiratorial dwelling 'Guttenberg' was unavailable because the owner was hospitalised, a brief meeting took place at Oederan.

The informant was consulted only on the matter of the Wiedemann defection, and stated the following:

On the evening of 6.7.64 he visited the Wiedemann family, because he is very well known to Dieter Wiedemann and his parents. Only the father and (?) were at home. The father told the informant that he was very shaken by what Dieter had done, and would never have thought it possible. Through his actions Dieter had brought shame on the family and destroyed the career of (?), because he certainly wouldn't be permitted to ride any more races abroad.

The informant believes that the words of the father are honest and from the heart. He was very shaken up and you could see the grief in him.

Speaking to other people in the neighbourhood, the informant learned that on 30 June 1964 Wiedemann withdrew a considerable sum from the bank in Flöha.

Furthermore, the mother has often bragged about Wiedemann's friendship with a female person in West Germany. The informant is therefore of the opinion that the mother had prior knowledge of the defection.

In the coming days the informant will return to the Wiedemann household when the mother is present, and try to talk to her alone.

A further meeting is arranged with the informant on 9.7.64 at conspiratorial dwelling 'Hanna Hilbert' in Karl-Marx-Stadt (17.00)

Lieutenant Langklotz

MfS383/65 bd1, BSTU0073

Re: The defection of Dieter Wiedemann

Comrade (?), resident in (?), Flöha, employed at VEB (?), states the following: 'During the mushroom season of 1963 she and her husband observed, from their apartment close to that of the mother and father of Dieter Wiedemann, that he and a young girl went through a gap in the fence in the direction of the forest. Because Dieter Wiedemann was wearing rubber boots they assumed that they were looking for mushrooms. Further, it is known that this young girl from West Germany was visiting Fritz Diersche at the behest of the Wiedemann family.'

Comrade (?) suspects that the girl is a member of the Jehovah's Witness sect in West Germany and is thus connected to (?)

Lieutenant Hellmann

MfS383/65 bd1, BSTU0083

Ministry for State Security Object Administration 'W' Karl-Marx-Stadt

Department B

Karl-Marx-Stadt 7.7.64

Department II/AG Postal Customs Investigation

Order to initiate postal customs investigation

On:

Wiedemann Karl, Flöha, Wiesenstrasse 15

Wiedemann Marianne, Flöha, Wiesenstrasse 15

Wiedemann (?), (?) Flöha and (?) Karl-Marx-Stadt

Command level: C

Name and telephone number of requesting officer:

First Lieutenant Eichler, Department B

Tel: 545 or 544

Head of the Object Management
Head of Department B

Colonel Zuschke
First Lieutenant Münzner

MfS383/65 bd1, BSTU0074

Flöha, 8.7.64

Flöha District Service Unit

Line XX

<u>File memo</u>

On the accounts of the Wiedemann family

Wiedemann, Dieter	Acc.no. 4178	Balance	0
	Acc.no. 10826	Balance	34DM
Wiedemann, Marianne	Acc.no.10825	Balance	7DM
Wiedemann, Karl	No account		
Wiedemann, (?)	Acc.no. (?)	Balance	(?)

Dieter Wiedemann withdrew 1,200DM on 29.5.1964, and 700DM on 30.6.194. The account balance was 19DM in credit.

The accounts of the parents and younger brother have remained untouched for many years.

The accounts were audited by the Flöha Savings Bank.

Sub-lieutenant Stolpmann

MfS383/65 bd1, BSTU0075

Flöha, 8.7.64

Report

Re: Statement from Mayor Hense of Flöha, on the
defection of Dieter Wiedemann.

At nine o'clock today, 8.7.1964, the subject
arrived at the District Service Unit, and issued
the following statement:

At 7.45 this morning the Wiedemann family
were waiting for me in front of the town hall.
They were talking with (?), from the housing
office. Mrs Wiedemann asked to see a copy of the
newspaper article which said that Dieter had
fallen into the hands of 'headhunters'. She said
that it wasn't true, but that it was probably
related to the tension between the SC Karl-Marx-
Stadt and DHfK Leipzig riders, and to what had
happened at Greiz.

After this, Mrs Wiedemann wanted to know about
the fridge that Dieter had received from the town
council and other organisations in recognition of
his Peace Race achievements.

The mayor told her that the fridge is Dieter's
property, and that a payment is out of the
question. The fridge should somehow be sold,
and the monies placed in a frozen bank account.
Then, should Dieter return to the GDR, he will
be able to access the account. After this Mrs
Wiedemann said that she would be suspected of
being guilty, but if anyone was to blame it was
the functionaries. Ninety per cent of the athletes
were on Dieter's side. All you need do is ask them
properly, but they can't be trusted because they
are under pressure from the functionaries.

It was explained to her that Dieter had enjoyed
great trust among the population, even as far
as the central committee, and it's questionable

whether he would enjoy such status in West Germany.

In response to this, Wiedemann's father said it's best to wait and see what happens. Mrs Wiedemann then questioned how Dieter can have faith amidst all of these disputes.

The mayor stated that he wanted nothing more to do with the matter, and said that he stood by what he'd said at the beginning. Mrs Wiedemann said that if other agencies wanted to interview her, she would only give information in the presence of her husband.

The mayor asked to be informed in the event that Dieter wrote a letter and asked questions, because they had been friends before his defection. The Wiedemann family agreed to this, and left.

Mayor Hense then stated that there was a discussion among the populace to the effect that if Dieter returned within eight days he should be immune from punishment, but that if he didn't he should be punished.

First Lieutenant Liebusch

DIETER

They refused to give my mum the birth certificate at first. Defection was a treasonable offence, so they were hardly going to hand it over just because she asked for it. They were determined to make life difficult, but eventually someone she knew there made a copy. I don't know how, but somehow she managed.

DIETER

The threats started straight away. They said, 'You won't be needing all this space now that he's gone. We'll probably move some new people in to share with you, because there are a lot of people needing housing.'

MfS383/65 bd1, BSTU0113/0114

Flöha, 10.7.64

Re: The defection of Dieter Wiedemann.

The family Wiedemann has a single-family house with six rooms. Three rooms are located on the ground floor, and three more upstairs. Two years ago, a single woman lived in two rooms on the upper floor, but moved into a care home.

Because Dieter Wiedemann was a top athlete, the Wiedemann family were given six rooms for their own use. In view of the current situation, the council housing committee recommends that the two first-floor rooms should once more be occupied. The occupancy will not take place until it has been agreed by us what form it will take. Mayor Hense agrees with this measure.

The Wiedemann family has never decorated the house on political holidays, or for other political events. The parents show no interest in civic life. Only the (?) takes part in some events. The Wiedemann woman is considered to be the so-called king of the house. Even her husband has become subordinate to her ideas. Known links to other Flöha citizens are to (?), who lives on the corner of (?) Street and (?) Street. Also, a certain (?) of Flöha is linked to the wife.

Furthermore, one of our informants has very close links with the Wiedemann family, with a particularly good connection to Dieter for five years. Trainer (?) should also be a good connection. He and his wife have visited the Wiedemann family several times. They were seen there during this year's Peace Race.

Dieter has an aunt living in the USA. No further information is available at this time. It has not yet been determined whether parcels or letters arrive. The existing informant knows nothing either.

At 3.15 p.m. on 6.7.64, vehicle XL36-66 was seen in front of the Wiedemann house. On the same day (?), the Chairman of the LPG Flöha type I, was twice seen at the Wiedemann house.

Mrs Wiedemann sells eggs through the VEAB.* As a result the family has a lot of visitors, and it may be difficult to determine who among them are visiting in respect of the Dieter affair. The names of people who visited the Wiedemann family on 6.7.64 have already been communicated to comrades of Object Administration 'W'.

The executive director of SC Karl-Marx-Stadt is a godparent of Dieter, though it's not known to what extent he fulfilled the role.

The father asserted that it's no wonder the athletes have no confidence abroad, when a delegation of fifteen athletes is accompanied by forty handlers.

The telegram to the family Wiedemann was most likely sent by his girlfriend. The girlfriend lives in Mitterteich, Bavaria. There is no post office there, so the telegram was sent from Tirschenreuth.

The Wiedemann family had western visitors in 1962 and 1963. Dieter Wiedemann appeared on the 1962 submission. In 1963, a certain Diersche made the request due to an alleged silver wedding anniversary. However, there was no silver wedding anniversary in the Diersche family at this time, but the Wiedemann family celebrated a silver wedding anniversary.

The application for the permit was therefore clearly fraudulent.

First Lieutenant Liebusch

---

* VEAB (*Volkseigener Erfassungs und Aufkaufbetrieb*) was a state-owned purchasing company. Smallholders sold eggs, poultry, fruit and vegetables through it.

DIETER

A delegation from the sport club went to see my mum and dad and proposed a meeting. They said, 'He's bound to be missing home, and he probably realises he's made a big mistake. Let's arrange a meeting with him and see if he wants to reconsider.'

They assumed that when I saw them I'd be homesick, and that seeing my parents would persuade me to go back. My mum wrote to me and told me, but I wanted nothing to do with it.

The other thing to bear in mind is that it was probably a trap. I'd committed a criminal act, so I'm pretty sure that had I gone back they'd have made an example of me. I would probably have ended up in jail anyway, but, regardless, my mind was made up. It was hard, but I needed to concentrate on building a new life.

MfS383/65 bd2, BSTU0128/0129

Transcript

Flöha, 13.7.1964

Report from the conspiratorial dwelling 'Tulpe'

Ref: Wiedemann

In the local neighbourhood the following has been discovered about Wiedemann:

The family Wiedemann is associated with the family (?), living in (?) street, Flöha. Both are (?). He is (?). Their attitude towards the state is opaque. There are further associations with the family (?) living in (?) Street.

The (?) family has a negative attitude towards our state. The wife (nee (?)) has connections with the west via relatives. In 1961 (?) wanted to abscond to West Berlin. He was picked up by the police and sentenced.

A few weeks ago a female from West Germany visited Wiedemann. She is said to be the girlfriend/fiancée of Wiedemann. It is not known if there are any connections with West Germany via relatives. Mrs Wiedemann has expressed the opinion that her son absconded because he was not awarded a car after the Peace Race and that generally he was not at all satisfied with his rewards.

Mrs Wiedemann only voted at the last election after being summoned by Mayor Hense. This gives rise to suspicions that she is a Bible basher.

Associations in the local neighbourhood were not known, the same goes for parcel traffic/exchanges with West Germany.

'Tulpe'

MfS8963/69 BSTU0030/0031/0032/0033

Berlin, 14.07.1964

Meeting report

Source: Informant 'Hildebrand'

Date: 13.07 15.00-17.00

Location: 'Vineta'

In accordance with his orders, the informant reported about the behaviour of the athletes specified to him.

Regarding rider (?) he again stated that he had behaved very well, and in political discussions has a good attitude towards the GDR.

(?) also behaved very well. The informant has already reported on the visits he had in West Germany. The behaviour of the Dynamo cyclists (?) and (?) was impeccable. During the course of the meeting the informant reported that on the basis of a conversation he'd had with the trainer from Karl-Marx-Stadt, rider (?) had been looking for an opportunity to defect. The trainer from Karl-Marx-Stadt told the informant the following about the behaviour of (?) in Giessen:

During the final lap in Giessen the West German rider (?) who had defected from Halle a few years ago tried to persuade (?) to also stay in West Germany. He said to (?) 'Do like Wiedemann, you'll do much better over here!'

At the end of the race in Giessen the order was for all riders to go back directly back to the hotel. Immediately (?) passed through the finish, two West German cars came up him from behind, handed him Coca-Cola and beseeched him, 'Stay here!'

(...)

On the subject of Wiedemann's defection, the informant reports the following:

W. sent a telegram to his parents with words to

this effect, 'I've found the woman of my dreams …'

To this the informant comments that a female person from West Germany visited Flöha twice, and Wiedemann was instrumental in these visits. The informant was told this by trainer (?).

During a conversation with the secretary of the cycling federation, comrade (?), the informant was told that W.'s mother had attempted suicide and is in hospital.

On the issue of the cycling qualifiers, the informant reports the following:

On Saturday 11.07 the former GDR athletes (?), (?) and (?) were in the bar of the Erfurter Hof hotel with West Germans. The West Germans were staying at the Erfurter Hof. The informant could not say with whom these three were talking because he couldn't enter the hotel himself as he's too well known there. He adds that it would have been better had somebody from the MfS who is familiar with the situation been there to resolve certain things there and then.

Furthermore the informant is of the opinion that stricter controls on West German sports delegation should be implemented by our border agency because they are in a position to determine who comes into and goes out of the GDR. For example when the West German athletes came in on Friday they brought with them three radios of Japanese origin. When questioned by our border agents they explained that they were walkie-talkies but they couldn't use them because they'd forgotten the relay bases. This does not correspond to the facts and only during a meeting with the president of the German Cycling Federation were they informed that they could not use them because their use contravened our laws. The legal regulations for the import of such apparatus stipulate:

Check who owns the apparatus

That import is approved

The frequency approval has been granted according to regional post and telecommunications authorities

The fact of the matter is that no data was taken at the border, even though subsequent consultation with the chief of Police in Erfurt confirmed that this equipment should have been destroyed.

Furthermore, west zone television came to Erfurt with their own cameras, even though the export of film material is forbidden to all countries. In Giessen we had had to take the west zone feed. The informant stated that the import of the Japanese transistor speaking equipment which has a range of eight kilometres, allied to the West German cameras, is a sign of the lack of diligence of our border agency.

A West German commissar, accommodated in one of our team cars as per the agreement, provoked our comrades throughout the whole race. He agitated against the GDR so that after the end of the race, the mechanic (?), who was travelling in the same car and is normally very calm, said to this person, 'We won't say "Till next time" because we hope there won't be a next time.' The name of this West German commissar is unknown to the informant.

The informant further reports that it is absolutely necessary to keep West German journalists under control, because in his opinion their ID is the only genuine thing about them. For example, about ten journalists came to Erfurt, though only four covered the race.

(...)

Lieutenant Müller

DIETER

There were only two professional teams in West Germany but one of them, Torpedo,[*] was based in Schweinfurt. That's only about 190 kilometres from Mitterteich, so I wrote to them with a list of my results from the GDR. I told them I had some bureaucratic problems to resolve, but I asked if they'd consider offering me a professional contract for the following season. They replied straight away. They sent a cheque for 200 marks to cover the travel expenses, and told me to go for a meeting as soon as I had my paperwork sorted out. In the meantime Sylvia's dad got me a temporary job at a plumber's yard.

When they granted me asylum they gave me 100 marks and a voucher for a new suit. More importantly, it meant that I was free to come and go as I pleased, without having to report to the police station every day.

---

[*] 'Torpedo' was the brand name of the bicycle hubs manufactured by Fichtel & Sachs.

MfS383/65 bd1, BStU0147

Flöha 17.7.64

Flöha District Service Unit Line II

Memorandum

On 17.7.64 the owner of the conspiratorial
dwelling 'Kaufmann' stated the following in
respect to the defection of Dieter WIEDEMANN:

The mother of W. was recently at the dairy in
Rudolf-Breitscheid-Strasse, Flöha. Here she was
asked by customers the reasons for the defection
of her son. W. answered to the effect that she's
been asked several times already, but that she'd
been told to keep quiet. If people continued to
nag, however, she would come clean with the full
story.

The owner of the conspiratorial dwelling heard
this from a neighbor, who was on the premises
at the time. The owner of the conspiratorial
dwelling said that the defection is attributable
to the poor education of the parents. The
Wiedemann woman was the only one who, during
the Nazi times, demanded that the owner of the
conspiratorial dwelling greet her with 'Heil
Hitler'.

Lieutenant Scharl

MfS383/65 bd4, BSTU0089

Berlin, 20 July 1964

Government of the German Democratic Republic

Ministry for State Security

Main Department XX

HA XX/6/I/5634/64

Ministry for State Security Karl-Marx-Stadt

Object Administration 'W'

Department B

Karl-Marx-Stadt

Wiedemann, Dieter

Please find attached a report for information
and operative evaluation.
It has become known to the German Gymnastics and
Sport Federation that the mother of W. has made a
suicide attempt and is said to be in the hospital.

Further that W. already became engaged last
year. We ask you to examine these issues and to
inform Main Office HA XX/6 of the outcome.

Lieutenant Colonel Volpert

DIETER

One day a couple of journalists from *Bild* turned up offering me quite a lot of money for my story, but I said no. I didn't want it to become a media circus, and I had no intention of allowing it to be used as a propaganda instrument.

I'd left my friends and my family behind, and I didn't want my name associated with anything which suggested that the east was inferior or that the people were ignorant. In *Neues Deutschland* they always portrayed the FRG as immoral, and so I assumed the West German press would be the same.

The other thing is that I was still living in fear of the Stasi. I knew they had agents in the west, and I couldn't afford to rub their noses in it. I didn't want to provoke them because for all I knew I might have been putting my own life at risk. Then there was always the hope that the border would be opened again, and I didn't want to compromise my chances of going back if that happened. I just closed the book on it and got on with my new life as best I could.

Bild published a story anyway. Apparently in the GDR they were saying that when I'd defected I'd stolen their bike.

MfS383/65 bd2, BSTU0178

Sportclub Karl-Marx-Stadt

Sections: Boxing, Ice Hockey, Ice Skating, Football,
Weightlifting, Bowling, Field Athletics, Cycling
(Track, Road, Indoor), Swimming, Water Polo,
Gymnastics

Oberfrohnaer Strasse 27, Karl-Marx-Stadt W30
20 July 1964

To:
Area Command
German People's Police,
Department 'K'
Hainstrasse 142
Karl-Marx-Stadt C1

Re: Defection of Dieter Wiedemann
  We hereby file charges against the former
cyclist of SC Karl-Marx-Stadt, Dieter Wiedemann.
Previously domiciled: SCK Dormitory, Zwickauer
Strasse 485, Karl-Marx-Stadt W30.

  This person is a defector and has in his
possession 1 complete racing bicycle excluding
saddle. The bicycle is the property of SC Karl-
Marx-Stadt.

  The costs amount to:

  1 frame with 1 set of wheels and all components
= DM 1,035.00

  Payment should be made to our account no. 30369
Stadtsparkasse (town savings bank) KMST W 30

  With sporting regards

  Representative of the Chairperson
Finance Leader

  Sportclub Karl-Marx-Stadt (Secretariat)

MfS383/65 bd4, BSTU0093

13.7.64

Dieter Wiedemann
Jos. Werner Strasse 15
Schweinfurt
872
<u>To:</u>
The German Cycling Federation
Brüderstrasse 5-6
<u>Berlin C1</u>

Dear Sirs,

I hereby tender my resignation from the German Cycling Federation.

The racing bike provided to me has been sent to the address of my parents. From there it is to be delivered to you immediately.

I trust that the clothes taken from Giessen will also be sent to my parents. Many thanks.

With sporting greetings

Dieter Wiedemann

DIETER

I went to see Torpedo on 22 July, and they offered me a contract for the following season. They wanted to let the dust settle first, so they suggested I do some amateur races to keep myself fit until then. They gave me a job in the factory in the meantime, and organised a place for me to stay. I started work the following day, and they organised lodgings for me.

On a Friday evening I used to ride home to Mitterteich. I'd spend the weekends there if I wasn't racing.

EBERHARD

My birthday was 1 August, and they called me in again. They told me I'd have to leave the sport club and go back to work. They said I could ride, but that the state would no longer be supporting me. In defecting my brother had betrayed the republic, so there was no way I could carry on representing the country. They weren't aggressive at all, and they weren't threatening me. They just informed me calmly, and then I left.

I was heartbroken.

MfS383/65 bd2, BSTU0030

Sportclub Karl-Marx-Stadt
Oberfrohnaer Strasse 27, Karl-Marx-Stadt W30
13.8.1964

Karl Wiedemann
Flöha
Rudolf-Breitscheid-Strasse 51

Termination

We hereby confirm that your working contract,
dated 2 February 1963, will be terminated on
27 August 1964. You still have a paid holiday
entitlement of eighteen days, and therefore our
working relationship will conclude on 3 September
1964. The entire inventory must be handed over on
Wednesday 12 August 1964.

Motive

At present SC Karl-Marx-Stadt has no further
requirement for the work you do.

You have the right to appeal within fourteen
days of receipt of this letter, or you may go to
arbitration.

Signed

Schreyer (President)   Hess (Trade union)

Flöha, 5 August 1964

Karl Wiedemann
Flöha
Wiesenstrasse 15

Dear State Councillor

We kindly request an appointment to meet with you. We would like to talk about the defection of our son, Dieter Wiedemann. My other son, Eberhard Wiedemann, who turned nineteen on 1 August 1964, has been dismissed from SC Karl-Marx-Stadt, and I too was dismissed from my job there on 4 August 1964. I had been working there as a mechanic for six years. I think I did a good job, but now I have been dismissed.

Our son has given us the reasons for his having left the GDR, but he only told us after the defection.

On 31 July 1964 two sport club functionaries from SC Karl-Marx-Stadt visited us at our flat, and asked us why Dieter had defected. They informed us that Eberhard would have chance to talk to them, but that he had to present himself within an hour. Failing that he need appear at the sport club the following morning, 1 August, at nine o'clock.

We disapprove of the actions of our son Dieter, but also of the injustice done to our other son through the actions of the sports functionaries.

We cannot condone the actions of SC Karl-Marx-Stadt, because in previous instances where athletes have defected or tried to defect, there have been no consequences for their families.

I would therefore kindly ask you to consider the decisions taken, and to grant us an appointment to meet as soon as possible.

Yours faithfully!
Karl and Marianne Wiedemann

DIETER

As I understand it they interviewed my former colleagues, and they were dumbfounded by what I'd done. I know that Täve, for example, said I was the very last person he would have expected to defect.

To be honest, though, for the first six weeks I had very little contact with anybody, just letters from my mum. I had no idea what was going on.

GERHARD

I was a cyclist, and I knew Dieter and his dad because I lived near Flöha. Obviously everybody knew what had happened, but among the cyclists you spoke about it under your breath. You had to be very careful what you said because it was a political issue. You didn't talk about politics in the GDR because you didn't know who was in the party. You didn't want to lose your place in the sport club, so you knew better than to speak about it publicly.

Then I was one of five brothers, and our dad had died when we were young. We'd worked our fingers to the bone to be able to keep the family farm, and we didn't want to run the risk of having it taken off us.

RAINER

People might have *wondered* why he defected, but nobody talked about it. The only people talking about it publicly were party members.

MANFRED

It was a sort of moot point. They didn't tell us anything, and I guess it was because they didn't want it to become a *cause célèbre*. We spoke about it among ourselves, but only in passing and not when the officials were around.

MfS435/71 BSTU0132

Karl-Marx-Stadt 11.8.64

Report

A few days ago I had a chat with colleague (?).
We talked about the cyclist Dieter Wiedemann.
Colleague (?) said: Wiedemann is one of those who
wants to become a great rider at any cost. He
probably saw the offer as a chance to become a big
professional. I believe it wouldn't have cost the
West Germans much to convince Wiedemann. He's not
concerned about defection east or west.

(?) knows Wiedemann through cycling at SC
Wismut.

'Ursel'

MfS383/65 bd4, BSTU0103

Extract from operative plan, Leipzig Area
Command, Department XX/6, 12.8.64

Through informant 'Diamant', Leipzig Area
Command, Department XX/6, understands that not
only the road cyclist Wiedemann, but also the
following cyclists from SC DHfK:

Marks, Rainer

(?)

(?) and

Krause, Karlheinz

had, or still have, the intention of defecting
illegally by means of West Germany.

During conversations on 24.7.64 and 2.8.64,
Marks reported that the motive for their plans is
insufficient earning potential.

During the conversation on 2.8.64, (?) also
confirmed that Marks has already expressed his
ideas about an unlawful exit of the GDR for a
second time.

Original report: See GDR Cycling Federation
report

MANFRED

I don't know the upshot of it all because my cycling career finished in August. We were at the Tour of Yugoslavia, and we were doing extremely well. We'd won a lot of prizes, but then the trainer told us that there was a new rule. He said that from now on all the prizes would go straight to the federation instead of us, and they would decide whether or not we were given them. We were extremely upset, and I took it upon myself to have it out with him. It almost became a fight, and that was the end of my cycling career. I was twenty-five, and they said I should think about taking up football.

So all those things combined – the Melichow incident, criticising the training, being a Christian, not joining the party, not being one of the DHfK group – had ended up costing me a great deal.

AXEL

It was the Tour of Yugoslavia. Joop Zoetemelk was winning the GC, and I was second. He and I were much the strongest.

Ford were sponsoring the race, and the first three on GC were each going to get a car. The three cars were mounted on a truck in front of the peloton, so we saw them every day; it was a big incentive, as you can imagine. Then one of the GDR functionaries came up to me and said, 'You know that if you win the car you don't get to keep it? It goes to the GDR embassy in Yugoslavia, not to you personally.'

What happened? I finished fourth.[*]

DIETER

I hadn't thought for one minute that there would be any particular issues for my parents. I knew that a cyclist named Joachim Bässler had defected

---

[*]   Axel Peschel won the 1968 Peace Race.

in 1957 and there hadn't been any consequences for his family. I was the fifth Wismut athlete to leave, albeit the first since the wall had gone up. I knew that Ampler had been planning it as well. He had a brother in the west and he'd planned to defect while he was in Sweden. As far as I know they did some kind of a deal with him. They made him marry his girlfriend, and that was that.

So there hadn't been any particular consequences for any of them, and anyway the GDR constitution stated that everyone had the right to work in the profession of his choosing. That's all I'd decided to do. They had delegated me to Giessen in the first place, and I'd simply decided to stay there to become a professional cyclist. I still think they wanted to make an example of somebody before the Olympics, and I guess I handed them the opportunity.

Would I have defected if I'd known? I really don't know, to be honest.

EBERHARD

It was a difficult time for me, and also for my dad. He'd had the job he'd always wanted, and his dream had always been to see his two sons ride the Peace Race together.

He told me that an official from the town hall had informed him he ought to feel ashamed. He'd said he ought to feel like a thief because of what Dieter had done.

My dad was a very quiet person, very introvert. He never let anybody see the effect of what had happened, but he suffered terribly. He wasn't angry, no. He wasn't the sort to get angry, but he was hurting so much that it was all he could do to try to survive. He was sixty years old, and he ended up doing a nothing job in a bike factory. It was the end of his dream.

MfS383/65 bd2, BSTU0020/0021/0022/0023/0024

Karl-Marx-Stadt, 03.09.1964

Department B
Transcript from Original
Addressee:Mr Dieter Wiedemann
        16 Jaegerstrasse
        (872) Schweinfurt
Sender: None
Postmark:Karl-Marx-Stadt, 28.08.1964

28.08.1964

My dear boy!

Yesterday afternoon at around four o'clock we finally received the letter we have been awaiting for sooo long for - thanks. It's early now - 06.15. (?) has already been gone for a half-hour so I've had some coffee, seen to the chickens and will now use the time to write before I get started with other work. Dad's still asleep. He's only now just starting to relax. On 13.08 they served him his notice - so they've pushed it back from 04.08 to 13.08. That means he was at home on 14.08, and everybody said to him, 'Karl, first of all you need to calm down. It's already cost your nerves enough!' (...)

We think 90 per cent are surprised by the course of action taken against dad and (?). Believe me, dear boy, I've got enough copies of everything and perhaps you can still use them. Your (?) is keeping a keen eye on everything.

The alderman told a council worker that 90 per cent of Flöha was against the WIEDEMANN family, to which the worker replied, 'Bring me the 90 per cent then, perhaps it's the other way round'. Apart from that we've left no stone unturned and have done everything, but you know better than anybody that their arm is much, much longer.

Regarding the telegram from Berlin. We found out on 20.08 and all three of us went on 21.08. Of course you're only allowed to see an employee. They'd already received our letter fourteen days earlier, but believe me it was utterly pointless since some functionary had been feeding them lies. It could be that it was someone from the club or the German Gymnastics and Sport Federation, we don't know. (...) Please understand that I can't tell you everything. We just hope that we can talk about this some time. That's why there's no point writing. (...)

I'm sorry you had bad luck in the race and it didn't really turn out right. We also believe that you too are suffering a lot under this, but believe me we can't spare you everything. In any case we haven't told you everything because even party members are shocked, especially those who are human and have a bit of spirit. Unlike this guy from the club - thank God everybody's not like that.

And even if our skies are now darkened by storm clouds, the sun will eventually shine again. Dad has received some offers of work without having to go looking, because everybody in the area knows what has happened to us. He has more or less made his mind up already about one. Dad will probably earn 30DM per month less, but also no performance bonuses, but this is fine by him because he's scrupulous.(...)

Had we publicly condemned you in the most extreme way, we'd have been seen as righteous people. But how could we do such a thing? - dragging a decent man through the muck. Very few people are doing that - even those who knew you just as a sportsman. You are and will remain our dear boy and we hope that you will continue to give us joy.(...)

If you have a wish or need anything we'll do what we can to send what's permitted. You know

your mum, she'll try everything and do everything
possible. In my letter of 03.08 I asked if other
riders there are using Kowalit tubulars. (?)
said they are in great demand after the Erfurt
criterium, that he has bought some for you and
will send a new one and a second-hand one today.
However we are only allowed to send goods to the
value of DM 30.00.

Now to why you haven't written for some time.
We believe you when you say you haven't much
time, but at least send a small postcard and let
us know you're well. You can see that even H. has
been thinking about you and post is the only
thing keeping us together at the moment. (...)

For various reasons I will send post to the
company and only now and then to the new address.
I'll give you the reasons for this later. Caution
is the mother of wisdom. Please let me know the
company's address in your next letter. We were
also worried that we had no post from you and we
assumed it might not be getting through to us. So
we are going to get a book. (?) will see if he can
find yours – please be patient because we need
to get this right. In my letter of 03.08 I asked
how many light pyjamas you have, if you have any
white shirts or a cardigan. Please answer these
questions. (...)

Your dad has got out of bed now and is building
a bike. He has to build a completely new race bike
for (?)'s grandson. Dad doesn't mind building it. It
will cost whatever it costs. Even the new employer
has said to him, 'Karl, get yourself properly
better first!' and even the party secretary was
beside himself about everything we've been put
through. But we'll remember everything – they
can all be sure of that. So now to round things
off. We are all healthy and we hope you are too.
Do something for your nerves ... You've got enough
offers, and don't be mean with the money. You can
succeed bit by bit. We're also doing our upmost

for you. We wish you all the best in the coming races and remember we're with you in thought and are not angry with you, on the contrary we and sooo many others are glad about your successes. I don't like to go out shopping because I often get stopped and asked about you, and then when we go our separate ways they always send greeting and best wishes to Dieter. When it's less warm I'll send you a cake. Even though you can buy them, you won't refuse anything down from home.

Many greetings from your loved ones.

GERHARD

Once a month I'd deliver straw to Karl for his rabbits, and he'd call by while he was out on his bike.

He was a very quiet person, and he didn't tell you what he was feeling. I think maybe he just internalised everything. He had his animals and his smallholding, and he busied himself with those things.

He'd lost his work at the sport club, but I carried on taking my bike for him to fix. He never asked anything for doing it because he was someone who liked to help other people. I carried on taking my bike because I thought it was something I could do to try to make life a bit easier.

MfS383/65 bd2, BSTU0035/0036

Karl-Marx-Stadt, 1.10.1964
Department B
TRANSCRIPT
Addressee: Gertrud DIERSCHE, Gartenstrasse 3,
Flöha, near Karl-Marx-Stadt
Sender: Postmark Mitterteich, 21.09.1964
20.09.1964

Dear Auntie Gertrud and Uncle Herbert!
    We received your last letter with great joy, and
now I want to write you a few lines to return the
favour!
    I look forward to your visit – it will be a
party! I do hope it all works out!
    I can hardly believe it! He's here, and he'll be
here for ever more! It seems like a dream to me!
It was like in a fairytale and you've no idea how
lucky we both are, and I will never forget what
you two have contributed towards our happiness.
As soon as the dust settles over there I'll come
back to visit you in Flöha. The past doesn't
leave me alone though that which imprisoned me
over there is here with me. But I would like
once more to visit the little spot of land where
we were both very, very happy. What do I mean
were? We still are, but now it's something quite
different again! Now on the radio they're playing,
'The Place next to you belongs to me'. That's our
favourite song. Pretty, isn't it? You will soon
be able to put your arms around the good fellow.
We especially notice that the days are passing
quickly. We'll chew over the story of Giessen.
You'll have the best rendition!
    We plan to marry later, and we're already
saving hard! I'm cooking on Sundays now, sometimes
at home and sometimes at my gran's. I want to be a

perfect housewife, though I can see that I have a
lot to learn. I'll definitely do it, though. (...)

As a Christmas present I'm knitting us matching
ski pullovers. From wool as thick as your finger!
Fantastic! But please, not a word to Dieter in
your letters! It's supposed to be a surprise! Yes,
this year is going to be the best Christmas ever.

That's all for today! Please write to me again!
I'm thrilled by anything coming from Flöha!

> With warmest greetings,
> Your Sylvia!

(Excuse the handwriting!) _____.

First lieutenant Hörig

EBERHARD

I still maintain that Dieter must have known there would be problems for us, because as a GDR sportsman you were under close surveillance all the time. If they said you had to watch a certain TV programme you watched it, and they were always being schooled about how to conduct themselves in the west. For me it must have been clear to him that there would be consequences for the people left behind.

DIETER

I had no contact with anyone, just the letters my mum sent. I don't know how many were opened, nor whether they were intercepted. My guess is that they allowed most of them to reach me to remind me of how hard it was for my parents. That way I might be tempted to go back, to relieve them of the suffering.

It was a very harrowing time for them, because they were being made to pay for something they'd known nothing about. It was hard for me as well, because I was responsible for their being treated like criminals. That's why the letters from Sylvia are all gone. They destroyed them for fear of the Stasi using them as evidence against them.

SYLVIA

So the paradox was that he couldn't go east to see his family any more than he'd been able to go west with his old GDR passport.

At first we lived in fear that the Stasi would come for us, but there was no contact. The only hint I ever had that they were watching us was one time he came to pick me up from work. A car pulled up outside with a GDR registration plate, and so I just said, 'Look, don't pick me up any more; it might be dangerous.'

His mum sent him letters and food parcels, which was the only thing she was able to do. We were getting food parcels *from* the GDR, but they'd take two or three weeks to arrive. She'd send jars of jam, fruit, things like that, but by the time they showed up the jars would be broken and the fruit would be putrefied anyway. We'd have to throw them out, but it was the only contact she had with him.

DIETER

I got a letter from my mum. It said, 'They're coming next week to pick up the prizes you won.' My dad told me a guy he knew from the town hall had been instructed to do it, but he'd refused. Apparently he said he was retiring in a few weeks, and he wasn't prepared to start acting like a bailiff. In the end the mayor had to go and do it himself. The point is that they had no right to treat them that way. The GDR constitution stated that everybody was free to work as they saw fit, and I hadn't even been living with them when I'd defected. They'd forced me to change residence to the sport club, so they had no legal entitlement to anything from that house.

My mum was extremely upset, as you can imagine. She couldn't believe that they were being treated that way, and nor could a lot of the people in Flöha. Letters of support started arriving at my parents' house, but they were anonymous. I was a criminal, and people didn't want to risk being seen to support me.

Flöha 16 September 1964

Dear Dieter Wiedemann!

We are staggered by what Mayor Hense and his functionaries have done in visiting your parents' house and confiscating your prizes. Like you we are convinced that those prizes were for your results, and that it's only right they remain at your parents' house.

Previously those people who came to pick up the prizes were happy to celebrate your results with you. Furthermore, the way they are treating your father and brother is unfair. You can't imagine how many people in and around Flöha are still celebrating you, and are still proud of you.

We wish you all the best for your sports career, and above all for your continued good health. Our respect for you remains unchanged.

Greetings from the sportspeople
of your home town Flöha.

DIETER

When I'd left I was still owed a lot of prizes from the Peace Race. The way it worked was that in addition to what we were paid by the cycling federation, prizes were awarded locally. Companies, schools, local councils and sport clubs all across the route would donate things, and at the end they always held a big gala where the team was formally presented with what they'd accumulated. We'd been extremely successful so I was owed a TV, binoculars, crystal, porcelain … I'd say that the value of what they owed me was around 6,000 marks.

Normally you got it a fortnight or so after the race finished, but because of the Olympic qualification it was held over. Why? Well, having all four Olympic qualifiers was a big objective in the GDR, because cycling was one of the most prestigious sports. They promoted the idea that we had the best race – the Peace Race – and the best riders in Europe. The FRG had professional cyclists, so it followed that their best amateurs wouldn't be as good as ours, otherwise they'd have been signed by trade teams. Then they made out that we had the best coaches, the best support, all those GDR propaganda things.

I'd left the country, but it didn't alter the fact that I'd been one of the team. I'd contributed a lot, and they had a legal obligation to reward me. But when my dad asked for what was rightfully mine, they just refused outright.

Berlin, 5.10.1964

Mr Karl Wiedemann

938 Flöha

Wiesenstrasse 11

Dear Mr Wiedemann!

I received your letter from the administration office of the federation, but I haven't been able to answer you sooner because I've been extremely busy. Moreover, I had to double-check some of your statements and to conduct two further interviews, though those people requested that I don't disclose their names.

Now, however, I am able to reveal the findings.

Your son, Dieter Wiedemann, was a member of the Peace Race collective for 1964. Before the race the team agreed that all prizes would be divided equally between each of the members. Your son's good result was achieved only through the collective efforts of the team and as such, given that he shamefully betrayed the others, he forfeits the right to claim his share.

This decision is final.

German Cycling Federation

Heinz Przybyl

President

MfS4458/69 BSTU0051

Berlin 30.09.1964
Main Department XX/6/I

Proposal

To award informant 'Radler' reg: no. 16867/60 in celebration of the fifteenth anniversary of the GDR with a prize to the sum of 150DM.

Reason:

The informant 'Radler' was recruited in 1952 by Karl-Marx-Stadt Area Command and has worked well.

Because he was replaced as the trainer of SC Dynamo Berlin in 1954 the available documentation on the informant 'Radler' was archived.

In 1958 contact with the informant 'Radler' was re-established.

Informant 'Radler' always took the trouble to fulfil his missions diligently. In his unofficial collaboration he demonstrated initiative and responsibility. He provided us with valuable information about top sportsmen and his contribution towards the reconnaissance of these sportsmen is considerable.

In summary it must be judged that the informant 'Radler' is reliable and true to the cause of the working class.

Lieutenant Müller   Captain Voigt

IMMO

The Olympics were in October.* I went with Hoffmann, but obviously the FRG guys travelled independently. The official policy was that we weren't allowed to have contact with them, so we couldn't train with them beforehand. We'd maybe chat in the Olympic village in the evenings, but only when our handlers weren't around. So on a personal level there was no animosity, but we weren't a team. We came from different countries and we barely knew one another. During the race I crashed and had to change bike, so I only finished forty-fourth.

DIETER

One night in November there was a knock at the door. When I answered there were two BND† agents standing there, and they asked if they could come in. I said yes because I'd nothing to hide, and they started asking me about my activities in the GDR, why I'd defected, political stuff.

I remember thinking, 'Christ, it's happening again!' One of the reasons I'd defected was the Stasi meeting in 1962, and now I was being questioned by the *West* German secret police! I had nothing to hide, but when they left I was pretty pleased with myself for having avoided joining the party.

---

*   A GDR track rider named Jürgen Kissner also defected during Olympic qualification, in Cologne. Four years later the IOC recognised the GDR's national Olympic committee, so each of the German states fielded a team in Mexico. Kissner rode the team pursuit for his adopted country, and they qualified for the final.

They easily defeated the Danes, but a member of the GDR delegation issued an appeal because Kissner had 'pushed' one of his team-mates. The FRG admitted that there had been contact, but replays showed that it had been no more than a light, involuntary touch. It had made no difference whatsoever to the outcome of the race, but the FRG were stripped of gold anyway.

†   The *Bundesnachrichtendienst* was the West German intelligence service. It's widely believed that the majority of their 'informants' were double agents working for the Stasi, particularly in the 1960s. They have no record of having visited Dieter Wiedemann.

DIETER

There was something strange, and at first I couldn't put my finger on it. Then I realised that it was the total absence of politics. In the GDR you couldn't escape it, because the very foundation of the society and everything was based on it and built around it. You turned on the radio and you had socialism, you bought a newspaper and it was socialism … always socialism. All the billboards were about socialism, and all the big sports events were homages to it. There were flags everywhere, pictures of Karl Marx in shop windows, streets named after Lenin and Rosa Luxemburg. There were signs everywhere telling you about how you had a responsibility to build socialism, and about how the west wanted to start another war with us. Everything was politicised, so much so that you didn't even notice it any more. Socialism filled your life whether you liked it or not.

Here my life was empty by comparison, and I had to learn how to fill the spaces. I realised that my whole life had been spent being told how to behave, what to think and what to believe, and now all I was being told was which washing powder I should buy. Nothing was politicised, and nobody was interested.

I found it very hard to assimilate practically, but also culturally. The first thing was that the Frankonian people were different. They came from farming stock, and most of them had never been out of Bavaria. They were louder, but they were also less well mannered and less cultured. They said whatever they wanted, *about* whatever they wanted, whenever they wanted. I wasn't used to that, and if I'm honest I found them a bit coarse at the beginning. They were always shouting, grabbing hold of one another, full of themselves. They talked a lot, but they didn't seem to say anything and they didn't seem to *know* anything.

It was as if they'd never been to school. People here had more of everything – more fun, more money, more possessions – but they weren't at all educated compared to people from the GDR. They didn't seem to value education at all, nor culture. Sometimes it seemed that they almost took pride in being ignorant.

Of course it was me that was different, not them. It was hard for me to fit in, and I was being reminded of the differences all the time. Food was so expensive here, clothes, rent ... Everything cost a fortune, and I had very little money. Then there was the waste. I remember that they *threw food away*, and to me that was unthinkable. It would never have happened in the GDR, and I found it quite shocking.

I was having a hard time adapting, and those winter nights at the lodgings were sometimes very long. I was a German and the people around me were German, but I felt extremely lonely and extremely foreign. We spoke the same language, but at times I felt like I had nothing in common with them whatsoever.

A lot of people at the factory had communist sympathies, and they seemed to think that because I was from the GDR I would, too. They kept inviting me to political rallies, as if they wanted me to be some kind of mascot. I tried to ignore it at first, but in the end I said, 'Look, if you agree with communism so much, why don't you just go and live there and see what it's like? There's nothing stopping you ...'

Anyway, I worked in the factory for the rest of the year, and they were the longest five months of my life. Sylvia and I were engaged in November, and after that things slowly started to get better.

DIETER

At first the letters from my mum had come every few days, and her anger had been directed at the authorities, not at me.

Over time the letters became less supportive. Any relationship suffers if you don't spend time together, and in our case it was worse because of the circumstances. There were no telephones, and as time went by so we had less contact and less in common. I had the sense that it was breaking apart in front of my eyes.

SYLVIA

You couldn't rent a flat together unless you were married, and so we couldn't really make a start until then. We were walking past a church one day, and Dieter took me inside and proposed. Mitterteich is a small place, and everybody there knew our story. They made fun of me for marrying a guy with a bike instead of a big car, but I didn't mind that.

DIETER

Over time it got distilled down to anger and resentment on my mum's part. At first I suppose she hoped that I'd give up and go back, but when I got engaged that receded. As they saw it I'd rejected them, and indirectly I suppose they were right. I'd decided to start a completely different life, and because of the wall they weren't permitted to be a part of it. That wasn't my fault, but nor was it theirs. It was just the way it was, but they were still being made to pay for what I'd done. They were being treated like they were responsible, so when I told them I was going to get married it was almost the final straw. She started writing, 'How could you do this to us?'

MfS383/65 bd2,BSTU0140

Karl-Marx-Stadt 17.12.1964

Subject: Wiedemann, Dieter

The following came to light through the
evaluation of Department 'M' reports about
Wiedemann:

On 14.11.1964, Dieter Wiedemann became engaged to a
certain Sylvia.

In early December 1964 he changed position at
work to that of supervisor, and his hourly wage
amounts to 3.09 deutschmarks.

In January 1965, he will become a professional for
'Fichtel & Sachs'. He begins his training in early
January 1965.

He expresses to his family in the GDR that he
carefully considered the steps he has taken
as regards both his personal loyalties and his
professional development, and that he is content.
His parents should reconcile themselves to the
situation.

Since Wiedemann currently has no intention to
return to the GDR, it is proposed to suspend the
ongoing operative procedure. The operational
personal investigation remains in place, and will
report on any further intentions of Wiedemann.

Lieutenant Schulz

DIETER

When the letters started to become accusatory it was extremely hard for me. When I'd defected I'd known I'd lose everything I had, but that I'd gain something else. The problem now was that I wasn't able to get on with my new life, because I was racked with guilt about the one I'd left behind. I felt like I was in a trap, and I had to find a way to get out of it. The only way for me to do that was to try to switch off from everything associated with the GDR. I wouldn't say I compartmentalised my feelings *per se*, but I just put them in a box and tried to forget about them.

In the end you have to make a cut, and the fact is that if I'd continued carrying the GDR round with me there's no way Sylvia and I would have survived. There's no way I'd have been able to function.

GERHARD

It wasn't their fault, but they wouldn't let his parents visit. It was terribly difficult for them.

Dieter had gone, and I had the sense that Karl was looking for another person he could bond with.

I felt that I might be playing the role of a sort of surrogate son for him.

SYLVIA

I wouldn't say that my father didn't *like* Dieter, just that they had nothing whatsoever in common. I think he'd been expecting somebody he could go out socialising with, but in reality Dieter would come home at weekends and they'd have nothing to say to one another. Dieter wasn't one to go out drinking and socialising, and my dad wasn't interested in sport. Dieter got on well with Roland, and for my mum he was the perfect son-in-law, but he was just too reserved for my dad. He would say, 'He's too insular. You can't *talk* with him!' but that's because he didn't understand him at all. They came from different worlds, and at times at the start it felt like my whole life was a fight between east and west. It was uncomfortable, and if I'm honest it wasn't much fun. I loved Dieter, but it dawned on me that we'd had no idea of what being together was going to be like. I had to learn that as I went along, and I was only eighteen.

Anyway, as time passed he became less worried about the Stasi, and I'd say that within six months he felt pretty secure that they wouldn't come after him.

MfS144/67 BSTU0145

Received: 6.1.1965
Informant: 'Jonni'
<u>Staff sergeant Koepp</u>

Appraisal of (?) WIEDEMANN

I've known W. October 1964, since I've worked in the forge. Before Christmas I was in conversation with W. In answer to a question about his brother he said he's doing very well. He works at Fichtel & Sachs in Schweinfurt, and earns 3.80 west marks per hour. After Christmas he wants to become a professional, because he can earn more there.

His opinion about our cycling is that it's going more and more downhill. Since the top riders like Schur, Adler etc. are no longer active, there is a big hole.

'Jonni'

NEUES DEUTSCHLAND

ORGAN DES ZENTRALKOMITEES DER SOZIALISTISCHEN EINHEITSPARTEI DEUTSCHLANDS

Ten riders are included in the candidacy for the Berlin–Prague–Warsaw Peace Race, beginning 8 May and supervised by coach Roland Elste. These are the candidates for places in the GDR delegation: Klaus Ampler, Dieter Mickein, Bernard Eckstein, Harald Dippold, Günter Lux (all DHfK Leipzig), Lothar Appler, Eberhard Butzke, Axel Peschel (all SC Dynamo Berlin), Günter Hoffmann (ASK), Rüdiger Tanneberger (SC Karl-Marx-Stadt).

However, in contrast to previous years this doesn't mean that other riders may not be appointed to the Peace Race team. Whoever proves himself in the spring preparatory races can earn a place, even if he is not among the candidates.

Meanwhile, some well-known riders have retired from the national team but continue to race: Günter Lörke, Immo Rittmeyer, Manfred Weissleder, Egon Adler and Wolfgang Stamm.

Reprinted from 'Peace Race candidates', 22 January 1965

IMMO

When I got back to the sport club they said they would be taking away my support. The result in Tokyo hadn't been very good, but I still thought what had happened in Giessen had a bearing on it. They said it was because I was too old, but I was only twenty-eight.

EBERHARD

I went back to my BSG, but I wasn't about to give up hope. They tried to help by giving me two afternoons a week off to train, and I carried on. I wanted to be so good that they couldn't do without me, so in the winter I took myself off and did a training camp on my own. I cycled, did cross-country skiing and running, and got myself into the best condition I could.

DIETER

The rewards for what I'd done were Sylvia and the fact that I was now a professional cyclist.

MfS383/65 bd1, BSTU0243

Provisional race calendar 1965

6.3	Het Volk	Belgium
7.3	Tour of Limburg	Belgium
13.3	Dwars van Vlaanderen	Belgium
14.3	Hoeilaart-Diest-Hoeilaart	Belgium
21.3	Wevelgem	Belgium
27.3	Tour of Middle Flanders	Belgium
4.4	Henninger Turm	Germany
6-9.4	Tour of Belgium	Belgium
18.4	Dortmund Union	Germany
25.4	Paris-Brussels	Belgium
2.5	Meisterschaft Zurich	Switzerland
5-8.5	Four Days of Dunkirk	France
12-16.5	Tour of Holland	Holland
29-30.5	Tour de l'Oise	France
6.6	GP Gippingen	Switzerland
10-16.6	Tour de Suisse	Switzerland
22.6-14.7	Tour de France (no participation by us) France	
18.7	Road race in Stuttgart	Germany
29.7	German Championship in Dortmund Germany	
7.8	Munich-Zurich	Switzerland
21.8	German Hill Climb championship	Germany
22.8	Hill Climb in Bad Schwalbach	Germany
27-30.8	Paris-Luxembourg	France
5.9	World Championships in Spain	Spain
9-12.9	Tour du Nord	France
16.9	Grand Prix d'Orchies	France
18-19.9	Tour du Picardie	France

In addition there could be one or two more races in Germany (Bremen, Nürburgring, Hockenheimring) as well as some kermesses and criteriums in Holland.

EBERHARD

Dieter would send us a letter at the beginning of each season, with his racing schedule. I was always left wondering how I would have done had I been given the chance.

DIETER

The racing was totally different from what I'd been used to. In the GDR it had always been a fight from the gun, but here they rode tempo until the last fifty or sixty kilometres, and then it exploded. The feelings I had on the bike hadn't changed at all, though, and in that sense it was my pressure valve. Riding was a way to unburden myself of the stress, and to be me. The riders were all fine with me, and nobody in the peloton was bothering me with questions about my having defected. Regardless of nationality, politics, all that rubbish, I was being judged on what I did on the bike. I suppose if I'd been a champion that would have been different, but I wasn't. I was just another rider, and I liked that a great deal.

I didn't earn much money, but it was a working wage. I trained hard in the hope that I'd do well enough to get another contract the following year, and of course there was always the dream of the World Championships and the Tour de France. Both had been denied me in the GDR, and they were scores I wanted to settle. I suppose I was still angry about what had happened, and I resented having been forced to choose. I was desperate to make a success of it, and I didn't want them to have the satisfaction of seeing me fail.

The problem was that Torpedo didn't have a big star, and German cycling was a bit peripheral back then. So we got to race in France, but only semi-classics and smaller stage races. We'd do Het Volk but not Paris–Roubaix, and the Four Days of Dunkirk but not Paris–Nice. We did all the big German races, and we'd ride in Holland, Switzerland and Belgium. I never did a single race in Italy, because there wasn't enough money. Only the very best foreign teams got invited there.

In May we were sent to the Tour of Holland, a five-day stage race. I was riding with people I'd grown up dreaming about, and that was a big moment for me. I found myself alongside Jacques Anquetil, and I realised that I liked being in that world. I finished fifth, and it convinced me that I was good enough. The following month we rode the Tour de Suisse. It was a big race back then, and I finished tenth.

So I was one of the best in Torpedo, and I was starting to feel like I belonged. I realised that if I got the chance to ride some stage races I could maybe become a decent professional cyclist.

MfS8963/69 BSTU0067/0068

Berlin, 17 August 1965

Main Department XX/6/I

Meeting report

With: Informant 'Hildebrand'

Time: 17.8.65, 10.30–11 o'clock

Location: Conspiratorial Dwelling 'Vineta'

A further meeting took place with the
informant 'Hildebrand' in preparation for the
World Championships in San Sebastián, Spain. A
conversation took place during which he made
assessments with regard to the nominated riders.

Individual road race – Men

The informant reported that he has no concerns or
objections against the departure of the riders:

    TAUFMANN
    HOFFMANN
    KATZMIRZACK
    LUX
    ECKSTEIN

In relation to the nominated rider (?) of SC
Karl-Marx-Stadt, he remarked that it would be
his first journey to a non-socialist country. The
informant then made reference to (?) relations:

During the Olympic qualifiers, the fugitive
Karl-Marx-Stadt cyclist Dieter Wiedemann was
poached by Fichtel & Sachs from Schweinfurt.
Following his defection he found a good
position, and now rides for them as a contracted
professional athlete. The former Karl-Marx-Stadt
cyclist (?) is in the same team, having been placed
there by his uncle, (?).

Obviously there must also have been connection between (?) and Wiedemann before his defection. It is also known that Wiedemann and (?) were close friends. However, the informant doesn't know if there is currently a relationship between the two of them.

However, it is known that Wiedemann will ride for West Germany in Spain. The informant was charged with more detailed inquiries about (?) in advance of the next meeting. He proposes to speak with (?), the section head at SC Karl-Marx-Stadt whom he knows very well, at the Tour of the GDR. The proposal was adopted.

MfS383/65 bd2, BSTU0197/0198

Karl-Marx-Stadt 24.08.1965
Department B

Final report
On preliminary operative procedure XVII 235/60
(Wiedemann, Dieter)

The preliminary operative procedure was started with the aim of repatriating Dieter Wiedemann to the GDR.

It has been established that Wiedemann is riding as a professional cyclist for the company 'Fichtel & Sachs' and is also employed by this company as a controller.

Since the beginning of 1965 he's been taking part in bigger professional road races in West Germany and in non-socialist foreign countries. To date, however, he hasn't achieved any great successes.

He has been engaged for a year and intends to marry this September. A new-build apartment has recently been made available to him and he's in the process of furnishing this apartment with his fiancée. His parents send over various small household items.

The operative measures taken reveal that Wiedemann is not currently intending to come to the GDR and nor does he intend to take part in races in socialist countries. He has told his parents that he has settled in well and that he wants to build a life in West Germany. They should come to terms with the fact that they won't be seeing one another for some considerable time.

Dieter Wiedemann maintains postal correspondence with his parents and (?) in Flöha. His bride also takes part in the exchange of letters. Wiedemann seldom writes to other people. These letters are about personal matters.

From Dieter Wiedemann's exchange of letters it can be deduced that despite his professional

contract he's not doing particularly well
financially. Even if he doesn't write this
directly it's clear that he has his parents send
quite a few small items for furnishing his
apartment. He could acquire these items for very
little money in West Germany.

Since a repatriation of Dieter Wiedemann is not
currently possible, it is suggested to place the
preliminary operative procedure into the archive
with a blocking order.

Wiedemann is registered in the object process.

Operative postal control will be kept in order
to learn Wiedemann's intentions and if necessary
take the corresponding operative measures.

Lieutenant Schulz

DIETER

They selected me as one of the eight for the World Championships in San Sebastián, and so I finally got to experience it. I was riding for Rudi Altig, and I got round. Altig came second, but he didn't pay us. Tommy Simpson won it.

The GDR were allowed to send a team that year as well, for the first time in four years. I thought better of trying to have any contact with them, though.

MfS8963/69 BSTU0076/0077/0078/0079

Berlin, 13 September 1965

Main Department XX/6/I

Meeting report

Source: Informant 'Hildebrand'

Date: 11 September 1965, 10.00–11.00

Location: Conspiratorial Dwelling 'Vineta'

The informant 'Hildebrand' took part in the World Championship in San Sebastián, Spain, charged with keeping the cyclists (?), (?) and (?) under surveillance. Furthermore, he was tasked with reporting on the behaviour and appearance of the GDR delegation as a whole. The informant provided the following: (…)

The provocation over the flag issue, started beforehand by the West Germany embassy in Spain, where they negotiated directly with the host country, was such that the UCI had the commandos dig up the flagpole. (…)

Wiedemann – who likewise had no contact with our participants, and of whom our athletes stated that he did nothing and would have been better riding for us in the GDR.

Also the defector and former president of the Cycling Federation Scharch was in San Sebastián with (?) and (?). Presumably he was guest of honour of the West German Cycling Federation, because he constantly sat in the VIP box and was permitted to sit inside at the track events. The GDR team had no contact with Scharch.

According to the informant, (?)'s financial situation can't be very good, because he was sitting without a coat even in the pouring rain and his clothing was probably from his time in the GDR.
  (…)

SYLVIA

We were married on 18 October 1965, but Dieter's mum and dad didn't come.

DIETER

No, they didn't come to my wedding.

In normal circumstances people from the GDR could get a permit for the weddings and funerals of immediate family if the parish sent proof. Obviously it was different for me because I was a defector. There was no way they were going to grant them a permit.

My grandparents were the only ones who made it. The way it worked was that when people reached pensionable age they could visit family in the west whenever they wanted. They made out it was a reward for having contributed to the building of socialism, but it's also true that pensioners didn't contribute anything. They were a net cost, and some people believed they let them travel in the hope that they'd defect. My grandfather had relatives near Munich, and to be on the safe side they put in an application to visit them that weekend. It was accepted, and I picked them up from the train station so that they could be there.

SYLVIA

Imagine how he felt getting married without his parents! It was the happiest day of our lives, but there was also a deep sense of loss. It was profoundly upsetting for him, and for me as well.

MfS383/65 bd4, BSTU0117

Cycling Club 1889 of Schweinfurt
Graben 5
Schweinfurt 872
Tel: 2349
Schweinfurt, 24.11.1965

First Minister Walter Ulbricht
Berlin
German Democratic Republic

Dear First Minister,

The undersigned today permits himself to
trouble you with the following.

Last year, on the occasion of the Olympic
road cycling qualification in Giessen, Dieter
Wiedemann, who belonged to the delegation of the
GDR, stayed behind in the FRG.

I would like to point out here that he did so
not for political reasons, but for love. In other
words for his wife, whom he had met during a
visit she made from West Germany to his home town
of Flöha, near Karl-Marx-Stadt.

Because I now know Dieter Wiedemann to be an
outstanding person, I write today, without his
knowledge, to request an amnesty for him.

Dieter joined our club as an amateur cyclist,
and is popular with everybody as a quiet, decent
athlete. This year he has become a professional
road cyclist with my son, and on 18.10.65 married
his bride, for whom he had remained in the west.

It would be, First Minister, a very nice gesture
if you would issue a special amnesty as a wedding
gift, so that he would be in a position to visit
his parents in Flöha with his new wife. It's
certainly within your power to allow him to come
without molestation because of his status as a
defector.

I myself am now fifty-eight years old, and well remember when I found love at a young age. I also think that you, First Minister, would have done everything in your power as a young man to be with your bride, Lotte.

I assure you that Dieter has never once expressed dissatisfaction about the GDR. On the contrary, he speaks highly of the support he received as a GDR sportsman. Dieter attaches great importance to the fact that he isn't in the FRG for political reasons, but solely to be with his wife.

Dear First Minister, I beg you to place mercy before the law in these exceptional circumstances, and to give me a favourable decision.

With the greatest respect.
Josef Schulz

MfS383/65 bd4, BSTU0116

Berlin 11.1.1966

Ref:HA/XX/6/I 425/66

Council of Ministers of the German Democratic
Republic

Ministry for Sate Security

Main Department XX

Ministry for State Security

Karl-Marx-Stadt Area Command

Department XX

Karl-Marx-Stadt

Wiedemann, Dieter, Defected racing cyclist
Please find attached a transcript of a letter
from a West German citizen to the head of state,
for information and evaluation.

According to information received from the
Secretariat of the Council of State of the GDR,
the letter remains unanswered.

First Lieutenant Stange
Acting leader of Main Department XX

SYLVIA

The saddest thing of all was that it was becoming apparent that the GDR was going to be following us around. We were trying to build a future together, but we were struggling. We came from different countries, had different cultures and values, and there was always this terrible loss in the background. We were becoming aware of the extent of the damage to Dieter's family, and coming to terms with the fact that we were so completely different.

If I bought him a present – clothes, for example – he wouldn't wear them. One Christmas I bought him a pair of beautiful winter shoes, but he left them in the wardrobe. It upset me so I said, 'Why don't you wear the shoes I bought you?' He said it was because he already had a pair of shoes and that he didn't want to wear the new ones until they were worn out. He'd write the date on them and keep them in the wardrobe until he needed them. And I mean *needed* them.

All my clothes were tailored by my grandfather, and I liked clothes. I wasn't extravagant, but I liked to have nice things sometimes. Dieter couldn't understand that at all, and so it was as if our two worlds were colliding.

At the beginning it was very, very hard, and I remember thinking to myself, 'I don't know if I can do this.' There was no way back, though. We'd made our bed and we had to lie in it.

DIETER

The hardest thing about my new life was that I was suddenly responsible for everything I did. That may seem strange to you, but in the GDR everything had been taken care of on my behalf. The state decided everything. They decided what you earned, and they provided work and a roof over your head. Now I had to build a life for me and Sylvia, and the quality of that life depended on me and me alone. Of course there were all the administrative things, but it was more the fact that there was no safety net.

In the FRG I had to make decisions all the time, and choices all the time. I wasn't used to that, and so life was quite daunting. The idea of renting a flat from a private individual, for example, was completely alien to me. In the GDR if you wanted a car or a flat you were put on a list, and if you were lucky you got the same one as everyone else. Here there were lots of cars to choose from, and lots of everything else. I wasn't used to choosing, and I wasn't used to consuming. In the GDR you hadn't been able to buy a house, or an expensive car, and you hadn't been able to choose to go on expensive holidays. I struggled with those things a lot, because I'd been conditioned to act in a totally different way.

It wasn't so much that I didn't *want* to spend money, more that I didn't know *how* to spend it. Growing up in the GDR we hadn't had any, and the whole of society was geared around being frugal with it. Here people liked to *show* that they had money, and they did that by buying expensive things. If I'm honest I didn't actually understand that, and I found it disorienting.

SYLVIA

I moved to Schweinfurt and became a housewife, and he concentrated on being a professional cyclist. He was away a lot and I didn't know anybody there at first, but I soon made friends. We'd have a holiday together in the winter, and after all it was what we'd always wanted. I understood that with his career we'd have to wait to start a family, and so that's what I did. You have to get on with it, don't you?

Anyway I loved him, and gradually I started to understand him. It had been a struggle, but we were starting to find a way.

EBERHARD

They let me ride the Tour of the GDR in a mixed team, and I did well. I hadn't been able to train like the others, but I finished thirtieth on GC and fourth in the young riders competition. My results were actually better than a lot of the state-sponsored riders, so we appealed to the State Council again.

I was summoned to Berlin, but the general secretary of the federation told me that it made no difference. They couldn't help me, and there was no chance of me ever going back to the sport club. I qualified for the national 'B' team, but I knew I'd never be able to compete in international races. I tried again in 1966, but it's impossible for an amateur to beat guys who are training every day. So that was the end of it; I stopped racing at the end of the season and got on with my life.

The point is that I left cycling, but it never left me. Even today when I see somebody cycling the feeling is still there.

DIETER

In 1967 the format of the Tour de France was changed. Previously it had been run along trade team lines, and as a German it seemed that I'd never get to ride it. Now they reverted back to national teams and I finally had my chance. I was a domestique for Hennes Junkermann, the best German rider. I had no ambitions beyond helping him as best I could, and getting back to Paris.

The Tour was much longer back then. It was 4,800 kilometres,* more than twice the distance of the Peace Race. We had the best bikes, but they were nothing like the ones they use today. I rode over the Aubisque, Mont Ventoux and Galibier on a steel bike with 46x24, where today they use carbon bikes weighing almost nothing and 39x27.

---

* The penultimate stage alone was 359 kilometres. The longest stage of the 2014 Tour was 237 kilometres.

I was in decent shape when I arrived, and I only had one really bad stage, the second. We lost Kunde and Oldenburg that day, but somehow I made it round.

Junkermann told me to start Ventoux slowly, so that's what I did. The heat was incredible, but to be honest I felt reasonably good that day. I remember one of the British guys – Hoban, I think it was, or Denson – with a bottle of red wine. He said, 'This wine is the exclusive property of the British team!'

I was climbing reasonably well, and I was behind Simpson when he started zigzagging across the road. I watched him fall, and I saw them pick him up. As I rode past I looked in his eyes and you could see he was in a terrible state. I said to myself, 'There's no way he's making it to Carpentras'.

There was doping in professional cycling, and they say it had a hand in what happened to Simpson. For my part I just took whatever they put in the water bottle. I didn't ask questions, and nor did anybody else. You were given your *bidon*, you rode for 160–180 kilometres, and then there was a feed and you got another one. It was sort of assumed that you wouldn't get to Paris otherwise, so you just got on with it. Sorry if that's not what you want to hear, but that's about as much as I know.

Anyway, six of the German team didn't make it back to Paris, but four of us did. I was fifty-second on GC, but I think I did reasonably well considering it was my first Tour. I'd weighed seventy-two kilograms when we started, and sixty-seven when I got home. Had I been riding for myself I'd probably have placed quite a bit higher, but that was academic to me.

So in answer to your question, the Tour was the realisation of the impossible dream. It gave me some of the greatest moments of my life, and some of the saddest. I wouldn't say that it justified the defection in itself, but none of the other GDR riders will ever know what it feels like to ride into Paris.

The Peace Race was huge, yes, but the Tour was the Tour. Aside from my family it's probably the most valuable thing I have.

MANFRED

Wiedemann rode the Tour de France? Really? In 1967? I never knew that.

Dieter Wiedemann?

Are you sure?

Did he finish it?

RAINER

There was nothing in the local paper about him riding the Tour de France, absolutely not. They would never publish something like that. He was a class enemy.

DIETER

And that was pretty much it. They told us they were shutting Torpedo down at the end of the season. I had some meetings with Batavus, but I turned it down. I desperately wanted to do another Tour de France but they were only prepared to pay us for eight months of the year. So for me to continue would have meant Sylvia going back to work, and I didn't want that.

MfS383/65 bd4, BSTU0120

Zittau 1.8.1967
Area Command Dresden
Zittau District Service Unit
Daybook: 1524/67
Area Command Unit Dresden
Department XX
Dresden

Defection of Dieter Wiedemann – Peace Race participant

Through the operational handling of a West German citizen in the operational procedure (?) it became clear that he met with Wiedemann in Cologne on 30.7.1967. A meeting had already taken place beforehand, close to Düsseldorf.

If operational interest in Wiedemann exists on your part, we request consultation and definition of common measures.

Sergeant Lehmann
District leader

MfS383/65 bd4, BSTU0119

30 August 1967
Main Department XX
Object Administration 'W'
Department B
<u>Karl-Marx-Stadt</u>

<u>Defector and racing cyclist Dieter WIEDEMANN</u>
In a letter to us dated 1.8.67, Dresden Area
Command informed us that Zittau District Service
Unit is possessed of unofficial possibilities
which may be useful in respect to the operating
procedure of the defector Wiedemann. Zittau
District Service Unit therefore requests
consultation for the definition of common
measures. We ask you to get in contact directly
with Zittau to make the necessary arrangements.

First Lieutenant Keinberg
Leader, Main Department XX

DIETER

So my cycling career finished when I was twenty-six years old, and I'll never know how good I could have been. I was never a champion, but I think I could have been a reasonable GC rider at the Tour. With time I could maybe have made the top ten or fifteen.

I got a job instead, and with the overtime I earned we were actually better off. Instead of 400 marks a month for eight months I was earning about 500 for twelve.

I carried on training at first, but after a while it started to seem a bit pointless. Later I got heavily into cross-country skiing. We'd go to the Dolomites and I'd do sixty-five-kilometre races, marathons. That was brutal stuff, but I loved it. I guess that when all's said and done I'm just a crazy person.

SYLVIA

In some respects his career had put everything on hold. He'd come in the summer of 1964, moved to Schweinfurt straight away, and we hadn't lived together until we married the following autumn. As a professional cyclist he'd always been on the road, so we'd never really built the foundations of a life together.

I wanted children, but I hadn't wanted an absent father and nor had he wanted to be one.

DIETER

Our first daughter, Nicole, was born in 1969, and Nina and Alexandra came along in 1971. My dad was a pensioner by then, so there was no reason for him not to come. We'd known they wouldn't allow my mum and brother to come to the baptism, but they refused him a travel permit as well.

RAINER

The thing is that we felt German. We weren't envious of the west as such, because Flöha was our home. Our family was here, and our life was here. I think people just resented the fact that we couldn't go and see for ourselves. We knew we'd never be able to visit the west, though. We'd no relatives over there, so it was pointless even trying.

MfS511/80 BSTU0088/0089/0092/0093

Karl-Marx-Stadt 28.7.72

Summary
Of the available operative material on the
trainer of the cycling section of BSG Wismut

TÜRKE, Henry (nickname 'Honey')
Born 9.3.1927 in Chemnitz
Addr:Karl-Marx-Stadt (?)
Occupation: locksmith
SGAG Wismut, KRB, Chief mechanic
Organisations: Free German Trade Union, Society
for German-Soviet Friendship, German Gymnastics
and Sport Federation
Not party affiliated
Personal File Number XIV 0053359
Personal ID Number 090327428275
Police Notes:
5.4.1957 (?)
3.9.1964 (?)
22.5.1970(?)
1.3.1972 (?)
Trainer and training leader in the cycling
section of BSG Wismut Karl-Marx-Stadt

T. comes from a working-class family. He
attended elementary school from 1933 to 1941 and
industry school in Chemnitz until 1944.During his
time at industry school he learned the trade of
mechanic.

In 1944 he was drafted into the reservists and
in October that year joined the Wehrmacht. In
1945 he was taken prisoner by the Americans. He
was released in January 1946 from the Rheinsberg
camp in Münster. Before returning to Chemnitz in
May 1946 he stayed in Leumershagen near Bielefeld
with an acquaintance from the prison camp, and
worked as a car mechanic in Lübbediesch. From
June 1946 to 1950 he worked as a car mechanic

at Auto Repairs Strauss in Chemnitz and from
1950 to 1952 at the Köhler company in Chemnitz.
Subsequently T. worked until 1953 as an employee
at the Otto Grotewohl Stadium in Aue. T. has
worked at the former Object 37 of SDAG Wismut
since 16.5.1953.

T. has been active in cycling since 1943 and
took part in youth races in Chemnitz in 1943 to
1944. After a pause due to the effects of war,
T. took up cycling again in 1949 and in 1952 won
100-kilometre GDR team time trial championship
as part of the Wismut team. He took part in
three Tours of the GDR as well as numerous other
significant races within the GDR, where he placed
well without reaching the absolute top places.

As a top GDR sportsman he was then employed at
the Otto Grotewohl Stadium in Aue.

According to information which can no longer
be proven, T. also raced several times in the
FRG. Local area reports on T. show that he was
intending to defect at a road race in the FRG but
instead returned to the GDR.

This information could neither be confirmed nor
substantiated by sources in Department VIII.

In 1956 T. retired from top sport at SDAG Wismut
and since then has been working as a trainer or
training leader in the cycling section of BSG
Wismut South, the current version of BSG Wismut
Karl-Marx-Stadt.

As is common in the GDR, T. is known to cyclists
by the nickname 'Honey'.

With regards to work performance, T. was below
average in his time as an active top sportsman.

Even after he gave up being a top sportsman
his work was somewhat lacking in organisation,
which was improved only following some stern
face-to-face conversations. He is now considered
to be a helpful, comradely colleague who is always
fit for service. Even if he's still not exactly
one of the fastest workers, what he does is done

carefully and to a high standard.

T. does not smoke or drink, is sociable and is valued by colleagues as a wise old fox who knows the ropes. In his work and also in his local neighbourhood he appears friendly although his overall behaviour is opaque.

(...)

In his personal behaviour towards work colleagues and long established acquaintances T. is trusting and tells them things 'in confidence'. To what extent this behaviour could lead to loose talk cannot yet be judged.

In connection with (?), T. told both informant 'Günther' and the chairman of the BSG Wismut Karl-Marx-Stadt that (?)is a distant relative of the road cyclist WIEDEMANN, who defected years ago.

TÜRKE further explained that a committee for enticing GDR sportsmen and women, in which both (?) and WIEDEMANN were key players, was active in the run-up to the Munich Olympics.

(...)

The result of this is that T. is speaking with several sources about the activities of WIEDEMANN and (?). It is suggested that a face-to-face with T. take place with the purpose of clarifying these discussions, and if his behaviour is in order, to contact him with a view to his working as an informant.

It is suggested that the meeting be held at Object Administration 'W'.

First Lieutenant Enzmann

NEUES DEUTSCHLAND

ORGAN DES ZENTRALKOMITEES DER SOZIALISTISCHEN EINHEITSPARTEI DEUTSCHLANDS

The Volkskammer voted unanimously to ratify the 'Law on the contract between the German Democratic Republic and the Federal Republic of Germany on issues of transport of 26 May 1972'. This is the first treaty between the GDR and the FRG, as highlighted by the Minister of Foreign Affairs, Otto Winzer, in the explanatory memorandum. […] Furthermore, the deputies accepted the 'Law regarding issues of nationality.' […]

The Minister for Foreign Affairs informed the deputies that it was an initiative of the government of the GDR which finally led to the agreement on traffic. This first treaty between the GDR and the FRG is a major step on the road to normal, good neighborly relations between the GDR and the FRG. He hailed the agreement as a real contribution to pan-European security and cooperation, and underlined its binding in international law. […]

Reprinted from 'GDR initiative resulted in legal international regulation',
17 October 1972

DIETER

By 1972 Sylvia and I were happy, and we were a real family. Then in October they signed an amnesty treaty. It meant that former GDR citizens who had defected – people like me – were deregistered. The defection was therefore no longer classified as a criminal act, so I had the same status as everyone else.

In principle I was able to travel back without facing charges. I was undecided about whether to risk it at first, but the need to go back and reunite the family was stronger than the fear of what might happen. I made arrangements for Sylvia and the girls to be taken care of in the event that something bad happened to me, and we decided to go.

THE THIRD LIFE
OF DIETER WIEDEMANN
(and the Fourth)

MfS511/80 BSTU0150

Karl-Marx-Stadt 6.12.72

Commitment!

As of today I commit myself to support the
activities of the Ministry for State Security
through my unofficial conspiratorial activity. I
hereby commit myself to the best of my abilities
and with the required consistency to take up the
fight against the enemies of the GDR. I am aware
that I must maintain absolute silence about this
activity and anything to do with this activity
and anything I learn about the means and methods
of the MfS, to anybody, including members of my
own family. My unofficial activity for the MfS
will be carried out under the alias 'Seppel'.

Henry Türke

90 Karl-Marx-Stadt

MfS511/80 BSTU0003/0004/0005/0006/0007

Karl-Marx-Stadt 08.12.72

Meeting report

On 06.12.72 from 17.30 to 20.40 a meeting was held between informant 'Seppel', Comrade Senior Lieutenant Ermann and the undersigned in the conspiratorial meeting room in the clubhouse in Grüna.

The following things were addressed concerning the assigned missions:

Problem Wiedemann (?)
Problem (?)
(...)

To point 1

The informant had a conversation with W. (?) on 05.12.72. The informant spoke with W. and asked him if he had heard anything about his (?) To this W. replied that he still didn't know if his (?) was coming. W.'s father had already made three applications to travel to the FRG but each had been turned down.

W. thinks that W. Dieter is now afraid of travelling to the GDR because of his father's rejected applications. This argument was used for a long time by a certain (?), with whom W. is often in contact. The subject of the problem of coming into the GDR was discussed further. If somebody brings children up to the age of three years, they can come by car. W. said this was no problem, as D. has young children.

In respect to this problem the informant received from us the following concrete instructions:

He should have a one-to-one discussion with W. this week and state the following:

As an old acquaintance, the informant should advise W. that Dieter should not travel to the GDR, because it could backfire. Dieter has disappointed many functionaries from the club (SCK) and from Flöha.

If any of them see Dieter, they may lose it with him.

From his own personal perspective he would be pleased if Dieter were to come. That way he can finally speak with somebody who knows exactly what cycle sport in the FRG is like. He'd love to speak with Dieter about this.

Concerning the second action:
The informant is at a functionary conference in Greiz from Sunday 10.12.72 to Thursday 14.12.72. He should canvass the opinions of functionaries about how they would behave if a top sportsman who had defected were now to travel back to the GDR.

The informant suggested that he should do this in the political training session, since this would be the least suspicious.

(...)

A short meeting with the informant was then agreed for 09.12.72. At this meeting the informant would report the results of the conversation with W. (?)

The next meeting after this was agreed for the 20.12.72 at 19.00.

In the course of the meeting the informant made an open and honest impression. His reports are factual and he himself made suggestions as to how to tackle problems, especially W. (?)

He was rather shocked about the truth of the relationship between W.(?) and his (?) because the informant assumed that W. trusted him and therefore would tell him the truth.

Ruttloff

MfS383/65 bd3, BSTU0035/0036

Karl-Marx-Stadt, 7.12.1972
People's Police, Flöha: Personal review
Wiedemann Karl
Born: 3.12.1904, Flöha
Resident: Wiesenstrasse 15, Flöha
Wiedemann Marianne
Born: 9.3.1914, Siegmar-Schönau
Resident: With husband

Previous requests for transit to the FRG:
1.
26.9.70-23.10.70
To visit:
(?)
Resident: Wuppertal-Ronsdorf
(?)
Relatives in the FRG:
Wiedemann Dieter, son
Born 17.6.1941
Resident: Neue Schule 4, Geldersheim
In the FRG since 4.7.1964

2.
05.05.71
Ilse Hermann
Born: 26.2.1915
Resident: Kleinsiedlung 37, Mitterteich
Housewife

3.
07.11-04.12.71
To visit:
(?)

4.
04.05-31.05.72
(?)

5.
20.12.72–02.01.73
To visit:
Wiedemann Dieter, son
Born 17.6.41
Resident: 9 Hindenburg Strasse, Dittelbrunn.
Lathe operator, Fichtel & Sachs, Schweinfurt
(Requested following the rejection of 28.11.72)

All applications were made by Karl Wiedemann,
and each was rejected by the People's Police
according to article IX/22 sub-paragraph 9.4

In the last discussion with Mr Wiedemann, on
28/11/72, Lieutenant Neuhäuser, department head
at Flöha, explained that the application would
be rejected because his son had committed treason
against the GDR, and had inflicted great political
damage upon the GDR.

First Lieutenant Kade

Mf383/65 bd3 BSTU0043/0044

Karl-Marx-Stadt 11.12.72
Report

On the short meeting held on 9.12.1972 from 18.00 to
19.00 in Karl-Marx-Stadt with informant 'Seppel'

The informant 'Seppel' reported on the execution
of the assigned mission

Face-to-face meeting with WIEDEMANN (?), as
follows:

On 7 and 8.12.1972 a personal conversation
took place between 'Seppel' and WIEDEMANN
(?) during which 'Seppel' again tried to get
information about the possible entry into the
GDR by WIEDEMANN Dieter. In accordance with the
mission, 'Seppel' was having serious misgivings
about a possible entry and visit by WIEDEMANN
Dieter because this could be taken badly by
the functionaries and active sportspersons of
the SC Karl-Marx-Stadt as well as the general
population of the area. These serious misgivings
were repeated during the two conversations on
7 and 8.12 and W (?) took the same view as in
previous meetings, that it was not certain that
WIEDEMANN Dieter would be visiting and that his
opinion is that his(?) would not be coming.
He was not worried about a possible visit by
his (?) because neither functionaries nor active
sportspeople would want to approach WIEDEMANN
Dieter or other such persons. Doing so would put
them at risk of being thrown out of the club.
WIEDEMANN (?)and his (?) would themselves have
felt the impact of the regulations with their
dismissal from the club following the defection.
The discipline of not maintaining contacts
with capitalist countries, which was imposed on
sportspeople and functionaries, would result
in W. Dieter being left completely unmolested

during a possible visit. This would also mean that
during such a visit he could devote all his time
to his relatives and to sorting out his personal
problems.

In a further conversation between 'Seppel' and
(?), a work colleague of W (?), he repeated W's view
that a visit by his (?) was not a certainty and
that his (?) would not be coming to the GDR any
time soon.

'Seppel' said that (?) does not know the actual
details and that W (?) does not give anything away
at work. Otherwise (?) would know all about the
personal problems of W (?).

The next meeting with 'Seppel' will be held on
Weds. 20.12 at 19.00 in Grüna, after his training
course.

W(?)is aware that 'Seppel', as he does every year,
will be with his training group in Oberwiesenthal
from 25.12.1972 to 7.1.1973, where they will also
bring in the New Year.

During the conversation with W (?) 'Seppel'
mentioned that he was personally interested in
meeting WIEDEMANN Dieter to talk about cycle
sport in the FRG and that his having contact
with WIEDEMANN Dieter would not cause him any
problems.

W(?) gave no reaction to this at all.

                    Senior Lieutenant Enzmann

MfS383/65 bd3, BSTU0048/0050/0052

Karl-Marx-Stadt   19.12.1972
Daybook Number: VIII/1760-II/1336/72
<u>Confidential!</u>
Council of Ministers of the German Democratic
Republic
Ministry of State Security
Administration: 'W' Karl-Marx-Stadt
Department: VIII
Sub-department: II
Clerk: Sergeant Meinhold
Telephone: 5288
Main department: XX
Area Administration: 'W' Karl-Marx-Stadt
District Officer: Ufw Ruttloff
Daybook Number: XX/1972/72

                    Investigation report
To be investigated: Wiedemann, (?)
Actually investigated: Wiedemann, (?)
Born: (?)
Address: (?)
Occupation: (?)
Place of work: (?)
Personal File: (?)
Personal ID #:   (?)
National Army: (?)
Visits to socialist countries:(?)
Arrival in West Germany: WIEDEMANN,
Dieter and Sylvia

(without application)
   In the local neighbourhood it has been
discovered that the person to be investigated
works at SDAG Wismut. Precisely which activities
he is involved in, e.g. working hours, the persons
asked could not say. It was occasionally observed
that he left home together with his wife between

06.15 and 06.30 a.m. On another occasion he went to work alone in the morning. In the afternoons he mostly comes home alone.

The wife of the person to be investigated,
Wiedemann,   (?)
Born: (?)
Address: (?)
Occupation: (?)
Personal ID #:   (?)
Personal File: (?)
Visits to socialist countries: (?)
is said to be an employee of VEB   (?).

As previously mentioned, she sometimes left home in the mornings with her husband and took the local bus to work. In the evenings she returned home between 16.30 and 17.00.

Meinhold   Meinhold
Captain   Sergeant

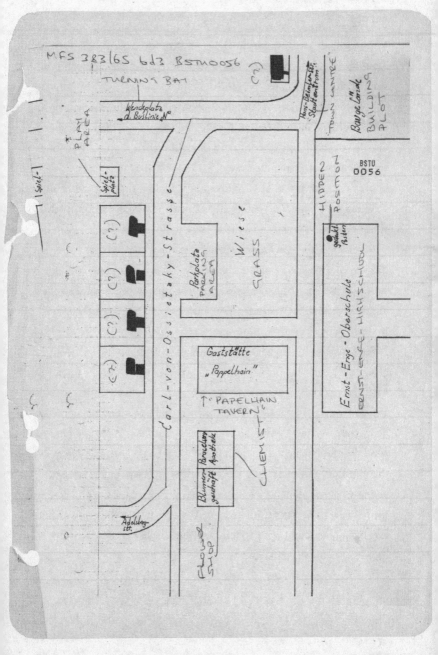

MFS 383/65 bd3 BSTU0056

TURNING BAY

Wendeplatz d. Buslinie N°

(?)

Hans-Beinlapratz, Stadtzentrum

TOWN CENTRE

Bauge Lände
BUILDING PLOT

PLAY AREA

Spiel-

Spielplatz

Spiel

Carl-von-Ossietzky-Strasse

(?)   (?)   (?)   (?)

Parkplatz
PARKING AREA

Wiese
GRASS

BSTU 0056

HIDDEN POSITION

gedeckt. Posten

Ernst-Enge-Oberschule
ERNST-ENGE-HIGH SCHOOL

Gaststätte "Pappelhain"

↑ "PAPPELHAIN TAVERN"

CHEMIST

Blumen geschäft   Bracelion Apotheke

FLOWER SHOP

Adelsberg-str.

DIETER

We appealed, and eventually they granted us a permit. It was 22 December, and our intention was to stay for ten days. My mum and dad were finally going to meet Nicole, Alex and Nina.

We set off very early because I was worried about what might happen at the border, but in the event they let me through just like everybody else. Given that it was Christmas I'd thought that there would be a lot of traffic, but we arrived quite early.

We decided it would be best if I left Sylvia and the girls in the car and went in first. That way I'd have a little time alone with my mum and dad. It had been eight years, and it made sense to do it that way.

When I got there my mum was still cleaning, and the first thing she did was chastise me for arriving too early. My dad was genuinely happy to see me, and he wanted to have a party because we were reunited after all those years. I knew straight away that it would be extremely difficult to make things all right with my mum, though.

She was jealous of Sylvia, and she was angry with me.

SYLVIA

We had wanted to unify the family, but there was tension immediately. They were angry with him, and angry with me. We'd spend hours sitting round talking, talking, talking … We'd be up until two o'clock in the morning, and everything would come out. It was hard for them to accept what he'd done to them, and it was very hard for them to accept me because I was the reason he'd left. We were trying our best to work everything out, but it was just terrible. Deep down I always knew it was broken with them, you know?

MfS383/65 bd3, BSTU0059/0060/0061/0062

Karl-Marx-Stadt   27.12.1972
                                          Confidential!

Council of Ministers of the German Democratic Republic

Ministry of State Security
Administration: 'W' Karl-Marx-Stadt
Department: VIII
Sub-department:2
Clerk: First Lieutenant Hupfer
Telephone: 5285
Main department: XX
Area Administration: Ruttloff
District Service Unit:
Daybook Number: VIII/1771/2/1339/72
Daybook Number:

Investigation report
To be investigated: Wiedemann, Carl
Actually investigated: Wiedemann, Carl, Max
Born: 3.12.1904 in Flöha
Address :   Flöha, 15
Wiesenstrasse since 10.6.59
Occupation: Car mechanic/
locksmith
Personal File: XIV 1599 407
Personal ID #:   031204426720
FE/Kl: 1 and 3
Permits to West Germany: Refused
   The person named above is not a member of
any party and does not appear in any form on a
socio-political level in his local neighbourhood.
Because of the defection of his son Dieter, those
in power in our society have not called upon him
for employment. Wiedemann does not express his
political views in any way and does not engage
in other conversations with other citizens. To

date he has supported the collection of donations for people's solidarity. On the one hand it could be said that Wiedemann is a politically disinterested person, on the other hand he could be unsympathetic towards our state. This can be concluded from his reticence and the less than friendly utterances of his wife.

In Wiedemann's case we are talking about a quiet and uncommunicative person. He is friendly to people but keeps himself to himself and does not get drawn into any discussions. He spends the vast majority of his spare time at home and in his garden. No complaints can be made about his morality. W. is of good repute but is not popular on account of his reticent behaviour.

Family relationships are in order. His wife: Wiedemann née Lang, Marianne

Born:	9.3.1914 in Siegma-Schönau
Address:	as per husband
Occupation:	Seamstress
Personal ID #:	090314526722
Personal File:	XIV 1599 723

is not a member of any party, does not belong to any democratic mass organisation and keeps herself away from socio-political events. She publicly expresses a negative attitude towards our state, even more so since the defection of her son, Dieter. However, Mrs Wiedemann expresses herself more to (?) and her comments lack a sense of purpose. For example, she complains about shortages in the shops and denies the truth of all our achievements. When her husband's applications for trips to West Germany were turned down she said 'When I start drawing my pension I'll give them what for.'

People we asked were of the opinion that, should she visit West Germany, Mrs Wiedemann would not tell the truth there, but would complain about conditions here. She is considered a non-beneficial person who belongs to reactionary forces in our society.

Mrs Wiedemann is a blabbermouth. She recently said that her son Dieter wants to come to the GDR soon. In this regard she also made public that her son defected because of a girl from West Germany. This female has stayed with relatives in Flöha, Wiesenstrasse (family DIRSCHE) and this is how Dieter got to know her. Mrs W. can be characterised as (?). On the basis of these characteristics she is not popular. Morally she is clean.

(...)

Contact with the son Dieter in the FRG is by post. The son regularly sends letters and parcels. One person we asked told us that earlier Mrs Wiedemann had met her son Dieter in Austria. Further details about this could not be obtained. Dieter W. was not seen again in Flöha.

The person to be investigated, W. Carl, made the following applications to visit West Germany, which were however declined:

```
from      6. 9.70 to 23. 10.70 declined
          5. 5.71 to funeral      "
          7. 11.71 to 4. 12.71    "
          20. 12.72 to 2. 1.73    "
```

The applications to visit West Germany are believed to concern
Wiedemann, Dieter   Son   (1972/73)
Born: 17.1.1941
Occupation: Turner at Fichtel & Sachs, Schweinfurt
Address: Dittelbrunn, Hindenburgstrasse 9

Hermann, Else   (1971 funeral)
Born: 26.2.1915
Housewife
Address: Mitterteich, Kleinsiedlung 37

```
(?)              (?) (?)
Born:            (?)  ·
Housewife
Address:     Wuppertal, (?)
```

Other foreign journeys of W. Carl

1959	Bulgaria
1960	USSR
1961	Tunisia
1962	Bulgaria
1963	Tunisia
1963	Bulgaria
1964	Morocco

Section leader

Hupfer

First Lieutenant

MfS491/63 BSTU0067

Flöha, 28.12.72

Flöha District Service Unit

Report on short meeting

With the informant 'Orion' in his apartment on 26.12.72.

(...)

On 25.12.72 Dieter Wiedemann came to visit him in his apartment. The informant had asked Wiedemann's mother to have Dieter call round if he was in Flöha over the holiday season.

Wiedemann brought his wife with him. During the conversation W.'s defection was touched upon. He said that he had no political reasons for his defection, that it was simply the fact that he wanted to marry his wife and this was the only solution he could see.

That aside, he was glad to get out of the house. He can't understand his mother because she has old-fashioned and bourgeois views and constantly confronts him with them. She hasn't changed at all and although he hasn't been home for a long time and has only been there a few days he's already had a few rows with her.

Wiedemann and his wife were well-dressed, though they did say that they both have to work in order to live well. They said nothing on the matter of politics.

(...)

Captain Langklotz

MfS383/65 bd3, BSTU0063/0064/0065/0066/0067/0068

MfS511/80 BSTU0010/0011/0012/0013/0014/0015
Karl-Marx-Stadt, 29.12.1972

Report

On the introduction of informant 'Seppel' into
the operative processing of Wiedemann, Dieter

In accordance with the agreed legend and
the pretext created, the informant 'Seppel' was
taken by car at around 12.45 on 28.12.1972 from
Oberwiesenthal to his garage in Karl-Marx-Stadt,
from where he was to take up personal contact
with WIEDEMANN (?). He then went to the latter's
place of work and, since he could not find him
there, went to his flat in (?) Street, Karl-Marx-
Stadt.

Before this, a telephone call had been made
to the informant's landlord in Oberwiesenthal,
pretending to be from the general directorate
of the working group for sport. It requested
that the informant attend an urgent briefing of
the general directorate concerning his planned
employment as a trainer with the BSG in Gera.
The result was that both his training group in
Oberwiesenthal and his deputy were under the
impression that the informant had been obliged to
go to the general directorate on account of this
urgent matter.

(...)

It was agreed with the informant that he should
visit Dieter WIEDEMANN at his parents' apartment
at 15 Wiesenstrasse, Flöha, at about 15.00.
Initially the informant encountered only the
mother of Dieter and (?). He briefly told her the
reasons for his visit. At first she was sceptical,
but having been given the details she opened up,
promised to help the informant and asked him to
come back around 16.30 as Dieter would be there

around that time. Dieter was planning a big night out that evening in Karl-Marx-Stadt with his wife, but should have enough time to address the matter.

The reason for her initial mistrust was that she wanted to know how the informant had known that Dieter was in town visiting. The informant replied that Dieter had been seen in a white car (BMW) on Christmas Day at about ten o'clock, on the road between Niederwiesa and Flöha. The informant stated that he had been on his way to Freiberg at that time.

Besides, the informant had already asked (?) several times about a possible visit by Dieter. He had not yet mentioned his problem to him but had resolved to do so. In this way, the initial reticence of the mother was completely swept aside and a general, personal conversation was struck up, further supported by the mother's assurances that she wanted to help.

At around 16.45 the informant came back to visit the family WIEDEMANN. This time he met Dieter WIEDEMANN and his wife, both his parents and his three children.

After a very hearty – and in the opinion of the informant genuine – greeting from Dieter WIEDEMANN, a conversation developed in the presence of the above mentioned persons. This conversation was occasionally disrupted by the children and cut short because the couple wanted to get ready for their night out in Karl-Marx-Stadt.

The informant presented the details of his son's attempted defection, his address in Karl-Marx-Stadt as well as the last time he was seen in Zingst.*

The informant said that he had little hope of ever hearing from his son again, since he knew of other such cases where attempts to defect across the Baltic had resulted in death.

---

* A municipality on the Baltic coast.

However, for his peace of mind he would put this matter to Dieter in order to use this one final chance in the search for his son. In this respect he explained that his father-in-law had lived in the FRG, but had recently died. However, for health reasons he hadn't been able to burden him with such a request. Neither could he use the acquaintances of the father-in-law on account of some longstanding personal tensions.

W. Dieter expressed some interest and promised to help him by writing to the appropriate tracing service and informing him in writing immediately he had initiated this.

The other persons present also showed understanding towards the problems of the informant and considered it a matter of course that they would try to be of help.

About three-quarters of an hour after the informant entered the apartment, WIEDEMANN (?), from Karl-Marx-Stadt, came in and was shown into the living room. Initially he was obviously startled and sceptical about the presence of the informant, and only after quite some time did he become more receptive towards the informant. The reasons for this behaviour are that (?) had strongly denied to the informant that Dieter would be travelling to the GDR this year. On the other hand he had told the informant that he had had no contact with Dieter, in order to avoid problems at work.

Both agreed not to mention the visit in any way, and nor the contents of the discussions at work.

At this point Dieter suggested that he would mail the informant without revealing the sender's details, so that the informant would not encounter any problems at work or with his sporting activities. To this the informant replied that he had been in postal contact with his late father-in-law without getting into trouble, and suggested that Dieter really should write the sender's details on any post to him.

It was finally agreed that Dieter would use the name and address of a neighbour or a family member living in the same block, since he was still well known in the GDR as a racing cyclist and in no way did he want to cause problems for the informant in resolving this important personal matter.

(?) was satisfied with this commitment.

In the course of further personal conversation it became known that Dieter is working as a lathe operator or fitter for the firm Fichtel & Sachs, is fully satisfied with this work and brings home enough money to live well according to western standards. His wife does not go to work because of the three small children.

He has completely given up cycling and hasn't ridden since 1967 when the three remaining pro-teams in the FRG all folded due to lack of money. On top of that, he had no time due to family commitments. He simply kept himself informed via radio and TV about cycling in the FRG and internationally, though information was scarce due to cycling's lack of popularity in the FRG.

On the subject of former cycling functionaries or active GDR cyclists who had fled to the FRG, WIEDEMANN, Dieter said that for a long time he had been in contact with the former GDR cycling functionary (?), but that this person no longer has anything to do with cycling in the FRG. He's already undergone three operations and during the third operation they opened him up and stitched him back up without doing anything because (?) is so hopelessly ill and doesn't have long to live.

Many a time he has been in contact with (?) (or similar), the defected cyclist from the Flöha area who now works as a trainer in a cycling club. Otherwise he has absolutely no contact with functionaries or active cyclists in the FRG.

Dieter is hopeful about measures taken by the FRG government to promote sport, whereby trainers receive grants from the state for training and developing juniors. However it's early days and it could be years before it bears fruit. The problem is that, just as in the GDR, cycling is not popular enough.

The family WIEDEMANN expressed their joy that entry into the GDR for Dieter's family had been approved, although they didn't say that this had been organised by the brother (?).

Dieter was fully occupied with visiting his relatives and devoting himself to his parents and with the exception of the informant he had not met with any former cyclists or functionaries. Just the former cyclist (?), who had openly refused to have contact with Dieter.

Dieter's father said that he had been very affected by this behaviour – i.e. open refusal of contact by former work colleagues and cyclists because of the defection of his son.

W. Dieter carried out his family visits in the areas of Flöha and Karl-Marx-Stadt using the car of his (?) so that he would not be so conspicuous in his own western car. He would use his own car only for the most basic shopping trips.

He let it be known to the informant that the reasons for his illegal departure from the GDR were that he had already got to know his current wife before then, and had wanted to build a life together with her. The informant noticed on several occasions that Dieter's wife can be noticeably pretty in appearance and he could understand Dieter's actions.

Dieter W. and his wife were receptive and accommodating towards the informant, and a further personal get-together was arranged for the coming year in the informant's apartment during Dieter's next visit.

Dieter saw no further opportunity to see the informant during his current stay because he didn't have time to travel to Oberwiesenthal and didn't want to cause problems for the informant by meeting in public.

None of the family members entered into political discussions or stated political opinions. This was obviously avoided, although the vast majority of the time available was devoted to the matter of the informant.

Dieter and his wife left the apartment to go out in Karl-Marx-Stadt just before the informant. Again they used the car of (?).

In a brief conversation between the father and the informant, the father stated that, though he's sixty-eight, he still works as a mechanic or fitter at the sewage works in Flöha. He still works three days a week, and the work gives him great joy. The rest of his time is devoted to his garden, and to cycling. From a physical perspective he feels completely well, and looking at him you would say he's a man in his early fifties.

In summary, it must be concluded that the informant fulfilled his mission by sticking to the legend, and has initiated contact with Dieter WIEDEMANN which can be built upon in the designated way.

In his preparation for and evaluation of this mission the informant made an open and honest impression. He visibly made efforts to fulfil the mission, and found it valuable to be instructed again before taking up contact as planned with (?) and his visit with Dieter.

In his evaluation of the implementation of the mission, he said it had not been easy to achieve his objective in accordance with the legend, and that he appreciated that carrying out missions can be difficult. The next meeting with the informant was arranged for 17.1.1973, 18.00 in Grüna.

The informant will be working as a trainer until 14.1.1973 in Oberwiesenthal, where it will be difficult to approach him without raising suspicions. His wife will be in Oberwiesenthal from 30.12.1972 to 17.1.1973.

At about 20.30 the informant was driven from Karl-Marx-Stadt back to Oberwiesenthal. The return journey, like the outward one, took place without complications.

The informant was dropped off in Oberwiesenthal around 23.00 without incident.

First Lieutenant Enzmann

MfS491/63 BSTU0075/0076

Karl-Marx-Stadt, 11.1.73

Report

At 10.00 on 26.12.72 I was visited by my former friend and classmate Dieter Wiedemann, who defected in 1964. He was accompanied by his wife and daughter. In answer to my question whether he'd had any problems visiting the GDR he answered no. He also said nothing when I asked him what he thought about his remaining in the FRG. Wiedemann and his wife were very open. W. said that he was working at Fichtel & Sachs in Schweinfurt. He is a turner in the test department for shock-absorbers. W. came to the GDR in a BMW 1600. He said he'd put his car in a garage to make his visit inconspicuous. I am to extend his greetings to all classmates because he doesn't have time to visit many people. According to W. he'd only visited his former club comrade (?) in Niederwiesa. I've told W. that I am organising a class reunion at the town café in 1973. I am going to invite other defectors from our year to this reunion. In previous years W. has had contact with (?). When asked about his mother, he said that she's an acquired taste. You always have to be careful what you tell her. On 31.12.72 I went to visit W. at his parents' apartment. W. was not there. In conversation with his mother she said that W. had had invitations from many friends but she'd warned him against going. In her opinion he could be asked provocative questions about his defection which could put him in trouble. You never know what many people's real intentions are. Wiedemann wants to write to me when he comes back to the GDR. He also wants to keep in touch about the reunion.

'Orion'

MFS 383/65 Bd3 0057   4

KITCHEN *Küche*

BATHROOM *Bad*

Flur ENTRANCE

LIVING ROOM *Wohn-zimmer*

BALCONY

Bal-kon BEDROOM *Schlaf-zimmer*

Wohnung des Wiedemann ▉▉▉
HOME OF WIEDEMANN (?)

MfS511/80 BSTU0020/0021/0022

Karl-Marx-Stadt 24.1.73

Report

On 19.1.73 and 22.1.73 a private, one-to-one
conversation with (?) Wiedemann was held at
his workplace. The first thing to state is that
(?) is open with me and in no way reticent,
and therefore understands the problem we
discussed when I visited Dieter and considers me
trustworthy. In our conversations we touched upon
Dieter and (?) stated the following about Dieter's
stay in Flöha:
(...)

At the beginning of the visit there was a
certain tension between (?) and Dieter which
only dissipated somewhat during the course of
the visit. As previously reported this tension
is related to Dieter's defection and the personal
consequences for (?)'s sporting development.
Tensions were also triggered by the behaviour
of the mother, who, despite the age of both sons,
still tries to treat them like children. (?) didn't
go into any further detail about the family
relationships during Dieter's visit. On the
behaviour of Dieter's wife, (?) said that nothing
pleases her and she can seem very feisty. She has
an answer for everything. Dieter went a number
of times with his wife on visits to Karl-Marx-
Stadt and once went dancing at the Hotel Moscow.
(...)

'Seppel'

MfS383/65 bd3, BSTU0072

Karl-Marx-Stadt, 14. 2.1973

Application to bar entry

It is proposed that

Wiedemann, Dieter

Born: 17.6.41 in Flöha

Address: Schweinfurth, Josef-Wurm-Strasse 15
turner with Fichtel & Sachs, Sweinfurth
be barred entry to all areas of the GDR.

W., Dieter a top sportsman of the GDR, defected in July 1964 during a race in the FRG. With this defection W. inflicted social damage upon the then national team of the GDR and his defection had a negative effect on his former club and local neighbourhood.

The behaviour of W., who until then had received every possible form of support for his development, was widely condemned. Approval for entry into the GDR was also widely condemned by the GDR public.

During the New Year period, W. entered the GDR by using his relatives to circumvent the existing entry bar, introduced in the district of Flöha. This could not be prevented.

During this time in the GDR, W. visited the cyclist Wolfgang Lötzsch,[*] who has been de-delegated from the Sport Club Karl-Marx-Stadt, in whose house no proof of an illegal border crossing could be found and who, until then, had denied all contact with capitalist countries.

W. further visited his former trainer in Karl-Marx-Stadt, who on account of W.'s defection was dismissed from Sport Club Karl-Marx-Stadt.

---

[*] Lötzsch is Wiedemann's cousin.

In the case of W.'s parents, we are dealing with people who have a negative attitude towards the GDR, and these negative attitudes are publicly aired by W.'s mother in particular. She tried to boast of her son's material development in her local neighbourhood.

As a result of this, it is proposed that W., who by the aforementioned act of defection as one of the most well-known former cyclists in the GDR, caused considerable political damage, be barred from entering the GDR.

Department XX Leader

Major Schönherr

MfS383/65 bd3, BSTU0074/75

Karl-Marx-Stadt 26.2.73

<u>Confidential!</u>

Council of Ministers of the German Democratic
Republic
Ministry of State Security
Administration: 'W' Karl-Marx-Stadt
Department: VIII
Sub-department: II
Clerk: Lieutenant Mueller
Telephone: 5286
Main department: XX Karl-Marx-Stadt 26. 2.1973
Area Administration:'W' Kmst
Daybook Number: VIII/158-II/124/73
District Officer: Ufw Ruttloff
Daybook Number: XX/129/73

Investigation report

To be investigated: Wiedemann, Carl
Actually investigated: Wiedemann, Carl, Max
Born: 3.12.1904 in Flöha
Address: Flöha, Wiesenstrasse 15
Place of work: VEB Services/Town
Technical
Occupation: Motor mechanic

In the local party area, W. Dieter is depicted as
a traitor. The comrades of the local neighbourhood
show absolutely no friendship towards him. It
could be said that a large number of the comrades
were shocked when W. Dieter turned up with his
car and his family. It is inconceivable that such
an arrival (from the FRG) would go unnoticed.
Another part of the population expressed
incomprehension about it. As a racing cyclist, W.
had had 'sugar blown up his arse', he'd been given

gifts by the state (TVs, radio sets and various
other presents). People are wondering why, despite
the treacherous act of W. Dieter, the state organs
of the GDR are permitting entry.

Other opinions are that it is better to allow
W. Dieter into the GDR than to allow the father,
W. Carl, to visit West Germany. The father would
portray our GDR in a bad light and cause trouble.
Such a case could cause political damage.

In general all local people were astonished that
such an entry from the FRG is possible.

First Lieutenant Hopfer   Lieutenant Müller

MfS383/65 bd3, BSTU0080

Flöha District Service Unit, 29.11.1973

Dieter Wiedemann – FRG

On 12.8.1973 I had a class reunion at Flöha
town café. W. also took part in it. In answer
to a question from his classmates, he said he'd
ridden three years as a professional. The team
in Schweinfurt had then disbanded, and he said
he hadn't been able to find a good contract
elsewhere. He wasn't worse off in his present job
in the shock-absorber test department in Fichtel
& Sachs.

His income as a professional fluctuated
between 1,200 and 6,000 DM. W. said that since his
defection, there had been great political unrest
in West Germany. Over here, nothing had changed
in this respect. He could have thought that time
has stood still. He wouldn't enter into political
discussions.

When (?) of Karl-Marx-Stadt asked how he felt
the system in the FRG compared with ours, W. left
the reunion without saying goodbye.

At around 19.00 on 13.8.1973, W. came to my
apartment with 10 marks to settle the bill we'd
paid on his behalf. He said he wouldn't come to
any more reunions because he'd only come to see
his old friends, and not to discuss politics.

W. will next visit the GDR to see (?), who lives
in Flöha on (?) Street. In my opinion W. has a good
relationship with (?) in Flöha.

'Orion'

RAINER

When he came back he and I became friends again. At the class reunions he'd never talk about himself, though, or about having ridden the Tour de France. That's just the way he was.

NICOLE, ALEX AND NINA

Those trips to the east were a bit strange. We always used to look forward to seeing our auntie and uncle, the grandparents and the rabbits, but nobody seemed to have any fun.

We had quite a good standard of living here. We had a bedroom of our own, a car, holidays. There was colour in our life, you know? The problem with GDR was that there just wasn't any. Everything was grey.

The yoghurt. The yoghurt was strange. The food was always really bad, and the pollution was terrible. Of course as a kid you don't understand that, but you understand that your breathing is different. You could *taste* the air there.

They burned brown coal, and the smell was awful. It made your clothes smell really bad.

RAINER

Everybody watched western TV, even though it was technically illegal. The problem was that Flöha is in a valley, so there was no reception. I set up a group, we got about 500 families to pay ten marks each, and we organised everything. We dug channels, cabled the town, got a helicopter and managed to get the antenna installed. We wanted a different perspective, and we were interested in politics. What you did was specify that it was for 'international' TV, as opposed to 'western' TV.

Prior to that I'd often walked to the station with the mayor, and we'd chatted about this and that. After the business with the antenna he never spoke to me again. He just completely blanked me.

DIETER

When you visited the GDR you had to deposit money for each day you were staying, and they gave you eastern marks in exchange. The rate was 1:1, which was ridiculous, but the upshot was that if I went for two weeks I gave them about 1,000 western Deutschmarks and they gave me about 200 back. Of course that was the whole point; the GDR was using it as a mechanism to get foreign currency.

The way it worked was that you had to spend the money you'd exchanged on entering. Things were much cheaper, but there wasn't much that you wanted to buy. It was also forbidden to export eastern marks or eastern products. You'd have wanted to buy things like Meissen porcelain, but they didn't want westerners going over and exploiting the fact that prices were subsidised. So ultimately it was just easier to leave the money with my mum and dad.

Equally, GDR visitors to the west were only allowed to take a minuscule amount of money. They wanted to limit their spending power, and the result was that the FRG government gave all GDR visitors welcome money, 100 marks.

One time we were on our way home, queuing in the exclusion zone at the border as usual. It was always extremely stressful, a dreadful experience for me, Sylvia and the kids. The guards were invariably pretty unsavoury people, so you just kept your mouth shut and hoped they wouldn't single you out.

You had to fill in a document declaring how many western marks you had in your wallet, and hand it in to them. I did that but as we got close to the crossing itself – I think we were the fourth car or something – one of the guards came up and said, 'Pull over to the side.' So I did and he asked for all of our documents. He took them off and then he came back and said, 'I know who you are and I know what you did.' I said, 'I don't know what you're talking about – it happened sixteen years ago and there's been an amnesty for eight!' Anyway, we had to follow him into this big garage, a grey concrete block with no windows.

We had to wake the twins and remove everything from the car, and then they set about taking it to pieces. They were rough with the car, and with the contents. There was nothing, but I'd bought a pair of shoes while I was there and hadn't declared them. Everybody did it, but they'd decided that they were going to make me pay. I'd already declared that I had seventy western marks because that was what I needed to fill the tank. He therefore gave me a fine of 120 marks, knowing full well that I couldn't pay it. I said, 'You know I don't have the money, so what am I supposed to do?' and he said, 'Well, look around you, you're surrounded by your wealthy western friends! Look at all these Mercedes and BMW's! It looks like you're going to have to ask one of *them* to lend you the money, because otherwise you're going to be spending the night in a cell.'

I therefore had to ask a complete stranger to lend me money. I had no ID because they'd taken it, and no way of proving that I was an honest person. I had to find somebody to lend me the money, and all I was able to give him as security was my word. Eventually I found someone, but the whole thing took three or four hours. It was the most degrading thing that ever happened to me, which of course was the whole point of the exercise.

Sylvia had had enough. She never went again, and the kids never went again. I only ever set foot in the GDR once more, a school reunion in 1985. It just wasn't worth it.

NICOLE, ALEX AND NINA

He never discussed his cycling career, his GDR life or the defection, not ever. Nobody knew about that.

We had a happy childhood. Everything was built around the family, around being together and staying together. So our mum didn't work, and we always had breakfast together. On Sunday we'd be off cycling together, or hiking, and holidays were usually built around hiking, skiing or swimming. We had wonderful family holidays in Austria, Italy, on the North Sea and in Denmark.

We had a lot of exchange students to stay with us, kids from other countries. Our parents were both very open-minded like that.

SYLVIA

People in the GDR weren't living in poverty like they had been before. The standard of living wasn't as high as in the west, but nor was it like Russia. There was no unemployment, and the state provided everybody with a place to live and enough money to live on. What they didn't have were the brands that you could get in the west, and so of course they were even more sought-after there.

By the time Dieter's mum reached pensionable age there was a thaw in relations between the two governments, and she started to visit here. She'd drag me around the shops for hours and hours, trying to get the best price for the things they wanted.

You remember the angora rabbits Dieter told you about at the beginning? Well, his mum used to send us the wool, and I would sell it to a textile factory nearby. The money would go into a separate bank account, and when they needed something I would get it for them using the wool money. Dieter's brother and sister-in-law liked to have western brands, and it was a way for them to have the things they couldn't get. So things like coffee, shower gel, decent quality tights for Eberhard's wife, cutlery.

It became a way of life, and I think it was like that for a lot of divided families. You couldn't have day-to-day contact, and so you ended up almost as trading partners. It cost us money and time, but it was Dieter's family and I felt a duty to help. The problem was that it became progressively more time-consuming. They wanted more and more stuff, and it started to undermine the relationship between us. It was fragile enough anyway, and the trading just put it under more strain.

As they saw it we had a responsibility to provide because we were in the 'golden' west. Notwithstanding the fact that we had three kids and only one income, they assumed we were rich. They thought we could just send whatever they wanted.

So I always felt put upon, and all I got out of it was the feeling that I couldn't do right for doing wrong. When the factory stopped buying the wool it was a blessing, to be honest.

Dieter's dad was a good man, but they used to send him lists of the things they wanted. It started to feel like we were just there to help them get the things they couldn't get at home.

DIETER

The paradox of GDR communism is that it actually created an extreme form of capitalism.

DIETER

It broke down completely in 1981. They had bad pollution in the GDR, and Eberhard's wife suffered with asthma. They couldn't get the medicine they needed, so Sylvia had to go to the doctor and ask him for a favour. We explained the situation and he gave us the medicine, but the problem was that she needed a repeat prescription. It wasn't her fault, but there was no way the doctor could give her it without examining the patient. So getting the medicine would have involved cheating the doctor, cheating the health insurance, cheating everybody.

My dad came to see us and the first thing he said was 'Listen, you need to go to the doctor and get her the prescription. If you don't I'm going home and that will be that'. That was the final straw.

DIETER

So now you know how it all ended, and of course everybody blamed everybody else. I blamed my mum, she blamed me, and my poor dad was stuck in the middle of it all.

Looking back, I suppose we were all victims. I hadn't seen my family for all those years, and no relationship could survive that without being seriously compromised.

RAINER

There was always a kind of inner contact between me and Dieter. I guess it was because we'd grown up together and because, indirectly, I'd been partly responsible for his having met Sylvia. Even after all those years it hadn't left us.

MfS XIV09038811 BSTU00007

12.4.82

My dears,

I'd like to take pen to paper and write to you. Many thanks for Rainer's letter. We're glad that Rainer's mum was able to spend a few nice days, and hopefully this can happen more often. Obviously you're aware of how things are between me, my parents and my brother. Unfortunately it can't be patched up. But let's put that to one side.

One of the things to come out of this situation is that I'm giving away the prizes from my sporting career to certain people. My parents know and are handing the following items over to you:

1 silver canteen of cutlery for six people
1 lead crystal vase, 16 cm high
1 couch
1 coffee table
2 armchairs
1 corner cabinet

Perhaps you can use these things for a weekend house. Otherwise give them away.

1 hairpiece for your wife Brigitte
1 pair of white ladies' shoes (Bulgarian)

Give them away if they don't fit.

1 set of bed linen (2 pillowcases/4 pillows)
1 rug which belongs to Sylvia and perhaps your mum can bring with her.

I hope that this will bring you a little happiness.

So that's all for today.

Many hearty greetings to you all, as well as Annemarie and Erich

From Dieter and family*

---

* Reprinted from Rainer Müller's personal file.

MfS XIV09038811 BSTU00009

Flöha 5 May 1982

Karl-Marx-Stadt Area Command

Flöha District Service Unit

<u>Department XX</u>

Departments M and VI of Karl-Marx-Stadt Area Command have made the following comments (...)

Furthermore, a connection between the Müller family and the former cyclist Dieter Wiedemann has come to light.

W. told the Müller family in a very personal letter dated 12.4.82 that he was giving them various sports prizes as well as other items.* (...)

Major Weiss

---

*   Reprinted from Rainer Müller's personal file.

RAINER

Of course I remember the wall coming down – everyone does. What did I think? I thought we were free.

DIETER

I only ever saw my dad once more, in 1991. I got a call to say that he was ill and that I should go quickly. He died two days later.

RAINER

Within eighteen months Brigitte and I both lost our jobs, because the VEBs we were working in disappeared. We were both in our late forties, and suddenly we were out of work. Everything just started closing down, you know? Psychologically it was a difficult time. An *extremely* difficult time.

We were lucky because we both managed to find work fairly quickly, but you still have high unemployment around here.[*] People see the images of the wall coming down, all those happy people flooding through.

DIETER

You ask if you can ever be free of it, but that's probably too simplistic. You get on with your life, bring your kids up, live your life as best you can. You try to be a good man and a good father, but I don't suppose you can ever be completely free of it. What happened obviously had a profound effect on me and my family, but I'm probably not qualified to articulate it.

---

[*] Flöha had a registered population of 13,200 in 1989. Twenty years later it was under 10,000.

NICOLE, ALEX AND NINA

He's an extremely quiet person, and he very seldom expresses his opinion. People mistake that for a lack of enthusiasm, or a lack of joy, but you have to understand the world he grew up in.

He's very intelligent and he can be quite expansive, but it takes time. If you put him in the middle of a group he'll wait until somebody comes up to him and asks him something. People say he's hard to know, but the few friends he has are friends for life. That's his character, though, not the fact that he's from the GDR.

Yes, but that character was formed in the GDR, wasn't it?

SYLVIA

It was the day after our silver wedding anniversary, and he came off his bike on his way to work. They operated, but it took him a year to recover.

RAINER

Dieter was very good to us. We had to build a new life, and he and Sylvia were always there for us.

We were lucky because we both managed to find work quite quickly. We survived, and Dieter came and helped me when I built this place. He's a good man, Dieter Wiedemann.

NICOLE, ALEX AND NINA

He always tried to keep his perfect little family together, and nobody from outside could penetrate it.

It was as if he was protecting his treasure trove.

He took early retirement when he was fifty-seven. He looks after his garden, they travel a bit, and he spends time with his grandkids. He has four of them, and they're his pride and joy.

SYLVIA

He's changed over the years, but change comes slowly, doesn't it? He's become less inhibited in the way he acts around other people, and they say that's typical of former GDR people.

DIETER

I last saw my brother in 2002, at a Wismut reunion. We sat together and chatted a bit, but that was all.

SYLVIA

After reunification they introduced a 'solidarity surcharge' for the east. It was supposed to last five years and yet here we are, twenty-five years on, and we're still paying it.

THE FOURTH LIFE OF DIETER WIEDEMANN

Two moments, both ostensibly innocuous. The first a conversation with Klaus Huhn, at his flat in East Berlin. In defending an ideology – or, more specifically, its interpretation and application – under which he thrived professionally and personally, he informed me, 'It's a shame that people are so fixated on this thing about the Stasi.' Klaus' assertion was that the Stasi was necessary within the context of the Cold War, but that in practical terms it was largely immaterial in the life quotidian of most GDR citizens.

Then Manfred Weissleder, on a dank autumn morning at his home in Weimar. The dashing, handsome, rapier-quick star of the 1960 Peace Race remained convinced that he'd never had any 'issues' with the Stasi. His having ridden for the apolitical SC Karl-Marx-Stadt had presented some practical difficulties, but not, *per se*, ideological ones. His assertion was that the DHfK riders were more engaged politically, ergo better placed to make political capital. However, he'd never felt that his lack of ideological conviction had directly compromised his cycling career. He'd been forthright at times, downright wilful at others, and, like any number of testosterone-fuelled young athletes, had challenged the status quo. He remained convinced, however, that the authorities he'd crossed swords with had been strictly of the cycling variety. He was adamant that the Stasi had played no part in his life, and that his sporting career hadn't been in any way conditioned by them.

Sad to say but the reality was entirely other not only for him, but for all GDR cyclists. And, by extension, for all the thousands of state-sponsored athletes who represented their country over its forty-year existence.

My starting position for this book was that it wouldn't fall into the Stasi 'trap'. I was broadly supportive of the socialist canon, and resolved that the narrative wouldn't become mired in what Klaus euphemistically termed 'The Flying Dutchman'. My conviction was that I would avoid making sweeping judgements about the GDR as a state, and it was precisely this conviction which informed my methodology in writing it. Put simply, I'd no intention of writing a treatise on GDR socialism, much less the Stasi. Rather, I would let Dieter and Sylvia tell their story and, with a fair wind, that of the sporting leviathan which was the Peace Race.

I wasn't deluding myself that the Stasi wouldn't have a part to play, simply because Dieter Wiedemann had defected. I was, however, utterly deluded in respect to its malevolence and reach, and to the politicisation of daily life in the GDR. The fact is that, notwithstanding its amorphous nature, the Stasi *was* everywhere, even in the formative years of the GDR. It was your former classmate, your coach and your colleague at the sport club. It was the shop steward at your place of work, your neighbour, as likely as not your very good friend. If the party – and its evident paranoia in respect to all things western – established the qualifying criteria for 'enemies of the state', the Stasi applied it more or less pejoratively. That much of its methodology was predicated on falsehoods was seemingly academic. In the GDR interpretation of socialism everything was subjugate to the *idea*, and all truths therefore transmutable. And therein, in its colossal hubris and arrogance, lay the cancer at the heart of the Eastern Bloc dystopia.

The obvious question, therefore, is whether Dieter Wiedemann was a 'victim' of the GDR or, like Klaus, one of its beneficiaries. Dieter's excellence as a cyclist afforded him the opportunity to travel, a basic human right denied to all but a tiny minority. In that sense he was extremely unusual and, amidst the lunacy of the Cold War, extremely privileged. By the same token it could be argued that he and his like – Täve included – were but pawns in a geopolitical game of chess. An obvious question, then, but one which isn't so very easy to distil. The GDR put a roof over your head and offered a job for life (at least until it committed political and financial euthanasia) just so long as you were suitably convinced, or suitably opportunistic. However, those who weren't, those who refused to subscribe to what amounted to a monumental self-deceit, were simply thrown to the wolves. The millions who saw no alternative but to play along, as often as not in order simply to be left alone, would have cause to contemplate their own duplicity. Their own moral bankruptcy. Hans Modrow, one of the GDR's few credible politicians, made reference to 'the deformation of character by ideology.'

Dieter Wiedemann will never know whether his mother attempted suicide in the wake of his defection, or whether it was part of the Stasi's bungled plan to repatriate him. She never spoke of it, and nor did his brother Eberhard when we met. Nor was Dieter privy to the desolation the Stasi visited upon their father, a good man in a horrific storm. What he does know is that his family was torn asunder as a direct conse-quence of his having fallen in love with a girl from Giessen, some 200 miles west of Flöha. However, only now, fifty years on, is he becoming acquainted with the full extent of the damage, and with the extent of the psychosis which enveloped the state he represented (if that is the right word) with such distinction. Peace Race rider or otherwise, he's not so very different from any number of former East Germans in that respect. Just like them he's trying to come to terms with his shadow life, and with the collateral effect of his decision to defect. Just like them he's having to find a new way to live, and to find an antidote for the venom contained within his Stasi file. Dieter Wiedemann is a Tour de France finisher. He is a man of resolve, but his road to redemption is going to be long, and not a little painful.

And the Peace Race? In Leipzig I met with Uwe Ampler, Klaus' son. He won the thing three times in the eighties and then, when the wall fell, rode the Tour de France for a professional team. When I asked him about his Peace Races he said, somewhat dolefully, that his victories were as nothing compared with his father's 1963 triumph. Uwe Ampler was a very fine cyclist, but by the end the event, the sporting synthesis of communism's great victory, had become a pale imitation of its former self. Though the racing was never less than thrilling, the idealism and optimism which had illuminated those early editions had largely dissipated. The proletariat had long since ceased to believe and so, well intentioned or otherwise, the Friedensfahrt served largely to remind them of their rulers' duplicity. It was an intrinsic part of the state apparatus, and the state was moribund economically, ideologically and, in the final analysis, politically. So yes, the perfect sporting metaphor right to the last.

It survived reunification, but ultimately became naught but another under-funded stage race in professional cycling's bloated calendar. The Peace Race became a parody of itself, a Cold War construct subject to the vagaries of the new world marketplace. It staggered on until 2006, but by then it had become an itinerant event, and a travesty. The final edition, won by an anonymous Italian named Gianpaolo Cheula, visited neither Berlin, Warsaw nor Prague. When the sponsorship dried up altogether, it put this once great spectacle out of its misery.

It spluttered back into some sort of half-life in 2014. Jozef Regec, a former Peace Race yellow jersey with political aspirations, acquired the rights, but inexplicably saw fit to dispense with the dove. Too heavy with Cold War symbolism, he blustered to nobody in particular. Regec then failed to garner sufficient political momentum for a relaunch, and the project was stillborn. A three-day under-23 version of the race still takes place in the Czech Republic each May. It's organized by Jan Svorada, the great Slovak sprinter who won the first post-communist Peace Race and later stages at the Giro, Vuelta and Tour. It's a nice event but, sad to say, almost entirely irrelevant.

The spirit of the Peace Race lives on, however, and the idea lives on. It resides in the hearts and minds of those who took part, those who bore witness and the few, like Täve Schur, who truly understood what it symbolized during those back-breaking post-war years. Täve, still tub-thumping for Marx in his mid-eighties, is very much in demand for book signings and personal appearances, whilst Klaus Huhn's appetite for communist invective is insatiable.

Elsewhere former Peace Racers gather each May at the Museum in Kleinmühlingen. They emerge from Poland and from Holland, from the Lebanon and from Russia. They speak different languages, come from different backgrounds, and have fashioned different 21st century lives. They share a genuine sense of kinship, however, engendered by their having contributed to the greatest annual sporting event ever created. For all that it became a political football, the Peace Race remains, at root, a thing of genuine wonder, the sporting synthesis of a beautiful, utopian ideal.

As I write Sylvia Hermann, the girl in the bedroom window, lies in a hospital bed in Düsseldorf. She is terminally ill with breast cancer, and it's touch and go whether she will see the publication of this book. Through the days, weeks and months spent trying to understand and then render this thing, I am reminded always of her unbreakable optimism, of her humility and forbearance. I'm reminded of the horror of the Second World War, and of the treacherous journey that the Hermanns – one family among millions – were compelled to undertake at the cessation. Theirs was, quite literally, a race for peace, and yet it merely presaged the geopolitical maelstrom of the Cold War. I think of Karl Wiedemann, a simple man trying, as best he could, to indemnify his family against the ideological madhouse which was the GDR. Like the Hermanns, he and his flock were the innocent flotsam and jetsam the psychopaths Hitler and Stalin left in their respective wakes.

Two families, each German, each entrenched in their country's age of torment. Two hundred miles between Giessen and Flöha.

Twenty-five years since the fall of the wall … Putin's 'freedom fighters' lay siege to eastern Ukraine, while his grotesque propaganda machine spins lies about 'fascists' in Kiev.

And so begins the fourth life of Dieter Wiedemann.

SELECTED BIBLIOGRAPHY

Applebaum, Anne. *Iron Curtain*, Penguin Books, 2013

Bruce, Gary. *Resistance with the People*, Rowman & Littlefield, 2003

–– *The Firm*, Oxford University Press, 2012

Ferenc, Jakub. *Sport w służbie polityki*, Wydawnictwo TRIO, 2008

Fulbrook, Mary. *The People's State*, Yale University Press, 2005

Ghous, Nessim. *The Conditions, Means and Methods of the MfS in the GDR*, Cuvillier Verlag, 2004

Gieseke, Jens. *The GDR State Security*, Federal Commissioner for the Records of the State Security Service of the former German Democratic Republic, 2006

Hönel, Manfred, and Ludwig, Olaf. *100 Highlights Friedensfahrt*, Sport Verlag Berlin, 1997

Johnson, Uwe. *The Third Book about Achim*, Jonathan Cape, 1968

Małcużyński, K., and Weiss, Z. *Kronika Wielkiego Wyścigu*, Książka i Wiedza, 1952

Martin, Mäik. *50 Jahre Course de la Paix*, Agentur Contrukt, 1998

Miller, Barbara. *The Stasi Files Unveiled*, Transaction Publishers, 2004

Riordan, James (ed.). *Sport Under Communism*, C. Hurst & Co., 1978

Schur, Gustav-Adolf. *Täve*, Neues Leben, 2011

Taylor, Frederik. *The Berlin Wall*, Bloomsbury, 2006

Tuszyński, Bogdan, and Marszałek, Daniel. *Wyścig Pokoju 1948–2001*, Fundacja Dobrej Książi, 2002

Ullrich, Klaus. *Fahrt der Millionen*, Sport Verlag Berlin, 1967

Wilkinson Johnson, Molly. *Training Socialist Citizens*, Brill, 2008

Zetzsche, Peter. *Friedensfahrt und Tour de France*